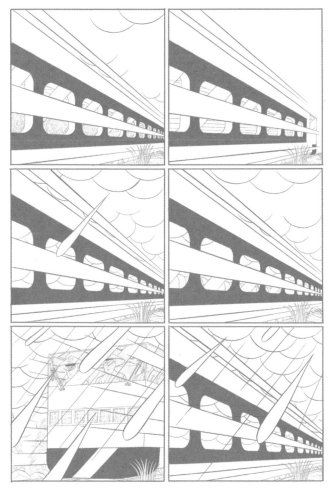

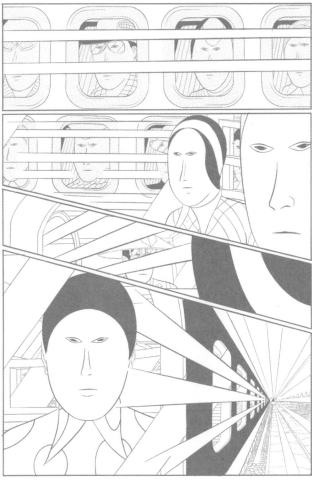

For Yuichi Yokoyama's commentary on *Travel*, see page 162.

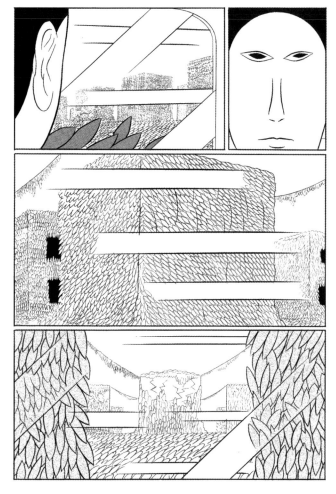

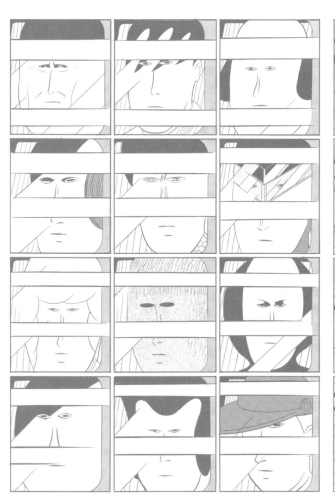

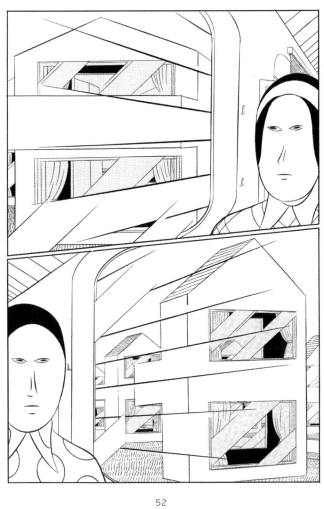

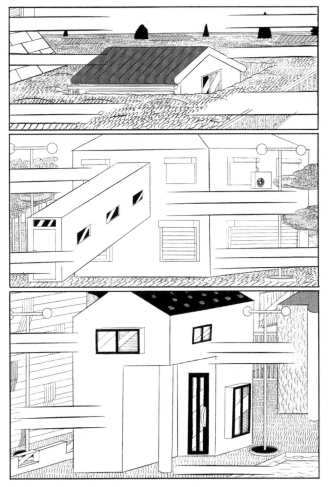

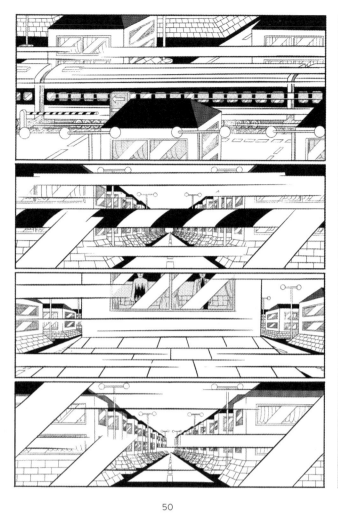

50

49

60

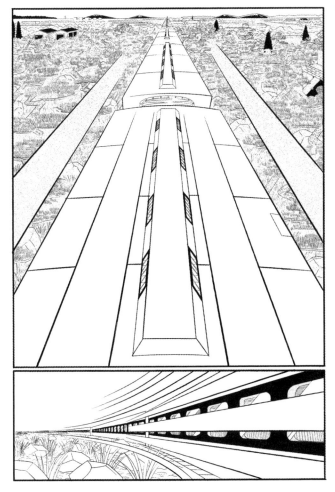

48

47

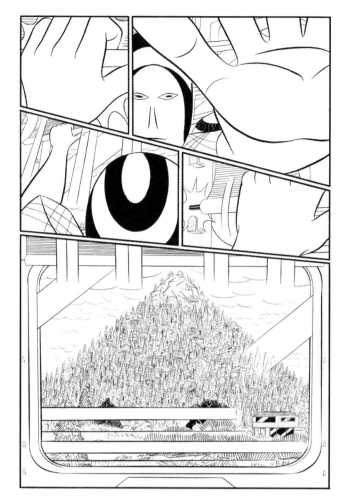

46

Grand Tour

Perspecta 41

The Yale Architectural Journal
Edited by Gabrielle Brainard, Rustam Mehta, & Thomas Moran

The MIT Press
Cambridge, Massachusetts & London, England

Perspecta, The Yale Architectural Journal is published in the
United States of America by the Yale School of Architecture and
distributed by the MIT Press.

Massachusetts Institute of Technology
Cambridge, Massachusetts 02142
mitpress.mit.edu

MIT Press books may be purchased at special quantity discounts
for business or sales promotional use. For information, please email
special_sales@mitpress.mit.edu or write to Special Sales Department,
The MIT Press, 55 Hayward Street, Cambridge, MA 02142.

ISBN: 978-0-262-51225-1
ISSN: 0079-0958

Designed by Rachel Berger & Lan Lan Liu
Printed and bound in China by Asia Pacific Offset

Titles, captions, and notes set in Abadi by Ong ChongWah
Main text set in Adobe Garamond, Robert Slimbach's digital interpretation of the types of Claude Garamond and Robert Granjon

The editors have made every effort to contact copyright holders
for material in this volume. Please contact *Perspecta* in case of error
or omission.

Send editorial correspondence to:
Perspecta
Yale School of Architecture
180 York Street
New Haven, CT 06520

Perspecta41@gmail.com

GRAND TOUR

being a treatise on
TRAVEL;

in which beginner and expert alike are shown the
mechanisms whereby **VOYAGING**
ennobles the architect's
HAND, MIND, and NAME;

in which **ROUTES** and **ITINERARIES** to sites
holy and profane are prescribed by the day's
sagest commentators;

in which **WONDERS LOCAL** are revealed
such that those prospecting to leave home might be
saved many hard labors;

in which the chiefest and most new techniques
for **SURVEYING WORKS** are considered;

in which the acquisition of **ARTIFACTS** and
PATRONS is discussed without shame;

& in which the **PAST** is known undiscriminatingly
alongside the **PRESENT.**

THE WHOLE forming a volume of utility to
men and women of words and deeds; on whose pages
expense was not avoided.

Why does London look like Rome? In the seventeenth century, the British reinvented their capital city based on their travels to Italy. Of course this is a simplification. Through equal parts copying, error, and interpretation, an entirely new architecture was created. *Perspecta* 41 asks how this process of borrowing and reinvention persists and how it has changed.

In pursuit of answers we employed a technique that has never let us down as designers: start with a familiar typology and push it to its limits to learn something new. As a type, Grand Tour constitutes a two-word answer to all of our questions about travel: where to go, what to do there, what to bring home, and what was to be gained. It is also hopelessly outdated and implies a limited class of travelers. We did not set out to update the Grand Tour by providing a replacement itinerary; we did seek to identify how the practices inscribed by the tour have evolved, maybe unrecognizably so. We also sought to expose the shockingly familiar parts of the historical tour that belie its dusty image. We hope the results are useful.

Gabrielle Brainard
Rustam Mehta
Thomas Moran

June 2008

Radical Inclusion!
(A Survival Guide for Post-architecture)

Michael Meredith Michael Meredith

0. Parable

If we are asked to think of architecture in terms of Humpty Dumpty[1]—as a complete, figured body of knowledge that fell and broke—if that is so, then the situation we find ourselves in, whatever you want to call it, is akin to arriving on the scene long after that well-formed egg shattered into little pieces. We never knew this supposedly beautifully intact egg personally, we didn't witness the tragic accident, and we're not upset. We just relish what's left. "Oh, look at the ornamental intricacy in the pieces, the complex field of tessellated egg fragments!" Who wants to put the egg together again? Maybe it was never together in the first place, maybe it was just a fable…

1. Intro

When asked to write about the Grand Tour, I was flattered but confused.[2] Why the Grand Tour, and why now? As a theme it appears reactionary, positioned against the contemporary amnesia of endless innovation. What we need is not a Grand Tour of the architectural canon but a map for today able to extend and produce relevant/useful architectural narratives.

Recent architectural production has been wholly uninterested in historical architectural referents (they're too "indexical"), focusing rather on dynamic shapes, variable patterns, new materials, new construction techniques, hybridized programmatic organizations—producing spectacular, idiosyncratic forms with novel aesthetic and libidinal effects. And a lot of the work is awesomely beautiful, almost cloyingly so—is this not enough? Are *Perspecta's* editors searching for yet another crisis, yet another anxiety-riddled moment of sentimental soul searching that seems to happen every so often, ostensibly marking the end of a period? Do we really need to resuscitate sturdy architectural models? On the other hand, if we take the narrative of the Grand Tour not as a rite of passage in the construction of a "discipline," but as an ad hoc model, one that works piecemeal through slow, accretive processes, that explores the tactile, embodied, sensual experience of architecture, the model might provide an apt alternative to the linguistic/theoretical mode of comprehending architecture, the legacy of postmodernism.

0. Parable

1 As far as I know, the Humpty-Dumpty metaphor was first used by Robert Smithson in "Entropy Made Visible" (1973) as a metaphor for entropic processes. Later it was used by Alan Colquhoun in an essay called "From Bricolage to Myth, or How to Put Humpty-Dumpty Together Again" (1978). Mr. Colquhoun, seemingly those egg parts didn't stick together as we have yet to reach a consensus on what defines the discipline of architecture.

1. Intro

2 I've found that self-conscious paralysis is associated with writing for *Perspecta*. Is it possible to write something like *Complexity and Contradiction* anymore? Texts don't have the galvanizing force/quality they once did, there are too many of them. Theoretical, ideological platitudes have no power to rally those revolutionary masses of architecture students in the architectural avant-garde…

2. Tour of the Discipline

3 Grand Narratives and the Grand Tour as part of the same era, the same episteme (of modernism, formulated philosophically by Hegel).

4 Classicism (the narrative of the primitive hut, Laugier), modernism (the narrative of the machine overcoming postindustrial production, Muthesius), postmodernism (the narrative of the vernacular and cultural specificity, Venturi and Scott Brown), deconstruction (the narrative of the act of reading and writing, Derrida), blobs (the narrative of the computer), parametric (the narrative of performance), postcritical (the narrative of the critical)… We're constantly usurping and dismantling previous groups as part of generational fervor and political power—the slash-and-burn agriculture of

2. Tour of the Discipline

For better or worse, I was born into a generation that does not overtly worship the architectural gods of modernism nor believe in those single-minded grand narratives[3] that have dominated the discipline within that reactionary ping-pong game of academic discourse.[4] For us, architectural education began after the "exhausted language"[5] of postmodernism and deconstruction. Raised on TV dinners of *petits récits,*[6] we sat in front of our computers and watched as an elegant, self-satisfied architecture of unifying formal construction—the last gasp of modernism's autonomy—became supplanted by ever-increasing anxiety, through a complex network of self-reflexive systems, from postmodernism to the postcritical. Now, we are left to oscillate between two extremes: the navel-gazing disciplinary "boudoir"[7] and an oceanic "field of cultural production"[8] synonymous with global capitalism, though we are indifferent to both.

Those who came before us were overwhelmed with language, with naming things, with situating and dominating architecture within the autonomous, internal games of connoisseurship—which in actuality spoke more about power and the authority of the reader/critic than about the pleasures offered by buildings. We have grown up watching the parade of ideological crises, only to eventually sputter and shift through academic fatigue toward the commercial and iconic savantism of celebrity artist/architects.[9] As a result, architecture became trapped between these two competing systems of evaluation—the academic/internal and the commercial/external.[10] At best, we reached a détente, sort of a new exhaustion, termed the postcritical, which tries by winking a lot to be both at the same time—esoteric and theoretical to those in the know, intelligent and iconic for the client.[11]

As formal autonomy became the Formalism Industry, the "critical" devolved, reversing the original intent by mystifying architectural production instead of clarifying it, a complete inversion of criticism espoused in 1968 by Manfredo Tafuri in his introduction to *Theories and History of Architecture.*[12] By now, criticism and demystification have become so elaborate and so contorted in creating alibis and rationale for architecture that the rhetoric of demystification is synonymous with mystification itself. Nowadays criticism's primary purpose (whatever is left of it) is a sort of spin, some hyperbole to rally generational fervor and create architectural constituencies.

Criticism and Pedagogy have, since modernism, conceptualized architecture through two-dimensional composition, while continuously referencing art, with its finer lexicon of illustrations for pictorial composition. This has become the default method of understanding architecture. When Colin Rowe convinced us to read Le Corbusier as part of a Hegelian art-history filtered through a metaphysical and idealized formal analysis of plans and elevations rather than as function or social program he stitched modernism to classicism, producing a continuous disciplinary narrative of architecture.[13]

Reduced to diagrammatic compositional structure, the works of Palladio and Le Corbusier do share a formal logic; within the project of disciplinary autonomy, they become very similar. If architecture once had utopian goals derived from material, economic, and functional efficiency, it abandoned these for an overriding logic of composition and organization of parts to whole. Rowe and Eisenman argued that functionalism and social narratives had turned the profession into a service industry. The established formalism as a dialectical opposite is

an attempt to open the discipline up, a way to get away from positivist functional-determinism.[14] Rowe was interested in placing architecture within an expanded cultural and historical dialogue. Ironically, today, the legacy of the "formal" compositional project has reversed

architecture. (There is a swing back and forth from conservative to radical, optimistic to rearguard, etc.)

5   See John Barth's "The Literature of Exhaustion" (1967), especially the parts about Borges's short story "Pierre Menard, Author of the *Quixote.*" Ultimately, I suppose, this is about an interest in architects working from the long-lost dead ends and moving onward from them instead of producing novel new territories and new dead ends.

6   Basically, this is the definition of Lyotard's postmodern condition: *"petits récits,"* or small narratives, our environment where there is the lack of a metanarrative, where everything is localized and dispersed. We have witnessed the transition from the Marxist dialectical model toward the complexity of Pierre Bourdieu's model of cultural production, where society is no longer analyzed simply in the sweeping terms of economic class structure, but as complex interconnected playing fields of culture made up of multiple forms of capital. The intellectual model of resistance from outside attacking the dominant condition has transformed toward a model of playing within the multihierarchical networked archipelago of culture, where there is no clear dominant model.

7   See Manfredo Tafuri, "L'Architecture dans le Boudoir: The Language of Criticism and the Criticism of Language," *Oppositions* 3 (1974).

8   See Pierre Bourdieu, *The Field of Cultural Production* (New York: Columbia University Press, 1993), 30: "The *space of literary or artistic position-takings,* i.e., the structured set of the manifestations of the social agents involved in the field—literary or artistic works, of course, but also political acts or pronouncements, manifestos or polemics, etc.—is inseparable from the *space of literary or artistic positions* defined by the possession of a determinate quantity of specific capital (recognition) and, at the same time, by occupation of a determinate position in the structure of the distribution of this specific capital. The literary or artistic field is a *field of forces,* but it is also a *field of struggles* tending to transform or conserve this field of forces. The network of objective relations between positions subtends and orients the strategies which the occupants of the different positions implement in their struggles to defend or improve their positions (i.e., their position-takings), strategies which depend for their force and form on the position each agent occupies in the power relations."

Bourdieu's original notion of "field" has continued to expand since it was introduced, encompassing larger constellations and networks of production. The limits and forces of cultural influence are impossible to define. They continue to grow the more you look at them.

9   "Towards an Academic Fatigue" should be the title of my manifesto, not illustrated with seductive images of new technologies but banal photos of classrooms and studio juries. In architectural discourse, this fatigue has become exacerbated through the constant, kvetching adjudication of architectural construction (as opposed to mere building): Oh, the anxieties! We are faced with the reactionary never-ending flip-flop, a Freudian return of the repressed. Ultimately, the problem with a truly autonomous language of architecture is there is no task to perform, no goals, there are only language games. Games for their own sake eventually get tiresome.

10   The internal disciplinary demands of architecture are contorted into disarray. External demands of the environment, celebrity success, and a renewed professionalism are the most pressing at the moment, but it is sure

to swing the other way soon. New Utopian desires of an elusive perfection with efficient high-octane performance, affordable radical economy, and/or sustainability is where we currently are.

11   Postcritical as described by Robert Somol: "The *critical* is always against a norm so it's reactive in that sense, but it also has to stand out and therefore demands visibility. It needs to produce that alienating, uncanny effect of putting some situation in quotation marks. What I'd like to advance is an alternative form of design that can withstand disappearing into the background, like Koolhaas's naked boxers on the nth floor, eating oysters in boxing gloves in *Delirious NY*. This is the kind of situation where there is nothing at all critical or notable about the architecture, but it's a spatiality that produces new kinds of relationships and effects. It doesn't demand rapt attention." Robert Somol, "Animate and Ambient Performances," interview, *Oris* 5, no. 21 (2003): 131. Somol is the best architectural writer/thinker/provocateur of his generation, but I'm sure there are two naked male boxers having hors d'oeuvres together in New York City right now and I doubt architecture either hindered or enabled two men to eat aphrodisiac oysters together in the nude.

12   Manfredo Tafuri, from his introduction to *Theories and History of Architecture* (New York: Harper & Row, 1980):

> The merging of the character of architect and critic in the same person—almost the norm in architecture, unlike other techniques of visual communication—has not entirely covered up this rupture: the split personality of the architect who writes and theorizes and also practices is commonplace.
>
> It is for this reason that the pure critic begins to be seen as a dangerous figure: and to be labeled with the stamp of a movement, a trend, or a poetic. As the kind of criticism that needs to keep its distance from the operative practice must constantly demystify that practice in order to go beyond its contradictions or, at least, render them with a certain precision, one sees the architects trying to capture that criticism; trying, in fact, to exorcise it.

Unfortunately, today this definition of criticism seems totally alien; it's about the political campaigns of artists (instead of parties or social groups) rather than demystification or precision.

13   Colin Rowe, "The Mathematics of the Ideal Villa," *The Mathematics of the Ideal Villa and Other Essays* (Cambridge, Mass: MIT Press, 1982).

14   See Colin Rowe, "Paradigm vs. Program," *The Cornell Journal of Architecture* 2 (1983) and Peter Eisenman, "Post-Functionalism," *Oppositions* 6 (1976). Modernism was never functionalist doctrine, but to their credit both Rowe and Eisenman produced a rhetorical oversimplification, in order to extend the narrative of architectural production, to open up architectural narratives, and to become more culturally engaged. Toward the end of "Paradigm vs. Program," Rowe's suggestion against architectural extremes (the formalists vs. the functionalists) is the detective novel—"constructing an architectural narrative from a series of seemingly incompatible references and facts."

15   "Art Into Life," Vladimir Tatlin's constructivist slogan.

16   See Hans Hollein, "Alles ist Architektur," *Bau* (April 1968). During the late 1960s and early 1970s, such figures as Archigram, Ant Farm, Superstudio, Walter Pichler, and the like, proved that we don't need to mean any one thing when we say architecture, but that the term has a legitimizing power all its own. Even more recently Diller + Scofidio built a career by producing apparatuses, machines, and accessories instead of buildings. Herzog & de Meuron produce urban perfumes, so we can all smell like, say, Rotterdam. (Yes, I mean that literally, they make perfumes. And why not, I suppose Gehry makes jewelry and everyone else makes horrible tea sets.)

itself producing a sort of false positivism—a formalism of pure technique, where endless computational scripts produce an architectural "automatic-writing," mind-numbing totalizing liquid spaces comprised of non-orientable NURBS surfaces or systemic and repetitive geometric techniques.

In today's art world, the grand narrative and formal lineage of painting composition has fragmented and receded. A quick survey of recent biennials and art fairs presents a strange array of objects within a collapse of historical narratives: the poor ad hoc, the non-composition, the minimal, the readymade, the ugly/abject, video narratives, performance, activism…everyone is trying to forget about the art-historical dominance of painting at the moment, and it's all sculpture, film, happenings, DIY, performance, expanding historical narratives by revisiting the marginal art practices of the 1960s and 1970s.

The same thing is beginning to happen in architecture, it's an old-school avant-garde tactic: you try to destroy the dominant status quo discipline to become more engaged in things in the world, in culture (for the new-school avant garde it is an engagement with the market). "Art into Life,"[15] etc. In this mode, working within and using cultural production, architecture is a pseudodiscipline. It is not rigorous; there is no authority. Architecture is a situation, a series of events, an established context or continuous conversation. If a discipline is an internal system of authority or a system of judging work against other work, it has never been systematic nor has it established methods of evaluation that are truly repeatable. The system of evaluation is based in the social; it is about authority and constituency, not something that can be hermetically codified or completely stabilized.

Without dominant ideologies or grand narratives, without the hegemony of clarity, we are left with an excess of possibilities. Like "Art," "Architecture" as a moniker has become so overused it's meaningless. It means everything and nothing.[16] This lack of direction along with the current disciplinary vagueness, where every dogmatic position appears flawed and inadequate, has created only guilty design pleasures. No contemporary discourse has produced a clear galvanizing ideology with illustrations. There are no more architectural fairy tales or holistic linear narratives to guide us.

Everything is OK, everything is complex, everything is easy, and as a result…architectural practice has flourished to become heterogeneous, broad, and fragmented. Similarly, discourse has been producing new terminologies and lexicons, an ever-increasing classification of work where architecture is divided into camps, tribes, and niches (in actuality, there are probably as many camps as there are architects). There are contingents of those interested in the material/technical, those interested in formal generative techniques, those interested in sensorial effects, and those interested in the social/meaning. Over the past couple years, there's probably a dominant population—the technical experts—but the practitioners of formalism and social/meaning persist. Of course, these camps are fluid constructs, people shift between them, straddle them, architectural cosmopolites and dilettantes alike. Our struggle is with the connectedness of everything.

3. Story Time: The Grand Tour

Once upon a time, between the sixteenth and nineteenth centuries, the Grand Tour was the primary model of studying architecture. Architecture was the activity of white, curly-haired, British, male aristocrats, who traveled for both education and pleasure on a sentimental Romantic journey toward Tuscany, a tiny epicenter of architecture only 8,494 square miles in size. The tour ended with the democratization of travel through the railroad, self-destructing through its own success—too many visitors destroyed the sense of place, and a deluge of imagery and souvenirs from the Grand Tour itself made a physical tour superfluous.[17] Souvenirs became substitutes for the experience; signification of knowledge and experience replaced real experience.

Today, travel is even more accessible; images and souvenirs precede any trip instead of resulting from it. Everyone has a completely themed and idiosyncratic itinerary set; they have seen the sites, eaten the food, and drunk the wine before leaving their house. The tension between the empirical knowledge of experience and the knowledge of imagery and signification has become part of the history of the Grand Tour itself. The codex of signification, of imagery, has triumphed over the empirical. During the Golden Age of the Grand Tour, architecture was meant to be seen and experienced; now it is a media event, a two-dimensional event. Its worth lies in what we say about it.[18]

If the Grand Tour existed today where would we go? There is no single itinerary.[19] Today's tour would either take the partisanship of a camp, each with its own set of canonic projects that could be adoringly visited, or it would encompass everything, taking an average of two minutes to flick through on the Internet.

If our current architectural moment is a continuation of modernism (late modernism[20]) that, like the Grand Tour, has unraveled due to its own success, through the constant pageantry of new formal and technical experimentation, architectural formal games (folded, twisted, repeated, crumpled, scaled, arrayed, etc.), which became meaningless and exhausted, then perhaps we're headed toward a neo-postmodernism. Possibly like the railroad, the computer has democratized design complexity to a point where sophisticated systemic and figural geometric games seem easy and/or empty, and we are left only with souvenir images of a design process. As during the shift from modernism to postmodernism, we need to search for new venues for complexity, but instead of digging further into architectural meaning, now we are pursuing computational aesthetics even further through parametric processes and tautological forms, which organize immense quantities of pieces/parts.[21]

Ultimately, the lasting legacy of postmodernism has been not the clunky beige pediment forms that have become our shopping malls and hotels everywhere, but the literal language, the way we talk, the way we legitimize architecture through a flattened index of images. Postmodernism established the notion of an articulated

As the production of the architect seems as loose and varied as ever (not producing buildings), the term itself, "architect," has been co-opted by computer programmers or information architects, network architects, etc.

3. Story Time: The Grand Tour

17   Mark Twain's *Innocents Abroad* is essentially about this.

18   Architectural survey courses are the flicker of PowerPoint presentations in a dark room, and design is about producing images to be included in that presentation.

19   The Tokyo tour for the Japanese modernists, the Middle Eastern vernacular for the Aga Khan camp, the Koolhaas-around-the-world tour for the Superdutch, slums for the activists, the German eco-tour for practitioners of sustainability…

20   Following Edward Said's *On Late Style: Music and Literature Against the Grain,* or the later "On Lateness," by Peter Eisenman, which insisted that we are at the tail end of modernism. Oddly enough, I made the same argument in 2006 through the curation of an exhibition titled *Beyond the Harvard Box* as evidence that our moment now parallels late modernism. The work being produced today looks surprisingly similar, flamboyant, and "anomalous," which is one of Said's characteristics of late work. You could say that a lot of the current architecture is about working with the leftovers from the 1960s and 1970s (think Buckminster Fuller, "green architecture," or inflatables, etc.). Said: "I've always been interested in what gets left out …I'm interested in the tension between what is represented and what isn't represented, between the articulate and the silent…" See *On Late Style: Music and Literature Against the Grain* (New York: Pantheon, 2006). For Said, those leftover/left-out parts are rudimentary aspects toward forming a style.

21   Evaluating the work addresses the problem of determining how much control you have over lots of pieces within the system, it is an internalized logic. Frankly, it's not enough to talk about outside of its own process. The alternative would be to escape a discourse built solely around the computer…

22   Today the distinctions are irrelevant as architects produce polyvalent objects—collapsing the scenographic, pure technique, and tectonic tactility.
See Andreas Huyssens, "The Search for Tradition: Avant-Garde and Postmodernism in the 1970s," *New German Critique* 22 (Winter 1981): 23–40:
> [T]he arts have nonetheless continued to gravitate, if not towards entertainment, then certainly towards commodity and—in the case of that which Charles Jencks has since classified as Post-Modern Architecture—towards pure technique or pure scenography…The American postmodernist avant-garde, therefore, is not only the end game of avant-gardism. It also represents the fragmentation and decline of critical adversary culture.

See also Kenneth Frampton, "Towards a Critical Regionalism: Six Points for an Architecture of Resistance," in *The Anti-Aesthetic: Essays on Postmodern Culture,* ed. Hal Foster (Seattle: Bay Press, 1983):
> [I]t is clear that the liberative importance of the tactile resides in the fact that it can only be decoded in terms of the experience itself: it cannot be reduced to mere information, to representation or to the simple evocation of a simulacrum substituting for absent presences…

architectural discipline, with inherently comprehensible rules of evaluation. It outlined the fundamental terms that frame the way we discuss and appreciate architecture: theory encapsulates and subjugates practice. The subject/object divide of architecture is split so clearly through the reading and meaning of architecture, where the meaning and signification of architecture is more important than the sensorial experience or social relevance. The production of architecture was and still is understood primarily as the production of signification, not the production of buildings or spaces, which is why the positions of Venturi and Scott Brown (democratization of architectural imagery) versus Frampton (against the semiotic project, for the tactile experience and the constructed-ness of architecture) in the 1970s

the tactile opposes itself to the scenographic and the drawing of veils over the surface of reality.

23 See Theodor Adorno and Max Horkheimer, *The Dialectic of Enlightenment* (1944, reprint: New York: Continuum International Publishing Group, 1972).

On "false needs": "The principle dictates that he should be shown all his needs as capable of fulfillment, but that those needs should be so predetermined that he feels himself to be the eternal consumer, the object of the culture industry. Not only does it make him believe that the deception it practices is satisfaction, but it goes further and implies that, whatever the state of affairs, he must put up with what is offered. The escape from everyday drudgery which the whole culture industry promises may be compared to the daughter's abduction in the cartoon: the father is holding the ladder in the dark. The paradise offered by the culture industry is the same old drudgery. Both escape and elopement are pre-designed to lead back to the starting point. Pleasure promotes the resignation which it ought to help to forget."

Adorno doesn't provide a way out. There is no escape from the culture industry because of its underlying hegemonic capitalist mechanisms. (Although today, capitalism has become like a second nature, it's just the background situation. There is no longer any Marxist dialectical alternative; there is no ethical problem with the system as a whole, only specific implementations and abuses of it. For better and worse, capitalism is something to be tweaked, not destroyed.) The immediacy of experience or the visceral, tactile pleasure of objects and environments could offer an escape from Adorno's negative dialectics—a true escape from false needs. (Think of the libidinal psychedelic aspects of late-1960s liberal politics. Could there be an architecture that operates as a sensorial drug?)

24 Jeffrey Kipnis, you know who you are.

25 Sylvia Lavin revels in this disposability in *Crib Sheets: Notes on Contemporary Architectectural Conversation* (New York: Monacelli, 2005), reducing entire discourses to consumable semi-representative quotes from within the architectural cultural field. As she suggests, maybe what we need is to forget everything, forget about architecture for a while and talk about something else. Don't be afraid of culture. Architects should stop taking themselves so seriously. Also, look at the progression of the *ANY* publications to the journal *Log*, in which critical discourse has become more discrete and individual, encapsulated within a multitude of small essays.

26 Geodesic geometries, Voronoi diagrams, hyperbolic surfaces, and projected geometries have all become a tiny customized button to be clicked in Rhino or other modeling programs. You don't have to understand their mathematic construction, there is little to no technical knowledge needed

are important to revisit. When postmodernism was being formulated, Venturi and Scott Brown won, and Frampton lost. That said, Frampton's "Towards a Critical Regionalism" (especially sections two, "The Rise and Fall of the Avant-Garde," and six, "Visual vs. Tactile") remains an important critique of an architecture which is understood primarily as just another visual commodity. It remains a prescient warning (and surprisingly relevant) for those who are ready to bring back asymmetrical haircuts, cobalt blue tank tops, oversized terracotta souvenirs from Tuscany, or a metatheory where broad linguistic referents trump a sited and specific operational logic. His provisional suggestion against a postmodern architecture of the "scenographic" or "pure technique" is a post-postmodernism (or whatever you want to call it) that engages the experiential and the tactile—things that are not so easily flattened or commodified.[22]

The educational model of the Grand Tour failed not because it was a bad idea but through its own overwhelming success, eventually becoming defunct through overuse with the democratization of travel for the masses. The Grand Tour transformed into a culture industry of tourism, cultivating and satisfying "false needs."[23] The slow empiricism of the journey—where you would spend months, sometimes years, surveying a building, drawing and dissecting it—was eventually replaced with speed, efficiency, and representation (prints, photos, and souvenirs).

We are facing the same problem at another level, where postmodernism has become so successful in producing new disciplinary terms and representation through which we discuss and frame architecture discourse and ideology, that ideologies themselves have become meaningless and disposable. In this vacuum, all that's left is pure technique and methodology, which have usurped all other architectural narratives. All critics can talk about is the intricate consistency of neurotic compulsive disorders, or the wonderful "post-indexicality"[24] and inscrutability of it all. In general, there is rarely strong relevant criticism, only relativism and so much of it that it never gains any traction. Read the majority of articles in architectural journals. Sure they are clever, but frankly I don't understand the relevance of most of them to architecture or architectural production. They are written for that moment, that so-called "flash in the pan," written to be forgotten almost immediately.[25] Their value is in wiping the slate clean and forgetting about history and discourse. Game over. Reboot.

Similarly, architectural representation itself has become an overwhelmingly disastrous success, as it's become easier to produce (especially in quantity). But most of my peers and students have become more and more skeptical of the campaigns of images, representation, and effects, ultimately preferring photography (or movies) of actual projects over drawings. Once you know how to make the self-similar Maya patterns, they're much less magical and are, frankly, superficial. It seems that almost everyone can make them with a few commands. Digital methodology is not a technical or disciplined technique any more than working with basic Euclidian geometries is. Modeling software has become a tool that requires little knowledge on how to construct these geometries.[26] There is nothing interesting or difficult about it; what is more important is what ends these formal techniques serve.

Perhaps the tactile, material, slow empiricism of the Grand Tour could be a way out, a valid alternative to the saturation of disposable ideologies and fast/easy representation, but again we're falling into the linear reactionary games of previous generations, another endgame in the continual search for an exit strategy. Currently there seems to be little possibility of constituting a new grand narrative or recovering an older one. Who would have the time?

4. Post-architecture toward Radical Inclusion

Today, there are no more singular galvanizing manifestos to bring about revolution; there are only minor texts of esoteric positions and tribal politics. There are no more disciplinary crises, only problems to be solved. Everything we've been taught is flawed. Every movement, "ism," "post," "de," and "pre" is associated with a series of fixed images and styles, each a totem of their looming failure. Once you have architectural illustrations for an ideology, the theory inevitably falters and fails because buildings are never complete or thoroughly singular enough to fully illustrate a theory.

Also, people are easily bored. There is no clear agency or relationship between theoretical narratives and form, no clear subject/object split, or hierarchy to things. Architectural rhetoric has become tired, frictionless, and ephemeral through the constant need to communicate and invent new words, new terminologies, giving an illusion of progress even though architectural forms and compositions haven't progressed much since the late 1970s.

Within this looseness, one way to establish order is to supplant the chaos of the open market with the hegemony of the "discipline." In the disciplinary model everything is evaluated through the specificity of shared codes or rules, which are problematic because, despite all of the discussion of the "discipline of architecture," there are no hard rules other than technical ones. We can always take refuge within the scientific certainties of sustainability instead of the artful messiness of architecture. Architecture is a pseudodiscipline. Architecture is simply a semicontinuous narrative conversation, a fable through the progression of rarefied buildings and design objects, and the referents could fall in and out of focus at any given moment.

Architecture is storytelling, and it depends on the interest and range of whoever is telling the story. Any building that sustains scrutiny and conversation is architecture. Nowadays the narratives of formalist techniques

and their spectacular forms seem to be winding down (there's not much left to talk about), but what comes after the fatigue of grand narratives, what happens after those disciplinary models of postmodernism based on imagery and two-dimensional compositions?[27] What happens after the compositional narratives of architecture?

Within our current architectural discourse (or lack thereof) we have to destroy (or simply ignore) those persistent dialectical architectural frameworks (academic/commercial, autonomous/contextual, etc.) in order to recover the specificity of architectural narratives; we need to be looking more at buildings, the particularities of their situation and history, unafraid of inclusion, *radical inclusion*.[28] Narratives of inclusion call for networked relationships of engagement instead of fortified boundaries. We can no longer construct those out-of-touch grand architectural narratives, but must simultaneously operate both smaller and larger. Nothing is to be expunged from the system. Instead of retreating into familiar postmodern historical models, we need to open things up further toward radical inclusion and

anymore, technical/geometric is just a style. The parade of so-called technique has been thoroughly exhausted and catalogued.

4. Post-architecture towards Radical Inclusion

27 The history of architecture is intertwined with the history of art and painting composition. (Typically, their histories are literally lumped together in academic settings.) The idea of the grid, the figure, collage, even animation, these all exist as imagery and are related to the dominant narrative of painting. It is hard to find an architectural example that doesn't have its parallel in art or music. Today, the narratives of painting and composition have expanded toward theater, performance, DIY, sculpture, social interventions. The literal frame of painterly composition is too removed from the world-at-large; current art practices are about establishing new social situations, working within a social space of cultural forces instead of just space. The compositional motivation of architecture has, like art, expanded to include a larger conception of "whole," an expanded concept of composition that includes architecture as a fragment of a larger, more complex organization.

28 Architecture should operate *inclusively* as a multivalent object for multiple constituencies. Inclusion is a quasi-pragmatist ideology, in an "instrumentalist," John Dewey sort of way, as a self-conscious synthesis: more than one reason to do anything, against the singularity of architectural thought and architectural production. It is for a more complex relationship between architecture and culture. (Inclusion is specifically against an older architectural model of resistance through self-satisfied singular formal devices, and for an operative practice, one that operates within the world, within multiple fields of production—something that can oscillate between being both autonomous and not.)

reorganization. Instead of referencing architecture, we need to use it.[29]

The system of evaluation in post-architecture[30] is social. It is about constituency; it is about those interested in a conversation about and through architecture. If language and form are constantly evolving, so is the system of evaluation. The dichotomy of "mass society" versus "alienated individual" no longer holds; the culture industry is no longer a totalitarian regime (sorry Frankfurt School). The new MySpace/Facebook/YouTube mass society is mainly comprised of alienated individuals who never come together completely, but form smaller constituencies and groups, each telling smaller and more specific stories. Everyone has become the media, happily stranded on their islands, in their niche, with their broadband connection. We're in a bottom-up, networked cultural model where anyone potentially has an authoritative voice, which means recovering a dominant architectural model or putting Humpty Dumpty back together again is frankly more impossible than ever.

29   The Spring 2008 conference at Princeton, "The Matter of Facts: Architecture and the Generation of Design Information," is one manifestation of this shift. As John McMorrough related in his opening comments, "recent architectural work seems unfettered by its categorical status. It sidesteps the historical divisions of autonomy and engagement and combines theoretical speculation with everyday work...This is a generational shift of focus, from the discipline of architecture to qualification of the world at large—from matters of form to matters of fact," though, in most of the work presented, autonomous architectural games have lingered as an afterimage.

30   While postmodernism posited an insistence on mechanics, semiotics, and techniques, the notion of a clearly defined discipline, with a set of codes and rules (a "discipline"), it was really a transcendental project. In post-Architecture there's no definitive discipline. And like Richard Rorty's "post-philosophy," in post-architecture (after the exhaustion of formal gamesmanship) what is needed is a multitude of inclusive narratives of use, those architectural (quasi-utopian, or micro-utopian) stories to provide relevance again.

WONDERFUL THINGS
The Experience of the Grand Tour

Gillian Darley

Group portrait of Members of the Dilet-tanti Society, after Sir Joshua Reynolds, 1812–1816. © The Trustees of the British Museum.

For additional images from the Grand Tour, see pages 25 and 28.

Pompeo Batoni, *Sir Watkin Williams-Wynn, 4th Bt., Thomas Apperley, and Captain Edward Hamilton*, 1768–72. © Amgueddfa Cymru National Museum Wales.

Giovanni Paolo Pannini, *Gallery of Views of Ancient Rome*, 1756–57. Erich Lessing / Art Resource, NY.

An elegant young man stands at ease, leaning by a column or posed against an antique statue, often in the company of a pedigreed hound. Hundreds of such portraits by Pompeo Batoni or his followers were crated home to hang proudly in the entrance halls and dining rooms of eighteenth-century country houses, frequently newly built and accurately modeled on the Palladian villas that their patrons had recently seen for themselves. The rigidity and conformity of the figure of the Grand Tourist, already tending toward caricature in the eighteenth century, mirrored that of his journey, which was taken in confined company and followed a strictly preordained route. But if such figures were archetypes, the reality was of far greater complexity and variety, reflecting divergent motives, exigencies, and preferences.

This essay is built around the Grand Tour as it was taken by Englishmen in the seventeenth and eighteenth centuries. It focuses on two men who had close if very different interests in architectural design. One, whose journey was an expedient self-exile from the Civil Wars of the 1640s, was a member of the gentry. The other was a working man's son, born more than a century later, who had strived for and won a scholarship to travel to Rome for his further studies. The journeys of John Evelyn and John Soane were both typical and atypical. In both cases, their own Grand Tours, while of limited duration, inspired them for a lifetime. The experiences of their near-contemporaries serve to illustrate how the tour came to serve such very different purposes and objectives.

In his essay "Of Travel," the late-sixteenth-century statesman-philosopher Francis Bacon considered overseas travel for the young, which provided education, and for the old, which provided experience. His list of topics for attention included the institutions of government, the law, commerce, and the church, as well as the artifacts, structures, and evidence of past eras and the present, ranging from cabinets of curiosity to fortifications. Architecture and the wider built environment served

not only to illustrate and embody history, but also as the expression of contemporary politics and society. To avoid distraction, Bacon warned the traveler to keep himself apart from his compatriots unless they offered first-hand knowledge. From them, usually diplomats, he should "suck the experience of many."[1]

Inigo Jones, scene painter, masque designer, and aspiring architect, avidly studied the detail and application of the classical canons, but initially only on the page (although he is known to have traveled abroad earlier in the entourage of patrons). Catholic Europe had been entirely off-limits for the English in the late sixteenth century, but James I's treaty with Spain in 1604 signaled the end of that isolation. In 1613–14, Jones returned to Italy in the suite of the Earl and Countess of Arundel. On this occasion, he had time on his side and the considerable advantages of traveling with Catholics. As such, the Arundels had exceptional freedom of movement, even in Rome, where they were licensed to excavate and found the first of the famous Arundel Marbles. The party went on to Spanish-controlled Naples and even considered going as far south as Sicily.[2]

Jones's tour of Italy was a purposeful architectural mission, since, at the advanced age of forty, he was about to become Surveyor to the King's Works— in effect, architect to the monarch. He drew and noted anything that caught his eye. The margins of his 1609 edition of Palladio's *Quattro Libri* are filled with dense handwritten comments, drawings, and corrections.[3] In a particularly direct borrowing, the double-height hall and balustraded balcony at the core of Vincenzo Scamozzi's Villa Molin near Padua are reflected in the central, dramatic cube within the Queen's House, Greenwich, for which Jones began preparatory drawings soon after his return to England in 1616. The party had stayed at the Villa Molin on their way south, but, more significantly, Jones and Scamozzi met in Venice, and the Englishman came home with several sheets of preparatory drawings for Scamozzi's *L'Idea della Architettura*

Universale, which was published the following year, in 1615.[4] Inigo Jones's journey, which led to the introduction of Italianate classicism to the British Isles, has been described as "arguably the most significant Grand Tour ever taken."[5]

Few early Grand Tourists had such clear purpose; most shared a wide range of interests, feeding the autodidacticism that infected much of educated British society in the seventeenth century. Young men briefly attended the universities of Leiden and Padua and toured the great palaces, private collections, and galleries of Paris or Rome. Continental Europe exposed even the most intellectually sluggish to new currents of thought and practice in the arts, literature, and the natural sciences. Some came home with trunks filled with the latest volumes from the printing presses of Amsterdam and Antwerp, Paris and Venice, as well as folios of prints celebrating the new architecture being commissioned by European ruling elites, civil and religious. Travelers could join a free-moving intelligentsia which might be found anywhere between the English Channel and the Mediterranean.

The seventeenth-century Grand Tour was initially an utterly bewildering confrontation with the unfamiliar, even for well-prepared young men who had read the available guides to the journey.[6] Entry controls were time-consuming and officials fraudulent; even the actual location of borders could be unpredictable. Once on the road, there were incomprehensible dialects to confuse even the best-prepared linguist, as well as the oddities in diet, currency, and, above all, religion. But the southern climate, the intensity and quality of light, and the heady richness of unfamiliar scents struck northerners most forcibly and transformed everything that they saw for the better—especially the remains of the classical world.

In this period, English Grand Tourists were quickly reminded that their own capital city was little more than a medieval shambles of timber-framed, jettied housing clustered round a collapsing Gothic cathedral, St Paul's. The handsome rebuilt areas of Henri IV's Paris, with its arcaded *places* and bridges unencumbered by superstructures, or the transformed Rome of Pope Innocent X, with its axial routes leading to pocket squares, or major intersections marked by Baroque eye-catchers—fountains, obelisks, and pirouetting church facades—provoked wonder and envy. Returning to England, travelers, from Inigo Jones on, were often invited to join the myriad commissions set up to control building and improve standards as London expanded. Ideally, London would be transformed into a masonry-built, orderly city, easily comparable to the best of modern Genoa, Lyons, Livorno, or Geneva, if not Paris or Rome.

Two young brothers, Nicholas and Henry Stone, sons of Inigo Jones's master mason at the Banqueting House, traveled to Italy between 1638 and 1642, and some sketches and notebooks from their stay survive. While their father's own architectural allegiances lay in Holland (Nicholas senior had worked for, and married the daughter of Hendrik de Keyser, master mason of Amsterdam), he pointed his sons firmly toward Italy. Arriving in Rome, Nicholas Stone went to visit Gian Lorenzo Bernini and received a hospitable welcome, in contrast to the weary indifference shown to the mono-glot Christopher Wren when he called on the grand old man in Paris in the mid-1660s. Stone had wisely assured that he was accompanied by an Italian speaker.

For some of the time, Nicholas Stone's patron, William Paston, joined him in Rome, and together they traveled out into the *campagna* to visit the Renaissance villas of Tivoli, Frascati, and Poggio Imperiale. At the latter, as Stone noted in his diary, "Mr Paston taking uery good liking to this housse desired leaue that I might come to take a modell of it, which was granted." Stone industriously measured and drew this villa, along with a number of others including the Villa Medici and the Villa Ludovisi, in plan, elevation, and fair copy.[7] All this was fodder for Paston's ambitious scheme to remodel his ancestral seat, Oxnead Hall in Norfolk. By familiarizing his future architect with his preferred models, Paston was planting the seeds for the classical country house, which he planned to build on his return. Unfortunately, the deteriorating political situation at home, followed by Nicholas Stone's early death in 1647, put an end to his dream.

John Evelyn set out from Surrey in 1643 on a route little different from that taken by one of Batoni's subjects. He headed for Paris, proceeded via the towns of the Loire and the Rhone to Marseilles, sailed to Genoa and Livorno, then pressed inland to Pisa, Florence, and finally on to Rome, with a diversion south to Naples. The actual moment of arrival in Rome was always thrilling. "I came to ROME on the 4th of November 1644 about 5 at night," John Evelyn noted.[8] His brother Richard, left behind during the Civil Wars to take responsibility for John's share of the family estates as well as his own, never had the opportunity to travel beyond England. He wrote enviously to John that Rome was "the only place I can imagine to please my melancholy humor and busie my wandereing fancy by reason of the vast number of Antiquities, a thing I have always delighted."[9]

John Evelyn shared lodgings in Rome with a Norfolk-born lawyer, Roger Pratt, who was educating himself

John Evelyn, Titleplate, *Views between Rome and Naples dedicated to Thomas Henshaw,* 1649. © The Trustees of the British Museum.

with great seriousness to be an architect. For Pratt, to become familiar with the Renaissance and classical antiquity was no mere mechanical exercise. As he put it with acuity, nothing could be "in the Intellect, which was never in the Senses." However carefully the aspiring builder had pored over the plates in the treatises of Serlio or Palladio in the library at home, Pratt recognized that there was no substitute for the sensation of running one's fingers along the stone grooves of huge fallen columns, slow-baked to warmth by the heat of the day, or perching on the corner of a broken altar, watching the sunset give way to moonlight over the Forum and the Colosseum.

Alongside the thrilling reality of Roman classical antiquity, still partially unexcavated and obscured by the vegetation, random structures, and agricultural routines that the Forum cheerfully harbored, was a rich selection of relatively modern buildings. Roger Pratt and John Evelyn were both greatly impressed by the Palazzo Farnese (like their peers, they believed it was the work of Michelangelo alone), but Pratt could not adjust his sights from the lofty grandeur of the Renaissance to the immediate turbulence of the Baroque. Despite Pratt's distaste for the Counter-Reformation, his prolonged stay in Italy gave him the architectural expertise to design and build the grandest Restoration mansion in London, the Lord Chancellor's short-lived Clarendon House on Piccadilly, before retiring to his estate upon marriage to follow the life of a seventeenth-century country gentleman.

The staunchly Anglican John Evelyn was surprisingly open to the explosive, curvilinear forms and plans of Baroque buildings such as Borromini's San Carlo alle Quattro Fontane or Sant'Ivo alla Sapienza. Evelyn's arrival in Rome coincided with the celebrations surrounding the inauguration of Pope Innocent x. Seeing the city in ceremonial mode, for which it was so well suited, may have made him more receptive to recent Baroque architecture in the papal city. In fact Evelyn's architectural tastes spread wide and he even hoped to sail to Constantinople from Venice, until Turkish hostilities with the Venetians prevented the plan.

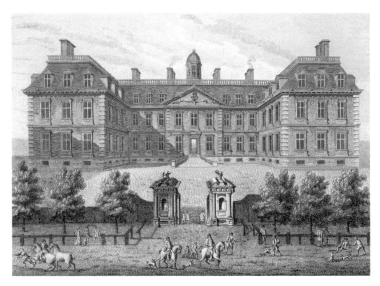

Albemarle House, formerly Clarendon House, London, published 1809 (engraving). The Stapleton Collection / The Bridgeman Art Library.

Despite Evelyn's thirst for knowledge in numerous fields, he often regretted how his weak grasp of mathematics, and geometry in particular, prevented him from properly recording and measuring the buildings of antiquity, leaving him without the requisite skills of an architect. His drawings, plans, sections, and elevations alike are competent but hesitant. Years later, he encouraged his son to make good these gaps in his own education, since "I exceedingly deplore my not cultivating them with more sedulity, when I had the opportunity."[10] In some ways Evelyn's time in Italy convinced him of his architectural limitations, usefully turning him into a clever and well-informed architectural observer, a theoretician rather than a builder, while at the same time reinforcing his aptitude for urban and landscape design, both of which he honed and practiced on his return. Evelyn's admiration for great European cities always colored his views on London, and he campaigned for a new approach to urbanism, arguing for zoning and a prototype Green Belt in his *Fumifugium* of 1661, an environmental pamphlet that was still in print three hundred years later. With the Restoration, Evelyn expected action and innovation from the new king, Charles ii. Believing he had the monarch's ear, he even entered the lists with a redesign of the City after the Great Fire. His scheme drew upon his admiration for the way in which major thoroughfares and important buildings gave emphatic form and focus to the urban frameworks of Rome and Paris.

Evelyn's diary, although written up many years later from his own notes as well as standard guidebooks, can be treated as an accurate guide to his preferences, tastes, and emphases. He devotes many paragraphs to the splendors of the palace and gardens of the Villa d'Este, and hardly glances at the ruined "Temple of Sibylla Tyburtina…a round fabric, as yet discovering some of its pristine beauty."[11] It was as an expert in the designed landscape of France and Italy that Evelyn returned, and he was able to apply the lessons of what he had seen overseas when advising Restoration statesmen and others on the disposition of their parks and gardens. Only the spectacular terraced garden at Albury, in Surrey, survives to show his capabilities. He remodeled it in the late 1660s for the grandson of his late patron, the Earl of Arundel. For Henry Howard, the future sixth duke of Norfolk, he made a Franco-Italian garden, steeped in classical allusion, comfortably set in southern England.

For John Evelyn, who had already visited the Low Countries in 1641 and who was to live in Paris with his wife, Mary, and father-in-law, Sir Richard Browne, the English Resident, from 1649 until early 1652, the experience of a Grand Tour was a period of continual enlightenment which he was eventually able to put to good purpose. As a bibliophile, his familiarity with the world of publishing in the Low Countries, Italy, and France, and his enduring friendship with several leading French printmakers, especially Abraham Bosse, was to be of great future use. His translation of Roland Fréart's comparative guide to the orders appeared in 1664, titled *Parallel of the Ancient Architecture with the Modern,* the first classical treatise in English to be illustrated with accurate, finely engraved plates. A second edition, with

Evelyn's greatly expanded preface, was published in 1707, a year after his death.

Evelyn's long and active life was continually informed by his awareness of the latest intellectual and artistic developments in Europe, particularly those in France. What began with his Grand Tour continued throughout his life, though he never left English shores after 1652. He updated his architectural information constantly, through contemporary prints and publications and verbatim reports from trusted witnesses—Christopher Wren, Samuel Pepys, and many more. Before Wren's official visit to Paris in 1665–66 to observe the building of the Louvre, Evelyn briefed him on recent work by François Mansart and Louis Le Vau and provided useful contacts. Once there, Wren reciprocated by reporting back on what he had seen, and promised more on his return.[12] Twenty years earlier, the "collector" earl of Arundel had provided an itinerary on what to visit north of Padua. Through Arundel, Evelyn had been only one remove away from, and one step behind, Inigo Jones, the English architect he most admired. In the same spirit, he took his obligation to pass the baton to new travelers very seriously indeed—even urging recalcitrant young members of his family on their own Grand Tours.

Evelyn's enduring interest in one particular building type, the military and naval hospital, was to be his greatest architectural legacy. As a result of the harrowing insights he gained as a Commissioner for the Sick, Wounded, and Prisoners of War during the second and third Dutch wars, he instigated a campaign to build premises where nursing care for the sick and aged could be provided for those who had served their country and were now ill or destitute. In the early weeks of 1666, with enthusiastic support from his colleague and soon to be close friend, Samuel Pepys of the Naval Office, he identified a site, drew up a scheme (albeit a somewhat rudimentary quadrangle) and lobbied energetically for a naval hospital to be built at Chatham, a Royal Dockyard on the River Medway.

Nothing came of it, since funds could not be found, but in the 1680s his expertise was central to the planning and construction of a hospital to the west of London for army veterans, Wren's heroic Royal Hospital in Chelsea. Finally, in his mid-seventies, Evelyn was rewarded with the post of Treasurer to the Royal Naval Hospital at Greenwich in 1695. The great palace for sick seamen on the banks of the Thames, east of the City, was closely modeled upon Louis xiv's Hôtel des Invalides, built in the 1670s, a magnificent home for the victims of war. Like Wren, the architect of the new hospital, Evelyn knew the Hôtel des Invalides almost as well as if he had been there, from prints and descriptions from friends and relatives who visited it on his behalf.

Evelyn's interest in current architecture never flagged. When over seventy, he carefully copied out a page from D'Aviler's *Cours d'Architecture* (1691). When almost eighty, in 1700, on inheriting the family seat, Wotton, in Surrey, he drew a "castle in the air" (as he called it in a letter to Pepys). He replaced the actual rambling Tudor house with a symmetrical lakeside villa, idealizing and claiming domestic classicism long before Lord Burlington, the father of English Palladianism, returned from the Veneto.[13]

Henry Stone, Page from a sketchbook of landscape and figure studies and drawings after Italian masters and the Antique, made during a sojourn in Italy, ca. 1638–42. Courtesy the Trustees of Sir John Soane's Museum.

The third earl of Burlington took four continental tours, two to Italy, in 1714–5 and 1719. A long procession of men of means came after him, educating themselves as architectural amateurs or becoming, at least, knowledgeable clients. They brought back editions of treatises and builders' manuals for their growing libraries, amassed collections of architectural prints, and commissioned buildings large and small, including galleries in which to house their handsome artistic trophies, which had been removed brusquely from the sites of classical antiquity. The pursuit of architecture soon came with a warning. Lord Chesterfield feared his son was becoming distracted and might lose interest in politics, as had others before him. He must concentrate his attention only on the very best, since "beyond certain bounds, the Man of Taste ends, and the frivolous Virtuoso begins." Chesterfield's emphases were clear: detailed knowledge of building ("the minute and mechanical parts of it") should be left "to masons, bricklayers, and Lord Burlington…who has, to a certain degree, lessened himself, by knowing them too well."[14]

When John Soane—he had recently added the *e* to a more pedestrian spelling—set out for Italy in his midtwenties, he had none of the assurance of an aristocrat or a member of the landed gentry, but a great deal more purpose and practical skill. The son of a rural bricklayer, he was now the proud winner of a Gold Medal from the Royal Academy schools. He had gained architectural experience in two leading Georgian offices: first, the younger George Dance's practice and then Henry Holland's, and he had considerable ambitions for his scholarship Grand Tour. Soane would come home with firsthand knowledge of the great monuments of classical antiquity as well as the social polish with which to cultivate contacts, and thus patrons.

Like John Evelyn's note of his arrival in Rome, Soane recorded the exact moment of departure on his Grand Tour. With a fellow architect, Robert Brettingham, he left London at 5:30 A.M. on March 18, 1778. Soane reached Rome on May 2, and in August apologized to a friend for being a desultory correspondent; he had been utterly immersed in "seeing and examining the

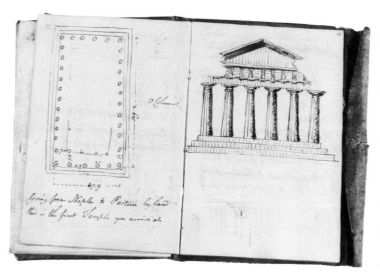

John Soane, Plan and elevation of the Temple
of Ceres, Paestum, from a sketchbook
labeled *Italian Sketches,* 1779. Courtesy the
Trustees of Sir John Soane's Museum.

numerous and inestimable remains of Antiquity." But
his friend would understand, being "no stranger to the
zeal and attachment I have for them and with what
impatience I have waited for the scenes I now enjoy."[15]
Soane's first surviving drawing from Rome, dated May
21, does not, however, show an example of classical
antiquity, but the ancient church of Sant'Agnese fuori
le Mura.

In addition to exposure to an almost complete text-
book of classical buildings and their sources, the
architectural Grand Tourist had unsurpassed opportunity for personal contacts along the way. Europe and
the well-trodden route of the Grand Tour was like
an immense drawing room in which aspiring architects
could rub shoulders with patrons as well as the towering
figures in their field. Soane visited the esteemed engineer
and bridge builder Perronet in Paris and fleetingly
encountered Piranesi in Rome. The fellow travelers who
grouped and regrouped along the way provided a length-
ening list of potential clients. Soane's career, initially
as a designer of country houses and then as architect to
the Bank of England, was almost entirely built upon
these contacts.

Soane's role as a Grand Tourist, given his lowly social
and financial status, often seemed closer to that of a
cicerone, a paid architectural guide. Thomas Jones, the
Welsh painter and landowner, whom Soane was to meet
in Naples, noticed that the Romans themselves classified
Grand Tourists into "three classes or degrees—like the
positive, comparative and superlative of the grammar-
ians." First were artists, second were "Mezzi Cavalieri"—
half-gentlemen or, in other words, gentry—third were
the "Cavalieri or Milordi Inglesi," who travelled with
a full entourage.[16] For those in the first category, both
the other groups might offer useful contacts once they
were home again. Soane made the most of all of them
while learning to negotiate his way along the tricky path
through an exacting social milieu.

One of his closest friends, John Patteson, did not fit
the social stereotype of the Grand Tourist either, since he
was enterprisingly combining the tour with trade calls
on behalf of his family's wool firm in Norwich. Since

the correspondence between himself and his mother survives almost intact, we have a disarmingly frank account
of his situation. He told his mother "business is despised
by the nobility in Italy," where, unlike England, there
were no "rich commoners." In return, his mother teases
that he will have become too grand for life at home
and will not easily "descend into a Norwich merchant."
After doing business in Leipzig and elsewhere, he moved
south and rewarded himself with a happy two months in
Siena, following Bacon's advice to stay away from his fellow English, living with Italians and seeing the country
for himself.

But once in Rome, Patteson found himself back on
the well-worn Grand Tour route. He wondered if there
was any point in keeping a journal, since everything
was so "exactly described" in books. As her son headed
for Sicily with Soane and other friends, Mrs. Patteson
avidly shadowed their party page by page through the
two volumes of Patrick Brydone's *A Tour Through Sicily
and Malta.* But he told her she must not take what she
read too literally: from "fine flowry descriptions of the
remains of antiquity about Naples…you form very high
ideas of the things themselves. But such is the surprize
of those who see them that they have scarce patience to
go over the beaten road and certainly would not, were
they not spurred on by fashion and the fear of being
laughed at." However thrilling for the student of classical architecture, long hours spent examining the ruins of
antiquity were not for everyone. On his return, Patteson
told his mother that he would be able to "make up
pretty stories" and persuade others that "I have seen such
wonderful things as in any travelling book they
will read of."[17]

For all his levity, Patteson's letters from Sicily show
how even a layman could not help absorbing the
language of the architectural treatise. His companions
taught him to appreciate the ruins of the temple at
Segesta, which "convinced us of the effect of proportion
and simplicity," but he could not resist enjoying "many
a good laugh against the others when they happen to admire a modern arch for an ancient one and such like."[18]
Meanwhile, Mrs. Patteson asked her son's friend Soane
for advice on reordering the house she planned to buy
outside Norwich. For every potential client met en route,
there was an entire family back in England.

For the true enthusiast, the journey might conjure
up romantic thoughts or intimations of the picturesque.
Thomas Whateley, politician and gardener, proclaimed
that "a monument of antiquity is never seen with indifference." But for most, literary and aesthetic associations
irresistibly led to thoughts of fallen empires, and, from
there, to observations on the sorry state of modern Italy.
"Some of the ruins…shew the variety and insignificancy
of that haughty pissmire [ant] man," Patteson mused in
Rome, looking at palaces now become vegetable gardens,
and temples become stables and cart sheds.[19]

For all the burgeoning editions of standard topographical and architectural guides, the most valuable
itineraries were those given as personal recommenda-
tions. John Soane's *vade mecum* had been a copy of a
letter written by Sir William Chambers to another architectural student, while Soane's mentor, George Dance,
spent six formative years in Italy. Soane himself offered

advice to his friend and fishing companion J. M. W. Turner as he headed for Europe after the end of the Napoleonic Wars. In thanks, Turner painted a grandiose scene of the Roman Forum for Soane.

For an architect on the Grand Tour, the object was not to copy the great originals in order to build them exactly at home, but to draw upon them as a source, freshly interpreted. Patrons might ask for facsimiles, but no architect worth his fee would agree without adding something of his own. Lord Charlemont never succeeded in building a replica of the Villa Rotonda in Ireland, nor did the fourth earl of Bristol, the Earl Bishop of Derry, manage to transplant his golden vision of "Tusculum," Pliny's villa, from southern Italy to northern Ireland. The bishop had taken Soane under his wing, guiding him to little-known sites around Naples, such as the aqueduct near Caserta and the Charterhouse at Padula, and then cajoled him to abandon his Grand Tour in order to return and transform The Downhill, the bishop's grim basalt-built mansion on a storm-battered headland in County Down. Within six weeks of Soane's arrival in Ireland, at the cost of a year of his Italian scholarship, the newly ennobled earl reneged on the project. In the wrong heads, dreams of Italy were mere delusions.

For Soane, certain buildings seen on the Grand Tour were talismanic, none more than the Temple of Vesta at Tivoli. The little ruin, to which Evelyn had hardly given a glance, was a leitmotif of Soane's entire career. He designed the Tivoli Corner for the northwest angle of the Bank of England, and made a special display in his house museum in Lincoln's Inn Fields, designating an alcove on the stairs the Tivoli Recess, in which he enshrined a cast of the entablature from the temple. Soane was of a generation to benefit from the extended itinerary of the Grand Tour, taking in the newly excavated sites of Herculaneum and Pompeii as well as the Greek temples at Paestum, south of Naples. Soane built a brick "Barn à la Paestum" for one of his contacts from the Grand Tour and included a cork model of it in his large collection, which also included the Temple of Vesta built to scale in cork.

Those architects who had not traveled beyond their own shores were rare—or unfortunate. Nicholas Hawksmoor never left England, while John Nash, born in 1752, did not reach France until 1814. Napoleon had cut the British off from firsthand experience of mainland Europe for the best part of two decades, and afterward the spell was broken.

Increasingly architects headed east, gaining their Greek Revivalist credentials and qualifying for membership of the Society of Dilettanti (for which a visit to Greece was a prerequisite). But a fatal sclerosis had overtaken the Grand Tour; the more of an institution it became, the narrower its emphasis. Antiquarian zeal, not architectural curiosity, now tempted the traveler off the beaten track. The Napoleonic blockade was timely; it allowed a period of topographical and architectural introspection and freed an entire generation of architects and patrons from the obligation to tread unquestioningly, and nostalgically, in their seniors' footsteps. By the early nineteenth century, the Grand Tour had been consigned to history along with the unquestioning veneration of the orders.

Architects had gained freedom of choice, both in destination and style. Setting out on quite a different itinerary, A. W. N. Pugin traveled almost annually to northern France, Germany, and Flanders, but he also continually visited the cathedrals at Lincoln and York and the medieval university buildings of Oxford. For Pugin, and the Gothic Revivalists after him, English Gothic architecture was inspiring in its own right. There was certainly nothing to attract Pugin south through Europe, leading to no more than a succession of "pagan" temples, as he put it.

Another generation on, Arts and Crafts designers, seduced as much by details of traditional tiling or masonry on a cottage or farm building as by the carving of the medieval masters, could find almost everything they admired within a short radius of home. It was their North American peers, men such as Charles Greene, who now came to Europe instead.

For those wishing to investigate the classical world, there was now the opportunity for settled periods of study in institutions in Rome or Athens, following the habit of the French, so long lodged at the Villa

Drawing made for John Soane's Royal Academy Lectures by Henry Parke, showing a student measuring the Corinthian Order of the Temple of Jupiter Stator (Castor and Pollux), Rome, n.d. (1814–20). Courtesy the Trustees of Sir John Soane's Museum.

Medici. Both the Architectural Association and the Royal Institute of British Architects considered setting up schools of architecture in Rome in the early 1900s, but nothing came of their plans. Instead, the British School at Rome opened in 1900, preceded by the British School at Athens in 1886. In 1912, it moved into Sir Edwin Lutyens's pavilion, originally built for the 1911 Rome International Exhibition. The American Academy in Rome followed in 1913. Both brought together fruitfully many disciplines, from the fine arts to archaeology. Architecturally, Lutyens's building makes a richly ironic conclusion to the story of the Grand Tour and its influence—a concrete adaptation of the upper order of the west front of Wren's St Paul's Cathedral, built amidst twentieth-century Rome.

1   John Pitcher, ed., *Francis Bacon: The Essays* (London: Penguin Books, 1985), 113–14.

2   Edward Chaney, "Inigo Jones in Naples," in eds. John Bold and Edward Chaney, *English Architecture Public and Private: Essays for Kerry Downes* (London: Hambledon Press, 1993), 31–53.

3   Giles Worsley, *Inigo Jones and the European Classicist Tradition* (New Haven, Conn., and London: Yale University Press, 2007), 16, fig. 5.

4   Ibid., 19–20, 102–4.

5   Edward Chaney, *The Evolution of the Grand Tour: Anglo-Italian Cultural Relations since the Renaissance* (London: Frank Cass, 2000), 208.

6   John Stoye, *English Travellers Abroad, 1604–1667: Their Influence in English Society and Politics*, rev. ed. (New Haven, Conn., and London: Yale University Press, 1989), 143.

7   Two sketchbooks, one by Nicholas Stone (with many pages missing) and one by Henry Stone, are at Sir John Soane's Museum in London. For the diary of the former, see Walter Lewis Spiers, ed., *The Note-book and Account Book of Nicholas Stone: Master Mason to James I and Charles I* (Oxford: printed for the Walpole Society by F. Hall, 1919).

8   E.S. de Beer, ed., *The Diary of John Evelyn*, vol. 2 (London and New York: Oxford University Press, 1955), 212.

9   Gillian Darley, *John Evelyn: Living for Ingenuity* (New Haven, Conn., and London: Yale University Press, 2006), 45, note 35.

10   Ibid., 47, note 43.

11   E.S. de Beer, ed., *The Diary of John Evelyn*, vol. 2, 397.

12   Described as "a letter to a friend," but clearly to Evelyn. Text in Lydia M. Soo, *Wren's "Tracts" on Architecture and Other Writings* (Cambridge and New York: Cambridge University Press, 1998), 103–6, note 12.

13   Gillian Darley, *John Evelyn: Living for Ingenuity*, 300 and plate 29.

14   Quoted in John Harris and Robert Hradsky, *A Passion for Building: The Amateur Architect in England 1650–1850* (London: Sir John Soane's Museum, 2007), 6.

15   Letter to Henry Wood, dated August 1, in Arthur Bolton, ed., *The Portrait of Sir John Soane RA* (London: Butler & Tanner, 1927), 16. See also Gillian Darley, chap. 2 in *John Soane: An Accidental Romantic* (New Haven, Conn., and London: Yale University Press, 1999).

16   Gillian Darley, *John Soane: An Accidental Romantic*, 25.

17   D. Cubitt, A.L. Mackley, and R.G. Wilson, eds., *The Great Tour of John Patteson, 1778–1779* (Norfolk Record Society, vol. LXVII, 2003), letter 75.

18   Ibid., letter 69.

19   Ibid., letter 72.

48

48
A SCULPTED WHITE AND PORTORO MARBLE BUST OF A ROMAN EMPEROR
20TH CENTURY
On a waisted socle
33in. (84cm) high

£2,200-2,800

50   49   51   52

49
AN ITALIAN ALABASTER URN AND COVER
POSSIBLY 18TH CENTURY
Of oval form, the cover with a pinched and stepped finial,
with moulded lip and tapering sides, each end with C-scroll
handles, on a waisted socle and moulded stepped base,
restorations
7¼in. (18.5cm) high; 10¼in. (26cm) wide; 6in. (15cm)
deep

£500-800

50
AN ITALIAN SCULPTED ALABASTER MODEL OF
THE COLISEUM
LATE 19TH CENTURY
On an oval plinth
7in. (17.7cm) diam

£300-400

51
AN ITALIAN SCULPTED ALABASTER MODEL OF A
TEMPLE RUIN
LATE 19TH OR EARLY 20TH CENTURY
From the Forum in Rome
12¾in. (32.3cm) high

£500-800

52
AN ITALIAN ALABASTER BUST OF A ROMAN
EMPEROR
18TH CENTURY
Mounted on a waisted polygonal socle
9in. (22.8cm.) overall

£500-800

For more on Sir John Soane, see page 46. For additional images from Sir John Soane's Model Room, see pages 92–93 and 170–171.

VRIESENDORP SYNDROME

OVERWHE BY THE GEOGRAP OF SENSA MEMORY, AND PLEN

Sam Jacob

We meet at Starbucks where a sign reads "Geography is a Flavor." It's in a shopping mall called Villagio, in the shadow of a sculptural observation tower in Doha's Sport City that looks like a gigantic vase on the skyline. We're with our client and here to meet an engineer, his assistants, and the mall manager. They are taking us to see a potential site for a high-end fashion store.

We are led through a grand barrel vaulted hall as though we are on our way to meet a Roman emperor, apart from the fact that one side has been slashed open to reveal an industrial-fluorescent lit Carrefour *hypermarché* so deep that we can't see its end. Ahead,

Images courtesy of Sam Jacob/FAT

a giant arch frames a view into an Italianate scene under a painted sky.

The name Villagio suggests an Italianified term for a type of settlement and explicitly reveals this mall's particular geographic flavor. Both Italian-ness and village-ness are exotic concepts in the accelerated nomadic-to-metropolis curve of Doha's Gulf coast urbanism. Out-of-time historicism and dislocated reference to place only serve to amplify sensations of unreality.

In the desert landscape, Italian-ness is expressed in the terra-cotta render and pan-tiled protrusions as the building writhes around within its tarmac car park. The interior offers a lightening quick tour of Italian-ness. Trailing our guide, we walk through a Tuscanesque town whose floor is so shiny that it looks like it has just rained. Through a pseudo-Verona full of balconies that no Juliet will appear from—unless that is, she's been working in the stock room. Then into a wing that is freshly Venetian, where miniature bridges cross a trough of mini-canal complete with motionless gondolas. Fine carved stone in Venetian Gothic style is set into quickly erected studwork.

The engineer opens a door in a temporary hoarding lit by tungsten-bulbed gas light fittings. And we step into a building site of an extension that is projecting out into the desert landscape fast.

While the engineer talks to the foreman, we get a chance to look around. We're in a street that seems to be modeled on Milan's Galleria, though it appears to have become bent. Above us is a giant oculus, whose center remains open to the sky. Along its length it transforms from being almost complete to a skeletal steel structure as though it were a diagram explaining mall construction principles. Scenography decomposes into desert.

This is soon to become Villagio's luxury brand wing. The manager tells us that tenants already confirmed include Prada and Dolce & Gabbana. Perhaps their leases were laced with irony upon finding themselves residing in an artificial Milan like captive animals in accurate simulations of their natural habitat.

However, Villagio's double-take sensation comes not from its attempts to replicate Italy but from how it recalls those famous desert-based grand-scale copies, the Venetian and the Bellagio. Villagio is a copy of Vegas, a replica that echoes replicas.

Maybe that Starbucks sign is right. Maybe geography really has become a flavor. Something that can be measured, mixed, and poured, made and remade according to recipes. Maybe there is a kind of geographic alchemy, a philosopher's stone that transforms place.

Is that what has touched fabrications such as Villagio, Bellagio, and so on? Maybe these massive replicas are attempts to cheat geography, to slip the constraints of place. In this way they may be more than a simple commercial response to the problem of marketing leisure industry behemoths.

In truth they are replicas not of places but of the mechanisms by which we collectively know these famous places. They are built from that most lowly, detached, disengaged, and aimless point of view: that of the contemporary tourist.

Tourism is a particular way of experiencing the world. It is an industry, a mechanism, and a point of view. Tourism's low regard is derived from the quality of the experience it delivers, as though at some point there was a more normal, natural, authentic way to be in the world that commercialization has interrupted. Maybe it was the feeling Captain Cook experienced when viewing Botany Bay, Edmund Hillary felt at the Everest's summit, or perhaps Neil Armstrong as he stepped onto the moon. Maybe Ansel Adams felt it photographing Yosemite, or J. M. W. Turner trembled with it as he looked out over stormy seas. These are moments that we imagine to be of sublime experience, of unique direct connection between individual and place that we experience vicariously.

Against these markers of authentic experience we feel that our package tour engagement with place is somehow emptier, more superficial and disengaged—devalued by the mechanisms that have delivered us to the point of the experience, that have turned the sublime into a commodity.

Souvenirs are perhaps the most pathetic symbols of tourist culture—exposing a total inability to engage with a moment or place. They stand in for a lack of immediate significant experience of our encounters with greatness, with history, the remarkable, and the unique. They embody, through their commodified reduction of significance, Douglas Coupland's phrase "bought experiences don't count"—which summarizes our distrust of the relationship between commerce and feeling, exactly the easy, uncomfortable relationship we have with tourism as an activity.

The souvenir simply proves that yes, you are, or were, there. It is the equivalent of not knowing what to say when you meet a favorite celebrity. Confrontation with experience demands some kind of reaction. And most likely, we are woefully under-prepared, undereducated, overtired, and overwhelmed by the experience.

You might call it a repressed or inverted Stendhal syndrome—the condition identified by Dr. Graziella Magherini, a psychiatrist at Florence's Santa Maria Nuova Hospital. She noticed that many of the tourists who visited Florence were overcome with anything from panic attacks to bouts of madness that lasted several days. She named the condition after the French novelist Stendhal, who visited Florence in 1817 and soon found himself overwhelmed by the city's intensely rich legacy of art and history. When he visited Santa Croce (the cathedral where Machiavelli, Michelangelo, and Galileo are buried) and saw Giotto's ceiling frescoes for the first time, he was overcome with emotion:

> I was in a sort of ecstasy, from the idea of being in Florence, close to the great men whose tombs I had seen. Absorbed in the contemplation of sublime beauty…I reached the point where one encounters celestial sensations…Everything spoke so vividly to my soul. Ah, if I could only forget. I had palpitations of the heart, what in Berlin they call "nerves." Life was drained from me. I walked with the fear of falling.[1]

Stendhal syndrome is an extreme example of how tourism affects our perception. It overtakes the content and warps our understanding. Tourism, rather than the

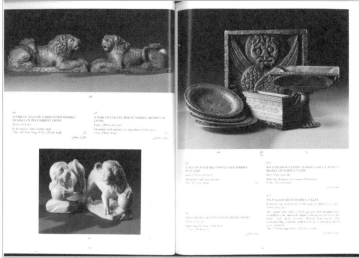

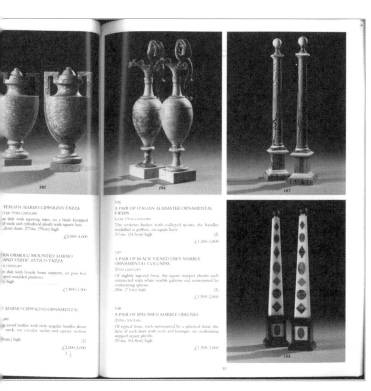

place we are visiting, becomes the experience. It may condense experience into something unbearably dense and rich—as in Stendhal's case—or it can wreath sites like a trivial fog obscuring the great and the remarkable, cloaking it in the shallow and insistent as we descend the steps of our coach tour to yet another site, thing, or place.

Stendhal was experiencing part of the Grand Tour—which became almost obligatory for young gentlemen in the eighteenth century. The Grand Tour packaged up classical civilization and offered it as an experience that could be bought, with the promise that exposure to it would transform those who took part. It's exactly the Grand Tour experience—the way it compresses and commodifies classical culture (the mechanism)—rather than the sites it revealed (its content) that threw Stendhal into light-headed reverie.

Young aristocrats would return from the Grand Tour a few years older, with a little more experience, a smattering of foreign language, having been immersed in classical culture (and having sown their wild oats), with a clutch of mementos in the back of a carriage. These mementos are what we now call souvenirs, and included portraits of themselves painted against a backdrop of Roman monuments, authentic ancient antiquities, continental works of art, as well as paintings, prints, and miniature models of ancient architecture. Indeed, the first recorded use of the word "souvenir" is in 1775, just as the Grand Tourists were beginning to circulate around Europe. Historian Marcus Kwint argues the term's direct relationship with the Grand Tour:

> The souvenir's roots spread throughout the collecting and valuation practices of many eras and societies, but it flourished under the particular conditions of western culture in the eighteenth and nineteenth centuries.[2]

The demand for these proto-souvenirs resulted in a thriving industry manufacturing objects destined for the stately homes of the touring aristocracy, especially in the hub of the Tour, Italy. Ancient antiquities and continental artworks, acquired as Grand Tour souvenirs, flooded into Britain. These objects reveal as much about the culture of manufacture and consumption as they do about the ancient world. They are a by-product of a new phenomenon, embodying the attributes, attitudes, and desires of Grand Tourists.

Flicking through a Christie's catalogue from 1998 concerning an auction of souvenirs from the Grand Tour, we see a selection of the kinds of objects manufactured for the Grand Tourists. In these objects, we see not only the subjects of the tourists' view but also other aspects of their contemporary culture—attributes of how they might have been looking, or what they might have actually seen. We also see the way that remaking these ancient objects as collectable souvenirs changed their nature.

Pages from *Souvenirs of the Grand Tour and Neo-Classical decorations* (London: Christie's South Kensington, 1998). © Christie's Images Limited.

We see transformations of scale and material. Small bronze Sphinxes, a golden Venus de Milo, miniature models of the temples of Castor and Pollux and Vespasian. There are slate models of Cleopatra's Needle at Alexandria, figurines of Mercury made in bronze, and plates transfer-decorated with the faces of Roman emperors.

In others, we see modern techniques reworking ancient motifs. We see engine-milled ornament in ivory vases with drill-fluted bodies on waisted socles with stepped plinths, clocks set into the bases of statuettes of pharaohs, miniaturized Corinthian columns retasked as modish home accessories such as candlesticks.

The everyday classical world is represented by replica *amphorae,* along with highly specific items such as figurines of Lorenzo and Giuliano de Medici (complete, like a child's doll, with their own to-scale collection of classical sculptures).

Certain antiquities are found in a variety of iterations. Trajan's Column was especially popular at the end of the eighteenth century. It features here in bronze or in rosso antico (as a pair with the Column of Marcus Aurelius) and as a 2-meter-high example by Luigi Valadier in marble, granite, lapis lazuli, gilt bronze, and silver gilt. Its popularity led to a post-souvenir version as Napoleon was inspired to commemorate the victories of *La Grande Armée* with a full-scale copy in the Place Vendome, this time featuring himself. Inevitably, this giant replica ended up being souvenir-ized itself.

Sometimes, the souvenirs depict things in as-new pristine form—as though frozen in perfection of antiquity—in others they are shown "as found," where the ravages of time are included in the representation— such as an alabaster model of the Colosseum in ruined form.

The souvenir as a personal record of the Grand Tourist's presence is also apparent in the portraits of young aristocrats painted by artists such as Pompeo Batoni (the volume of tourist trade is indicated by Batoni's 250 portraits of English travelers). Their role is similar to the photographs offered at the end of a rollercoaster ride: fixing your image forever as a tourist right at the moment of encounter with experience.

This mass of knowledge, artifacts, and culture washed up on the isolated island shores of British culture and had an almost instant impact. In the wake of the Grand Tour, England became enthralled with continental and historical exoticism, championing classical, historical, or literary subjects. It inspired radical changes in portraiture and landscape.

Inigo Jones, William Kent, and Lord Burlington all drew on their knowledge and experience of classical Italian architecture for inspiration. However, an original experience of the Grand Tour itself was not the only foundation of English classical revival. In the three great figures of English Baroque we see people whose classical knowledge comes once removed. Christopher Wren's only foreign trip took him to Paris; Hawksmoor never undertook a Tour and derived his knowledge from etchings; Vanbrugh's foreign experience (befitting his status as bad boy of the English Baroque) included two years locked in the Bastille—not a traditional stop on the Grand Tour. Their points of reference came

from the spoils of Tour-ism, from souvenirs such as the collections of measured drawings of classical architecture that were published, such as *The Antiquities of Athens* by Stuart and Revett, whose first volume was published in 1762. From this evidence, the English Baroque has its origins in what one might call Souvenir-ism.

In the eighteenth century, the souvenir was much more than an end in itself, more than a vessel that transported information from one place to another. It was itself an agent of change, a device pregnant with possibilities and bristling with virile intention. In the eighteenth century, these souvenir replicas, copies, and fragments of the ancient world provided the momentum for cultural change.

It is this that makes the landscapes of Stowe, the edifices of Blenheim, and the churches of post–Great Fire London such strange phenomena. They are evocations of distant places and times, and at the same time strong statements of their contemporary culture. Ancient architectural languages, cut loose from their context by the Grand Tour, liberated the architecture of the English aristocracy. The results are historical hallucinations that blur the line between souvenir, relic, replica, and reality, which merge an idealized past with contemporary expression.

Souvenirs too have mutated from their Grand Tour origins. Contemporary souvenirs are objects of almost no intrinsic value, formed from cheap, easily molded materials, mass-produced and made without craftsmanship. They have no vernacular connection to the place that they celebrate. They are stacked on shelves in multiples at a variety of scales. They seem the dumbest of objects, entirely inarticulate about the moment of encounter with their subject—if anything, obscuring the potential moment of encounter. Parasitic tourist retail trade flourishes to such an extent that it consumes its host. The tourist is overwhelmed, not by the sublime essence of place, like Stendhal back in Florence, but by the familiar relationship and easy transaction of tourist to souvenir as an alternative to the difficult task of comprehending a new and different place, finding solace in the souvenir store. Amongst the shops, stalls, and street vendors whose goods are arranged on a blanket, the souvenir-hunting tourist will find replicas and imitations of buildings and places arranged amongst novelty goods and counterfeit versions of designer sunglasses and handbags. Souvenirs exist amongst the lowest kind of commodities: copies, fakes, and jokes.

In an apartment in northwest London, Madelon Vriesendorp has amassed a vast collection of lowly touristic objects. Vriesendorp began her collection in 1972 in the U.S., where she lived with Rem Koolhaas until 1976. Together, they began to collect books and postcards of New York. She began to collect a specific kind of Americana, which she calls the "Wish You Were Here" series. These showed "the most devastatingly sad places: motels, lonely high-roads, tunnels, diners, the electric chair, cowboys, racist cards, etc., wherever American history was still raw and smarting."[3]

The collection was a device: a lens through which to see a culture: "Souvenirs are a great warts-and-all revelation about a country. Even in their jolliest attempt

For additional images from the Christie's catalogue, see page 27.

to present the glory days you are always on the precipice of the abyss with souvenirs. They are a giant step of memory-lapse, clinging onto yesterday's future."

Her collection began to appear as the cast in her paintings. Among these are those that she used to illustrate *Delirious New York*. "Although not done for the book specifically, they strangely fitted in…*Delirious New York* and collecting were parallel, one informed and inspired the other."

The collection fills surfaces, tables, boxes, suitcases, and shelves, vast enough to seem like its own world—a kind of desktop urbanism. Vriesendorp says: "I call my collection a city since it is constantly expanding, changing, and incomplete. I was forced to rearrange and reshape the city when it grew beyond its limits. I classified the collection into subjects and separated them into smaller groups, losing some of the original arbitrariness."

There are buildings to the left, body parts and fake food to the right. Each neighborhood has its own ghettos of self-similar objects—the Round Things area, for example, includes eyes, globes, clear bouncy balls with objects suspended inside, and egg-shaped things. Like a complex Venn diagram, the zones intersect: the eyes—squidgy ones, wind-up ones, and one that stretches into a shower cap—segue from "Round Things" to "Body Parts."

Vriesendorp describes the sensation that the collection has upon her: "Surrounded by it, I feel like a tourist who has been given the wrong directions, misunderstood them, and ended up in the right place." The collection is made up of so many familiar things, but gives the sensation that we have never seen them before.

Vriesendorp tells me, "My aim is to put together a wide range of incongruous and diverse items from different cultures which, through sheer accumulation, change their status. At its best the archive is a micro culture clash, a visual surprise, the least plausible depiction of an idea. It includes examples of accidental (or calculated) imperfection, objects of muddled origins (sometimes heavy with symbolic pretext), and rejects from an outdated (or never fashionable) artistic order, reinterpreted, misrepresented, bizarre, or mysterious."

Buildings are arranged in groups of formal similarity that she names "sets," like fragmentary acts from an urbanist's dream. A gang of Statues of Liberty hang out together—elegant ones, dumpy ones, and glittering ones. A washed-up Mr. Blobby has grabbed one of their torches in a final bid of Blobby fame. Nearby, there is a district made up of Empire State buildings including one of wax with a wick, flopped and fraying—the original *Delirious New York*.

There are abstractions that recall culturally specific ways of looking: a Great Wall of China zigzags in nonperspectival space recalling the spatial conception of traditional Chinese drawing. There are Japanese models depicting Manga-like city-crushing lobster monsters and a giant maggot in a plaza (like horror-genre public art).

Madelon Vriesendorp's "Object Archive."
Images courtesy of Sue Barr, Shumon Basar, and Charlie Koolhaas.

The collection assumes a quality that suggests the souvenirs are from places that we don't really understand—places that we've only just been to and have yet to fully take in. Their errors, misunderstandings, and mistakes mirror our own misconceptions, the gaps in our own knowledge. Vriesendorp's contemporary souvenirs make no pretense to erudition, education, or enlightenment.

Vriesendorp's collection erodes the singular intent of its constituent souvenirs through multiplication and juxtaposition. They are no longer about remembering a particular place (indeed, many of these are gifts from others). Massed, they talk about something else and offer a route out of the endless repetition of cliché that created them. Her souvenirs are mirages of culture, a record of the flickering shadows cast by buildings, cities, and people.

The idea of the collection has its own narrative—of cluster, group, selection, curatorship. It displays a concept of reach, the power that enables the gathering. And even if this is a poor relation to the aristocratic centralization of wealth and power witnessed in the amassing of Grand Tour booty, her collection displays the voracious scale and reach of contemporary tourism. Vriesendorp's collection comes from the things piled up in prosaic tourist shops, purchased in everyday ordinary tourist transactions. The massing of souvenirs is a technique to break down the power of the singular souvenir. These housebound, domestic objects are transformed through being collected. What one might think of as thoughtless gifts formed from lazy stereotypes become an artistic act through obsessive repetition. Arranged like this, they become more ridiculous and their intention is subverted. They no longer talk about place, but about lack of place. They remind us of nothing and nowhere, or everywhere and everything. Their agglomeration from singular object to hoard changes their meaning.

While Vriesendorp's concerns have been with the miniature, Koolhaas's have been with "Bigness"—as though the collection over the years has explored opposite directions. Each direction sheds light on the other. Though themselves tiny, souvenirs celebrate the large scale. Bigness abstracts while miniaturization concentrates narrative—a way of turning phenomena too large to comprehend into a consumable scale. Equally, ideas of uniqueness and generic-ness characterize both their work: while the souvenirs celebrate the special, the work of Koolhaas's firm, the Office for Metropolitan Architecture (OMA), has explored ideas of the generic. Though in topsy-turvy fashion, the souvenirs' mass production makes them generic, and OMA's concentrated logics turn generic-ness into iconoclastic specificity. Just as Grand Tour souvenirs echoed in the work of Soane and others, the New York souvenirs informed early OMA projects—perhaps for the same reasons.

Souvenirs are much more than representations of the past. They are both document and proposal, memories that allow us to glimpse the future. Souvenirs, as Wren, Hawksmoor, Vanbrugh, and Vriesendorp might argue, act like totems of something yet to come. They remind us not of what has happened, but what might, not of

places that you have been to, but places not yet invented. In the act of recording the past, souvenirs show that versions of the past can be manufactured.

The errors, shifts, and mistakes in the objects offer an escape from this false memory syndrome. They are cracks in the surface of seamless culture, jagged so that we might hold onto them and haul ourselves out of our particular hole. And as much as they release us from synthetic experience, the "mistakes" release the object from its singular fate. These possibilities occur because of the disappearance of meaning in the process of souvenir-ization. The souvenir is an articulation of an idea of "loss"—a way of visualizing the evaporation of cultural baggage. Their half-hearted telling suggests that the object is struggling to become something else—to escape its fate. It also suggests the souvenir is as unfamiliar with the place in question as the tourist. Perhaps that's why they share an affinity and why the tourist seeks their company.

Vriesendorp's souvenirs articulate a tension between uniqueness and ubiquity, between distinct place and homogenized globalism. These concerns in her collection mirror the real world.

Globalization erodes the exoticism of "other" cultures. Tourism envelops authentic destinations. In places such as Villagio, it manufactures its own destinations. Transport and communication mean geography is redistributed. The idea of place becomes looser and more fluid. Geography, as Starbucks tells us, becomes as instant an experience as flavor. It's something that might be called Vriesendorp Syndrome. Exoticism is less a "found" by-product of geography and increasingly a function of manufacture. That's to say the "exotic," "foreign," or "other" must be synthesized.

Vriesendorp's collection of captive buildings captures a sensation. With each displaced, off-kilter, malformed regurgitation, we find ourselves further from truth. The souvenirs are a document in which we can read the slippery effects of everything which creates them: ease of travel, mechanisms of mass production, marketing of "place," and tourism. In essence, it is a way of making visible the mechanisms of globalization and its effect on our experience and understanding. It is a description of the overriding context within which contemporary architecture is produced.

1 Stendhal (Marie-Henri Beyle), *Naples and Florence: A Journey from Milan to Reggio* (1817).
2 Marcus Kwint, "Material Memories: The Sentimental History Status of the Humble Souvenir." *Tate* 15 (1998): 44–49.
3 Madelon Vriesendorp, interview by author, March, 2007.

INTERVIEW WITH DENISE SCOTT BROWN AND ROBERT VENTURI

IS AND OUGHT

P41

DSB & RV

DSB   In the 1940s, the culture of English-speaking South Africa was dominated by England. As a child, I remember hearing English expats saying, "If you just look at that little corner of the landscape, it could be Surrey." And I remember thinking, "Why does the veld have to look like Surrey to be beautiful?" Political fault lines were everywhere in South African society at the time, but one issue was insidious rather than blatant. This was the tension between is and ought. As a recent colony, we were made to feel that we "ought" to be like the mother country, that English landscapes, for example, should be the model for our beauty. But I thought the African landscape—the "is" around me—was beautiful enough, and I didn't go along with the English oughts. I observed the same attitude in London in the 1950s, while I was studying at the Architectural Association. I learned that planning policy for postwar rebuilding was foisting a middle-class way of life onto bombed-out urban slum residents by moving them into new towns at the outskirts of cities. The "oughts" of middle-class planners were causing the people they planned for considerable suffering.

Given my experience of political schisms in Africa and England, I found the early rumblings of social revolution in America quite familiar when I arrived in 1958. But social critiques in the U.S. were more codified than those in England. Social scientists like Herbert Gans and Jane Jacobs and their followers, the social planners, dealt with the "is" and the "ought" in urban planning in a scholarly way. They were my mentors as I tried to make the social concern I had learned in Africa and Europe relevant professionally.

Mannerism in historical architecture was a parallel theme and an interest Bob and I found we shared when we met in 1960.

RV   I had arrived in Rome intending to focus on Baroque architecture but, just as my two years there ended, I realize that Mannerism was my main historical interest. This was a major conclusion.

DSB   It was, too, for me. The English New Brutalist architects who were trying to learn how city people really lived, came to see Mannerism as a model for the breaking of rules in urbanism. I agreed and felt a Mannerist outlook could help us confront the gap between is and ought in planning and design.

It sounds as though your youth preconditioned you to be sensitive to "foreign" experiences. Many people travel for no other reason than to experience something different—but, in your case, does travel have as much to do with coming home as with leaving?

DSB   Perhaps travel helps you learn what is inherently important for you. In a strange way, it sends you back to your own culture. When I got to planning school in America, I immediately began trying to interpret South Africa. I spent hours in the library on a term paper comparing public housing policy in South Africa, the U.K., and America. That's common with foreign students. They get a great interest in understanding their own culture and comparing it to other places. And I've wanted to do this ever since.

RV   That also applied to me. That's why I could come back to the U.S. and look at Main Street. I could love the Roman piazza, but after I'd seen it I could see the ordinary in America in new ways. I think it's significant that at that time, looking at history and looking at the everyday was something you really didn't do. Sure, you traveled a bit, but if you did, you looked at the modern stuff.

DSB   I went from Africa to Europe, let's say Rome—we've used Rome as a metaphor for Europe. Then from Rome to Las Vegas and from Las Vegas

Strip, desert, Venturi; Learning from Las Vegas studio, Las Vegas, 1968.   Scott Brown and Izenour with Yale students under the Stardust sign; Learning from Las Vegas studio, Las Vegas, 1968. Campus planning study, Tsinghua University, Beijing, 2004. Images © Venturi, Scott Brown and Associates, Inc.   Venturi and Scott Brown outside their Philadelphia residence with the editors of Perspecta 41, 2008. © Colin Montgomery.   Interior street; Mielparque Nikko Kirifuri Hotel and Spa, Nikko National Park, Japan, 1997. © Kawasumi Architectural Photograph Office.   Source materials; Mielparque Nikko Kirifuri Hotel and Spa. © Venturi, Scott Brown and Associates, Inc.

For photos from Denise Scott Brown and Robert Venturi's home, see pages 126–129.

Is and Ought   37

back again to Rome. We learned from Las Vegas to reinterpret Rome as symbolic architecture, not just as abstract space and volume. But there was another trip: Africa to Rome, Rome to Las Vegas, then Rem Koolhaas took over and added Las Vegas to Lagos. This leg completed my circle.

If Bob and I have a somewhat skewed view of things, it's because we see ourselves as marginal. Marginal people hear a different drummer. We feel this is why we can learn from Las Vegas as well as Rome. And Rem is marginal too—maybe because he grew up partly in Indonesia.

Is the marginal experience a prerequisite for developing a personal reading of a place? Or can architects be taught to think and look in these ways?

DSB It's probably not a prerequisite. Our childhoods may have given us a slightly skewed vision, but others could have had the same experience without that result. I don't know what causes it. It's probably more complex than simply feeling out of place where you grew up, but that's what it was for both Bob and me. We were put into WASP cultures, where we felt we didn't belong.

RV I was an Italian-American Quaker.

DSB And I was a South African Eastern European Jew set in an upper-middle-class WASP prep school. That will do it every time! But I think that today many people will have this marginal experience. As they live as expatriates, moving from place to place and among different cultures, they'll become, as we did, "visiting anthropologists." That's something that Bob and I wrote about in *Architecture as Signs and Systems: For a Mannerist Time*.

Would it be correct to say that travel gave you a set of intellectual tools with which you could come back and look at your home turf, rather than giving you fodder for your design work, as was the case with the historical Grand Tour?

RV I think it allowed me to open my mind and find relevance in a broad spectrum of things, opportunities, places.

DSB It *did* give us fodder for our work. We certainly learned from all we saw. But it also gave us swivel-tilted heads—we're always looking—and a particular way of looking. So when we visit some set piece of architecture, we tend to find its surroundings equally fascinating, for the context they give the monument but also for themselves. And we look intensely during our daily travels too. Our morning trip to work down Shurs Lane to Main Street contains the landscapes and buildings of an early industrial town overlaid by a twentieth-century infrastructure of rail, road, and power lines. The whole is a cityscape beautiful in a way no individual designer could have conceived, and constantly refreshing to us.

We want to ask you about travel as it relates to pedagogy. The trip you took with students to Las Vegas has now been institutionalized at schools like Yale. Yale's advanced studios have recently traveled to Iceland, Japan, India, Venice, and Abu Dhabi. Some people think it's ridiculous that studios travel for only one week, that this kind of travel can't result in academic research.

DSB I think that, as a professional, you should have a philosophy of how to look and a purpose in looking that dictates your subjects of study. We used techniques to analyze and visualize, most of which came from cartography, economics, and urban planning. We lifted other techniques from transportation planning, urban sociology, cultural anthropology, iconography, art and architectural history, and Pop Art. Our students set off for Las Vegas with a booklet this thick, asking, "How could you have written so many work programs for us?" But once they got there, they found our guidelines thin indeed!

At planning school, I was taught to see an urban problem as a complex of many variables, and to consider carefully which variables were appropriate to analyze. What are the salient variables, how do you find and depict them, how do you analyze them? Britton Harris used to describe the whale theory of collecting data. The whale opens its mouth and swims, swallowing whatever is in its path. But this doesn't work well where major data may lie off one's path. So how do you develop a sense of the issues of the study at the outset and establish its broad directions before you start collecting data? And what do you do with the information once you have it, to make it usable for design? These are questions to ask while traveling to research.

What do you think of the Harvard Project on the City? Rem Koolhaas has taken students to what some would consider unlikely sites for study, like the informal urbanism of Lagos. But he has also been criticized for dropping in and looking for intelligence in disorder, aestheticizing a complex reality.

DSB   Documenting "disorder" with an open mind is not exactly celebrating it. It's saying, "Is this really disorder? Let's look to understand it." A sociologist would ask, "Whose disorder?" I feel that being nonjudgmental, at first, is a very good idea. In the 1950s, we saw the human problems caused by architects, among others, making judgments too quickly. Holding back, not rushing to judgment doesn't mean you don't judge. It means you try to make sensitive judgments by learning about the thing you're judging—by asking, "Is this chaos an order we have not yet perceived?" Another question might be, "Can we ameliorate the problems of an area on its own terms, avoiding what's atrocious, but not losing what's good—and making sure we can tell the difference?"

These questions can take us from analysis to design. Researchers might ask them, or they might merely describe the conditions they see, and leave others to respond. They might apply the lessons to places other than where they were learned. So I'm not necessarily against merely searching. And aestheticizing, in the sense of abstracting this one variable for analysis, is approved scientific behavior. Criticism would be valid, however, if form-making were not combined with other criteria in synthesis—in design.

What are the political implications of looking at a place like Las Vegas or Lagos? When architects study a place do they tacitly legitimize or endorse it?

DSB   We architects cannot, in the main, choose our clients. They choose us, though we have the right to refuse and do so at times, usually for pragmatic, not ideological, reasons. But now and then, a project seems evil and we reject it on moral grounds. Are Las Vegas and Lagos to be rejected on moral grounds? Are they "politically incorrect"? I believe we should be politically correct—when we can define what that is. But I feel our choice of Las Vegas had that moral quality. It no more signified approval of gambling than studying Chartres Cathedral would be an endorsement of the bloodier actions of medieval Christendom.

Many firms have adopted a design methodology where research is used to generate unexpected formal solutions. Their methods depart from the same place as Learning from Las Vegas, but always result in form.

DSB   Although architects too often propose a building as the solution to all problems, it's not necessarily wrong to end up with a form. And whether form or function starts the process is not the issue either. Rather, the form should, in the end, take account of all requirements. At Penn's planning juries, Robert Mitchell, an architect turned planner, would criticize urban design students by saying, "You did a ritual dance called analysis. Then you closed that book and did whatever you wanted anyway." The idea is not to do that.

You decided to bring students' attention to Las Vegas for many reasons, some of which were personal, but the least of which was a desire to simply shock or provoke. Is there a danger of choosing research subjects for shock value, now that there is widespread acceptance for looking at the "wrong" thing?

DSB   We did have personal reasons. When I was four, my grandparents brought toys home to Johannesburg for us from Coney Island, and, oh, was that exciting! My father had a great love for places like Miami Beach, Atlantic City, and Muizenberg, which is a South African equivalent. My parents went to Las Vegas in the 1940s and came back with family movies. So it's been a long thing with us.

We also had aesthetic reasons. We went because Pop Art was very exciting to us. This, together with a Brutalist interest in popular culture, African urban folk art, and English Pop Art of the 1940s and 1950s, led to our welcoming of American Pop Art, and inevitably to Las Vegas. And when we got there it was an amazing love-hate experience.

However—and this has been difficult for architects to understand—we went to Las Vegas largely for *social* reasons. My teachers in planning school were the trigger. They said, "You architects are too arrogant about the way people choose to live. A little humility would help. You should study the cities of the American southwest open-mindedly. Don't just condemn them as sprawl. Go find out why they are the way they are, and why people flock to them, and not to architect-designed places." That's basically why we went. We chose the Las Vegas Strip because it was an extreme version and, being in the desert, it was easier to study than a strip laid over the patterns of an older city.

And we *did* intend to be provocative. This was because, for Yalies in the 1960s, we knew the research subject had to be "agin' the government"—in other words, iconoclastic—or they wouldn't have listened. But we had more down-to-earth reasons for going, too—getting architects to read, for one. I had learned from experience that the only way to entice architecture students into reading was to tie the material concretely to their design projects. The fact that they had to read in order to do their projects meant that they read. So our reading assignments were tuned to helping students pursue their research. But we hoped that, in the process, they would get grounding in subject matter we felt they needed in order to be sentient contributors within their profession. This applied, for example, in the "Learning from Levittown" studio, where we convinced architecture students to take on the difficult and opaque material of urban sociology.

RV   "Learning from Levittown" was more shocking to people than *Learning from Las Vegas*. Vince Scully was horrified by it.

Why?

RV   Because it was just too vulgar.

DSB   While Yale students were studying Las Vegas, Cooper Union students were making careful analyses of Le Corbusier. This seemed to challenge Herbert Gans's thesis in *Popular Culture and High Culture* that professionals would emerge from within the various taste cultures to serve their own group's cultural needs. Yet a broader social reading might suggest that upper-middle-class Yalies were secure enough to analyze Las Vegas, while for their more upwardly-mobile colleagues it was too close to home.

One member of our Levittown studio had grown up in row housing in northeast Philadelphia. His environment, as much as mine in Africa, was under attack from upper-middle-class "oughts," and he was fascinated to question this mindset and view his home in a nonjudgmental way.

RV   Was it the Levittown or the Las Vegas jury where a bunch of students from Columbia came up and heckled us?

DSB   It was Levittown.

RV   Bob Stern also came. He was a recent graduate then.

DSB   He didn't heckle, but he was not in favor. He took Scully's view. I felt they were thinking, "Denise is leading Bob in the wrong direction."

What about the fact that the studio wasn't an obvious opportunity to design a building?

DSB   Once, when I was planning an urban design studio, Penn's dean, Holmes Perkins, admonished me, "You're calling for too much analysis. The first love of these students is design. Don't take them too far away from it." So when we were first back from Las Vegas, I gave the students a brief sketch design to return them to what they loved. Well, they called it "that busywork Denise is getting us to do."

Is the research studio still valuable? Should there be a place in design schools for this kind of analytical design research?

DSB   The research studio is very valuable. But it is easy to do badly, in which case it's worse than useless. And to do it well takes knowledge, coordination, and many hours of preparation. It's like the interdisciplinary studios that were tried in the 1960s. They got a bad reputation, not because they were a bad idea, but because architecture faculty didn't have the background to handle them and couldn't spend the preparation time needed to make them succeed.

In gauging the value of research studios, you should consider which aspect of them you're discussing. They're multifaceted and they don't resemble traditional architecture studios. They require collaborative work, with coordination between groups and organized sharing of information. Students typically work in pairs, research is formally organized and supervised, and separate tasks are assigned to individuals and groups. And the studio programs must be prepared beforehand and revised throughout the semester.

For these reasons, research studios faculty must be collaborators as well as instigators, and searchers as passionate as the students. As in the traditional studio, they should teach design as the coordination of the elements of architecture, but they can also help students understand professional action as a terrain that includes more than form-making, and see research as a lifelong activity that architects do in the responsible performance of their work. And they can nurture professional commitment through the passion for the problem and the camaraderie that a good research studio induces. So yes, I feel that most architects during their training should have one research studio, but few require more than one—not because "this isn't architecture," but because there is no time for more given the brevity of professional programs. A core purpose of studio in architecture should be to give students experience in coordinating the elements of architecture, and this skill, like riding a bicycle, is best learned by repeated practice over time. But the group research studio can be critical in helping students prepare for individual thesis-level work, as well as for the collaborations of professional practice; and its structured workbook can support its students' future efforts as beginning architecture teachers.

Far from dropping the research studio, I feel architects should embrace it—carefully. We should institutionalize it but also limit its role in our pedagogy. And we should offer it to the wider university, because academic education could do with both an action-oriented model for its activist students and alternative pedagogies for its visual learners.

One theme we've noticed in researching this issue is the tension between taking time out of one's career to travel and develop ideas, and the need to practice. It seems like architects today don't have the time, literally and psychologically, to delay career-building for building an intellectual position.

RV   That's a good point. There's a real tension there, and you have to compromise in some ways.

DSB   Bob and I were lucky enough, after graduating, to spend time in study travel and work in Europe and elsewhere. And this was prolonged by our years of teaching. We've lived on the nurture and support from these experiences for more than forty years. We left teaching when we realized that our small, struggling practice needed our full attention, but in another sense we have never left. Despite being in practice, we've had a life of searching that started when we were students and continues today.

Much as I loved teaching, I have found the intertwined variables of practice, and seeing the physical results of my own conceptual thought, even more enchanting—to the point of addiction. Yet I feel lucky that we have been able to run a "mini-university" alongside our professional life. This means our work is a troika: we oscillate between looking-studying, designing, and theorizing-writing. And we keep up our travel for study and work. There can be no better way to see a foreign country than through working there. It's so much more rewarding than being a tourist. In short order, you're on close terms with strangers, sharing their efforts even when you don't share their language, and at work on things in life most meaningful to them and you. The cross-cultural and historical research and design we could do in building for Toulouse, France, and Nikko, Japan, were, to us, some of the great opportunities of our careers.

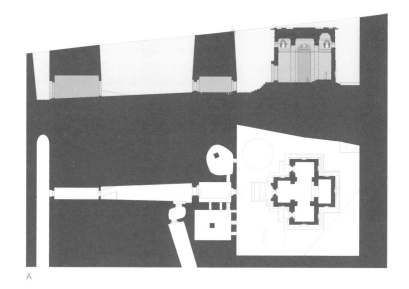

A

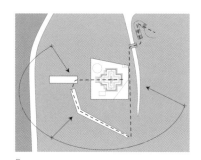

B

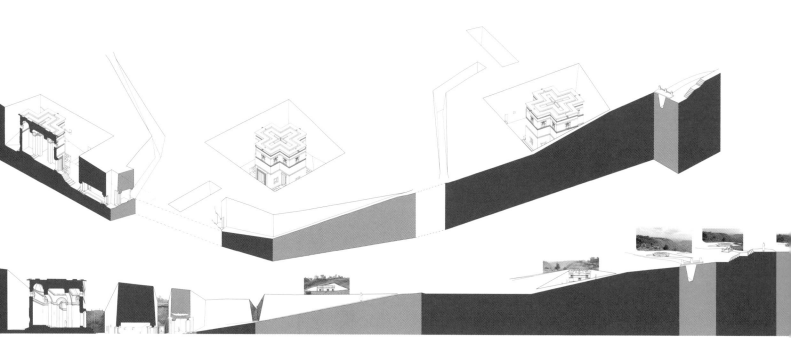

B

Seamless Drawing the Monolithic Churches of Lalibela, Ethiopia

Brook Denison

This project on the Ethiopian churches in the village of Lalibela began—as so many exciting things do—over a meal. On the wall of a stateside Ethiopian restaurant hung a faded tourism poster featuring an exotic church, hewn from the earth, surrounded by worshipers perched on the edge of a sacred pit. Christian since the fourth century, Ethiopian pilgrims gather and worship at the village's twelve churches, which are arranged in four compounds and thought to date to the twelfth and thirteenth centuries. They are composed entirely of deep red tuff, a smooth and seamless deposit of fine volcanic particles without bias or striation. Strikingly, the construction was a process of in situ removal rather than addition; the building is the remaining envelope after the surrounding rock is carved away and removed.

Searching the library, I found several books and articles. Numerous visitors have written about the churches, though none focused explicitly on the architecture. Most include narrative accounts illustrated with photographs. One set of sketches continually reappears in almost all of the publications. They are good, but, as sketches, their scope of investigation is limited to general spatial ideas. I was unable to find measured plans and sections, vital and necessary for beginning to understand a building in detail—which is where my project began.

This project took shape around two distinct desires: the first was to measure and record the plan and section of the church. This information is presented in an objective, straightforward manner with the hope that the building will be more comprehensible to others looking for information about what is there. In so doing, I hope to expose the churches to a wider audience. I can't explain why these unique and excellent buildings have remained at the periphery of architectural history, though the lack of available drawings has surely not encouraged wider exposure.

The second goal was to make a series of interpretative drawings. These drawings attempt to isolate an idea by biasing specific criteria within the drawing's space and presenting it at the expense of neutrality. I hope that by supplying objective orthographics alongside analytical

drawings, I will allow viewers to oscillate between the building's form and its concept.

With joint funding from the Herman Miller company and Jacqueline Nelson, I spent six weeks in Lalibela. Using a Leica Disto A3 laser measurer and sketchbook, I documented each of the twelve churches and their surrounding voids. What I had initially regarded as an exotic (even idiosyncratic) way of building was, in reality, a simple and straightforward expression so pure and consistent that I began to question traditional architecture's assembly of discrete elements. Rather than quarry and transport stones, they simply dug a void in the desired shape, leaving the remaining rock to define the building.

Through their seamlessness, these buildings return architecture—at least in a material sense—back to its most basic elements: void and mass. The buildings have a sense of inevitability. Their materials have been on site for thousands of years, awaiting removal of excess rock to expose what had always been with us. This method of building is one of the more original aspects of the churches. Without straying too far from the topic at hand, the formal origins of the twelve churches are likely rooted in two sources: the Byzantine centralized cross plan, and the hypostyle hall. Additionally, there are a few hybrids which borrow formal organization from both the centralized cross and the hypostyle hall to invent an original type. Saint George's—the subject of this investigation—is a perfect Greek cross of equal length on each of its four sides, with biaxial symmetry about its X and Y axes.

Returning from Ethiopia, I translated my annotated sketches of Saint George's into measured orthographics. In addition to accurately describing the size and shape of the plan and section, these drawings began to reveal—as only measured drawings can—the information I had initially sought. Walls' thicknesses (2 to 3 feet) emerged as I tracked out my measurements. The ceiling's depth—more than 7 feet—was an unexpected surprise (and one for which I have no hypothesis).

The orthographic drawings emphasize a figure/ground relationship unique to these subterranean churches. While most buildings divide the interior from the exterior, these churches have two closely connected rooms: one inside and one out. In St. George's, the interior room is relatively small and used primarily for storing sacred artifacts like the Coptic cross and several Amharic-language Bibles. The second room is outside of the building, formed by the void surrounding the church. It is here that services take place, the priest addressing the congregation from atop the church steps surrounded by parishioners filling the pit's floor, overflowing to the upper edge. I came to think of this space as a conventional church's nave, turned inside out. Open to the sky,

A *Void/Solid* (plan & section)
B *Procession* traces the path one follows to enter the church by unfolding the descending path into continuous segments. Photographs of the view from that segment are collaged into the sectional perspective, attempting to reveal what is difficult to see in images of St. George's central mass: the elegance of the entry as it slowly drops one's eye

below the surface and into the subterranean sacred space. Like Petra (in Jordan) the narrow and deep trench is a focused primer, transporting one from the many distractions of their surroundings into the singular focus of a narrow path before arriving at the climactic end.

it reflects the fact that relatively little happens indoors in Ethiopia.

While I mentioned two architectural sources for the churches' form, no precedent comes to mind for the exterior room surrounding the building. I am reminded of Pompeian houses' internal courtyards, though these hollow rooms maintain privacy and seclusion near the center of the building. Conversely, the Lalibela court-yards happen all around the buildings—which seems quite fitting for a program as public as a church. The surrounding void fascinates me for several reasons other than its originality: it required the majority of the work, comprising a volume exponentially larger (and therefore more laborious) than the interior of the church. How was its size determined? It had to be big enough to expose the subterranean church, but why did they con-tinue to enlarge the size beyond a moatlike form? Was it enlarged merely to provide an appropriate distance from which to view the church? Given the small size of the church itself, it seems reasonable to suggest that the sur-rounding pit was intended as the nave, sized to accom-modate the parish during services.

My time in Lalibela occurred during the rainy season, when the rains fall heavily on a near-daily basis. It is a welcome reprieve from the dry season, and is celebrated enthusiastically for its role in agricultural production and, by extension, human life. The desire to build below the earth's surface invites a series of engineering chal-lenges, the most burdensome being directly linked to the daily rains. Whether the idea for making underground churches was an extension of hydraulic engineering or was simply necessitated in response to the churches' design is unknown, but Lalibela's four compounds are connected by a network of channels and reservoirs that link the churches' surrounding voids. It isn't unreason-able to suggest that a civilization living atop a mountain in a climate with a dry season would seek to develop channels and reservoirs to collect water when it is abundant. And it is possible that this plumbing system inspired the churches, though I cannot prove it. Nev-ertheless, the hydrological considerations range in scale from the vast to the minute and are incorporated into every aspect of the building's design. A network of deep, narrow trenches slices through several mountain ridges hundreds of meters away from the nearest church. These channels quickly fill with water each summer afternoon, diverting flow away from the individual compounds with a moatlike network.

Beyond pragmatics, the channels, drains, and reser-voirs also have symbolic meaning. Liturgy incorporates the plumbing network, offering blessed "holy water" from a font carved into the ground of the outer yard and filled with the slow trickle of an artesian fissure across the courtyard. Each bout of food poisoning I endured (there were many) invited generous offers for sips of holy water from this sacred font. Presuming the roof's geometry was among the first shapes to emerge as construction began, the monolith betrays a chronol-ogy suggesting the high degree of importance plumb-ing systems play in St. George's design. The church's cross-shaped pattern (presumably among the first forms carved from the ground) is composed of connected con-centric rings, channeling water into long spouts reaching

past the plinth's edge before safely delivering runoff to the pit's floor below. Details like this suggest that water was at the forefront of the designer's concerns, even as a majority of excavation work remained. Then again, most suggest that St. George's was the last church to be built, so planning for water runoff could have been a residual lesson from the previous churches.

Another unique aspect of the churches is their low profile. Carved entirely below the ground plane, both the entry sequence and its visibility from afar are com-pletely different from a typical church, whose height and volume broadcast a silhouette which is always visible from surrounding areas and invites visitors with its iconic form and presence. In Lalibela, the subterranean aspect gives the church a humble approach: from a distance, one first spots the void surrounding the cross-shaped church as a dark sliver on the ridge's crest. Near-ing the edge of the pit, the church's outer walls become visible as the path tails to a slight depression. Single-file width at first, it widens as it descends, re-angling halfway down before reaching a series of small, dark rooms punctuated by extreme contrast in available light: bright, dark, bright. A larger room opens to the church's front steps, and one stands in the pit surrounding the church, looking up at the edge from where one stood a minute ago. Down here, the horizon is redefined by the pit's up-per edge, and the surrounding landscape is hidden from view. Like a James Turrell "skyspace," the simplicity of the walls and floor cast a meditative pall and emphasize the framed view of the sky, pulsing with each subtle shift in the atmosphere.

A

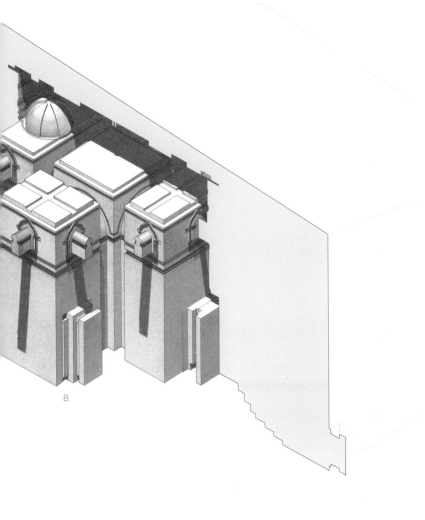

B

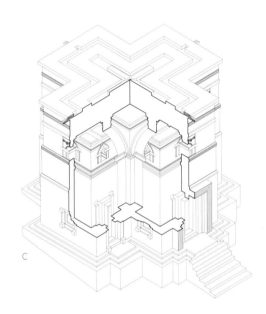

C

D

E

Sir John Soane's Model Room

Helen Dorey

Sir John Soane (1753–1837) was born the son of a bricklayer in Goring-on-Thames, near Reading, England. He began his architectural career at age fifteen, joining the office of George Dance the Younger in the City of London. When he was eighteen, he enrolled at the Royal Academy as an architectural student, attending the evening lectures given by the Professor of Architecture Thomas Sandby, and in the same year starting work for Henry Holland. It was during these years that Soane must have first encountered the antique world, and especially the buildings of ancient Rome that so inspired him in his later work: the Temple of Vesta at Tivoli; the Temple of Castor and Pollux in the Forum, hailed since the Renaissance as the most beautiful example of the Corinthian order in the world; the Pantheon; and the ruins of the Emperor Hadrian's Villa at Tivoli.

In 1776, Soane won the Royal Academy Gold Medal for Architecture, and as a result was awarded a traveling scholarship paid for by King George III. He set off for Italy at 5 A.M. on March 18, 1778, a date he remembered with nostalgia for the rest of his life. After arriving in Rome on May 2, Soane was soon writing to a friend that his attention was entirely taken up in seeing and examining the numerous and inestimable remains of antiquity, and of the "zeal and attachment" he felt for them. He asked his friend to imagine "with what impatience I have waited for the scenes I now enjoy."

Soane's time in Italy was spent visiting antique, Renaissance, and contemporary buildings from Genoa, Vicenza, and Verona in the north to Paestum and Sicily in the south. He often took detailed measurements of monuments by climbing to dizzying heights and dropping a plumb line or using a measuring rod, and he filled many journals with notes and sketches.

Soane returned to London in 1780 and set up his own architectural practice. He married an heiress, Elizabeth Smith, in 1784. Using contacts made in Rome to good effect, he rapidly made a name for himself. In 1788, he

was appointed architect to the Bank of England, a job he later described as the "pride and boast of my life." The Bank was his masterpiece—a miniature city within the City, with fortified walls, triumphal arches, courtyards, and vast top-lit banking halls reminiscent of Roman Baths. Soane remained as the Bank's Architect for forty-five years, only retiring at the age of eighty in 1833. His other masterpieces include Britain's first public art gallery, the Dulwich Picture Gallery; dining rooms at Nos. 10 and 11 Downing Street; work at numerous country houses; and the Soane tomb, one of only two Grade 1 listed tombs in London. Soane had a long association with the Royal Academy of Arts in London, where he was elected Professor of Architecture in 1806, a post he held for thirty-one years. In 1831, he was knighted by King William IV. Despite failing eyesight, Soane continued working until shortly before his death in 1837 at the age of eighty-four.

Soane is regarded as the father of the architectural profession in Britain, and his work still provides inspiration to architects across the world, from Arata Isozaki in Japan to Richard Meier at the Getty Center in Los Angeles to Richard MacCormac at the Ruskin Archive in Leicester. England's famous red telephone box was inspired by Soane's designs.

Sir John Soane's house, museum, and library at No. 13 Lincoln's Inn Fields, London, has been a public museum since the early nineteenth century. Soane moved into the square in the 1790s, when he bought, demolished, and rebuilt No. 12 (1792–94). After his appointment as Professor of Architecture at the Royal Academy, he went on to acquire, demolish, and rebuild No. 13, a larger property, to accommodate his ever-growing collection of architectural antiquities. When he was over seventy, he bought, demolished, and rebuilt No. 14 (1824–25), extending his museum premises across the rear of that house. Throughout the whole period, Soane also made continuous alterations to his "Museum," adding more objects to his arrange-

ments, seeking always to enhance the "poetic effects" and picturesque qualities of the architectural setting and to create didactic displays for the benefit of his students. One of the last of these alterations was his Model Room, created in 1834–35 in what had been his wife's bedroom on the second floor. The room housed imaginative displays in which historic and contemporary architectural models, including depictions of antique buildings in both ruined and reconstructed states, were displayed alongside one another, surrounded by framed drawings of Soane's own works.

In 1833, Soane negotiated an Act of Parliament to settle and preserve his house and collection for the benefit of "amateurs and students" in architecture, painting, and sculpture. The Act stated that the arrangements of objects must be preserved "as nearly as possible" as they were left at the time of his death. The Soane Museum, with its evocative displays, remains one of the world's greatest house museums.

Soane's friend Isaac D'Israeli wrote to him in a letter of 1835, "Your museum is permanently magical, for the enchantments of art are eternal. Some in poems have raised fine architectural edifices, but most rare have been those who have discovered when they had finished their house, if such a house can ever be said to be finished, that they had built a poem."

Soon after Soane's death in 1837 his Model Room was disbanded to make way for curatorial offices. This represented not only the loss of one of Soane's most evocative interiors, but also to some degree diluted the centrality of architecture to Soane's conception of his house and collection. The acquisition and restoration of No. 14 Lincoln's Inn Fields, next door to the Museum, has made it possible to plan the restoration of the Model Room as part of a program of works which, if fundraising is successful, will be completed by 2012 and will see the whole of the second floor, including Soane's Bedroom, Bath Room, Oratory, and Mrs. Soane's Morning Room, restored.

For images of Sir John Soane's model room and models, see pages 26, 92–93, and 170–171.

INSTEAD OF THE GRAND TOUR

Travel Replacements in the Nineteenth Century

Dietrich Neumann

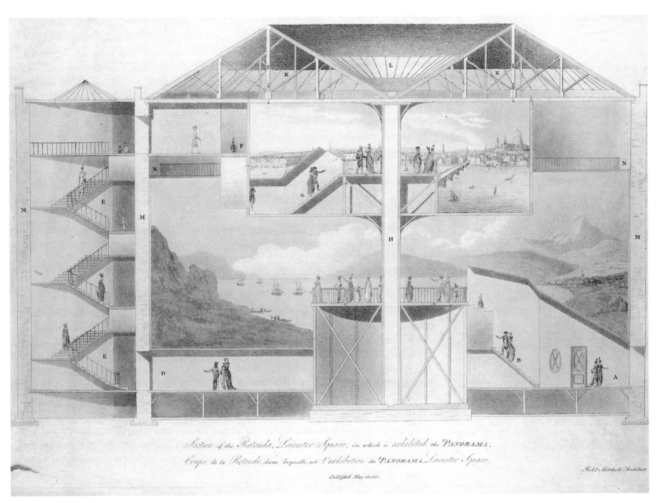

Barker's First Rotunda on Leicester Square where he showed his paintings of London and Spitheard, 1793. © The Trustees of the British Museum.

In his book *Le Paysan de Paris* (1926), French Surrealist Louis Aragon recalled that his friend Paul Valéry once described to him an agency in the old Passage de l'Opera in Paris "which accepted unstamped letters and arranged to have them posted from any desired point of the globe to the address written on the envelope, a facility that would allow the customer to feign a voyage to the Far East, for example, without moving an inch from the far west of some secret adventure."[1]

Perhaps it is no coincidence that the location of the Passage de l'Opera, which in 1925 was about to be demolished to make way for the eastern extension of the Boulevard Haussmann, was only a short walk from the Passage des Panoramas, in which three of the earliest panorama buildings in Paris flourished from 1802 until 1831. The panoramas fulfilled a purpose not unrelated to that of the agency in the Passage de l'Opera: their visitors found themselves temporarily transported to a distant part of the globe without having to leave the safety of Paris, and without spending considerable time or money. When the Passage de l'Opera opened in 1823, the panoramas nearby were showing views of Athens and Constantinople. The German architect Jakob Ignaz Hittorf wrote about the astonishing realism of these views: "Those who were lucky enough to have visited these famous cities believed they had never left them, and those who had not had the pleasure, thought they had been transported there."[2]

After its debut in London in 1793, the idea of the panorama building, a structure with a continuous, 360-degree painting on the inside of a cylindrical room, arrived in Paris with the help of the American inventor Robert Fulton, who later contributed significantly to people's ability to actually, physically, travel with the invention of the steam engine. Fulton had purchased the patent for the panorama building from the British inventor Robert Barker, and he commissioned several panoramas in Paris before selling out to a theater impresario.

The passion for travel that emerged in the nineteenth century was accompanied by the development of elaborate mechanisms for travel replacement at home, and in the process changed architecture's role and potential. Throughout the nineteenth century, countless panorama buildings existed in cities all over the world, in particular in Europe, the United States, and Japan, as perhaps the most significant form of visual mass entertainment and education. While in the first half of the century the subject matter of the giant paintings inside mostly concentrated on the depiction of faraway lands and bird's eye views, in later decades the panoramas' purpose changed to political and religious instruction through the depiction of battle scenes and biblical imagery.[3]

All panorama buildings had a similar spatial configuration. A visitor entered through a dark tunnel and emerged via a spiral staircase in the center of a circular balcony. Beyond this lay a continuous landscape in the round, lit ingeniously from above through skylights shielded from the viewer by a circular roof. Robert Barker coined the term "panorama" (meaning "see everything") for his invention, but it was actually not this quality that most fascinated the visitors. After all, seeing 360 degrees of one's environment was not an unusual experience. What made the encounter with the continuous

Passage de l'Opera, ca. 1920. Period photograph.

View of two panorama buildings in the Passage des Panoramas, 1814 (engraving). Bibliothèque Nationale, Paris.

panoramic painting so crucially different was the sudden, highly convincing passage into another world. As Charles Robert Leslie wrote in 1812, "I actually put on my hat imagining myself to be in the open air."[4] Many of the subjects of early panorama paintings were, in fact, the cities that travelers visited on their Grand Tours: Rome, Naples, Athens, and Constantinople.

Countless contemporary reports took delight in favorably comparing a visit to a panorama to the effort of actually traveling to a faraway destination, thus privileging the experience of artifice over that of reality. An article in *Blackwood's Magazine* in 1824 developed this idea quite succinctly:

> If we have not the waters of the Lake of Geneva, and the bricks and mortar of the little Greek town, tangible by our hands, we have them tangible by the eye—the fullest impression that could be purchased, by our being parched, passported, plundered, starved, and stenched for 1200 miles east and by south, could not be fuller than the work of Messrs. Parker's and Burford's brushes. The scene is absolutely alive, vivid, and true, we feel all but the breeze, and hear all but the dashing of the wave.[5]

A generation later, the critics' enthusiasm had not waned. A London writer noted on December 27, 1861: "There are aspects of soil and climate which…in great panoramas such as those of Mr. Burford, are conveyed to the mind with a completeness and truthfulness not always gained from a visit to the scene itself."[6] And the *Art Journal* agreed that the view to be had of Naples in the panorama in Leicester Square was "even more pleasant to look upon in Leicester Square, than is the reality with all its abominations of tyranny, licentiousness, poverty and dirt."[7]

Apart from views of distant lands, early panoramas often showed bird's eye views of an urban center, produced for and shown in the same city. Visitors delighted in pointing out familiar landmarks to each other and in understanding the expanse and overall form of their city. One of the earliest Parisian panorama buildings in the Jardin des Capucines showed a view of Paris from the Tuileries in 1799, and, in London, Robert Barker showed the city from the roof of the Albion Mills. Such bird's eye views anticipated the view from a tall tower,

Thomas Hosmer Shepherd, *Cranbourne Street Entrance to Burford's Panorama Rotunda in London*, 1858. © The Trustees of the British Museum.

or replaced the view from a hot air balloon, which was a pleasure (and danger) only very few people ever had a chance to experience. The Eiffel Tower in Paris finally fulfilled the role that the bird's eye views had prepared their visitors for, at least in the eyes of Roland Barthes, who observed:

> …architecture is always dream and function, expression of a utopia and instrument of a convenience. Even before the Tower's birth, the nineteenth century (especially in America and in England) had often dreamed of structures whose height would be astonishing, for the century was given to technological feats, and the conquest of the sky once again preyed upon humanity…the bird's eye view, on the contrary, represented by our romantic writers as if they had anticipated both the construction of the tower and the birth of aviation, permits us to transcend sensation and to see things in their structure…What, in fact, is a panorama? An image we attempt to decipher, in which we try to recognize known sites, to identify landmarks…to perceive Paris from above is infallibly to imagine a history; from the top of the tower, the mind finds itself dreaming of the mutation of the landscape which it has before its eyes; through the

Frederick Burnie after Robert Barker, *London from the roof of the Albion Mills*, 1792. Guildhall Library, City of London.

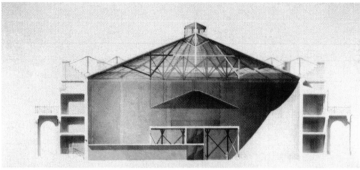

Johann Ignatz Hittorff, Charles Langlois'
Rotunda at the Champs Elysees, ca. 1839,
exterior and cross-section. Wallraff-Richartz
Museum, Köln; View of the dune of Pan-
orama Mesdag, The Hague. © Panorama
Mesdag.

Français in the Rue St. Honoré, and others followed in the Rue René Boulanger, the Rue du Château d'Eau, the Place d'Austerlitz, and the Rue de Berri. At any time during the nineteenth century, a Parisian *flâneur* (and his counterparts in London, Berlin, or New York) would have found several panorama buildings competing for his attention and offering, as it were, so many portals punctuating an imaginary map of the city, leading to worlds whose expansive spaces reached far beyond their buildings' actual size and location.

Contemporary descriptions of panoramas usually emphasized the breathtaking realism and verisimilitude of the large, continuous paintings rather than pointing out the shortcomings of the medium. After all, panoramas offered only a purely visual similarity; they lacked the ability to stimulate any of the other senses. Looking out over Cairo, one did not feel the heat of the Mediterranean sun or the dust-filled desert winds, nor hear the noise of camels trotting by or smell the food vendors at the base of the pyramids. And, of course, nothing in this scenery moved. The light did not change, and animals and humans were frozen in their tracks. But the panorama was still vastly superior to all other forms of imagery from exotic places that reached the interested public, such as black-and-white photography, etchings, and lithographs. Panorama paintings were much larger and they surrounded the viewer with their spatial, almost three-dimensional appearance, enhanced by the realistic middle ground between the viewer and the canvas, which usually provided a transition from three-dimensional objects in the foreground to the two-dimensional surface of the painting.

Few panoramas have survived unchanged to this day. In the United States, the Gettysburg Panorama in Atlanta has been seriously modified in order to cater to the expectations of a post-cinematic audience. Rows of seats are arranged on a turntable in the center of the circular room. The platform slowly rotates around its central axis, accompanied by taped explanations. The cinematic experience has intruded on its predecessor: *ceci tuera cela.* Other surviving nineteenth-century panoramas can be found in Sainte-Anne-du-Beaupré, Quebec; Altötting, Germany; Innsbruck, Austria; Thun and Lucerne, Switzerland; and Prague, Czech Republic.[9] Perhaps the most astonishing is the Mesdag Panorama (1881) in Scheveningen, a suburb of The Hague, Netherlands. Its creator, the then-famous painter of maritime scenes Hendrik Willem Mesdag, decided, contrary to all convention, to depict a spot very close to the actual location of the panorama—the beach at Scheveningen. At first glance, the scene could not replace travel in time or space, as other panoramas promised. But it offered something entirely different, and perhaps more lasting: by showing the view of the city from a spot on the beach that any city dweller could visit, Mesdag made visitors aware of the beauty of this particular place, which was threatened (and ultimately destroyed) by overeager development. At the same time, Mesdag demonstrated the visual and emotional power resulting from the transformation of a real scene into a work of art, suggesting, as the French architectural theorist Quatremère de Quincy remarked about panoramas in 1822, that "the world [seemed] to belong solely to the language of painting."[10]

astonishment of space, it plunges into the mystery of time, lets itself be affected by a kind of spontaneous anamnesis; it is duration itself which becomes panoramic.[8]

Even after the two panoramas in the Passage des Panoramas closed in 1831, an imaginary visitor to the above-mentioned agency would have been able to walk to one of numerous panorama buildings that existed in Paris throughout the nineteenth century. In that same year, the painter Charles Langlois opened a large panorama establishment near the Place de la République, and, after considerable success, commissioned the architect Jakob Ignaz Hittorf to build an even larger panorama at the Champs Élysées in 1839. Its size—40 meters in diameter—soon became the industry standard. Hittorf's structural masterpiece (boasting an early suspension roof) opened with a painting of the 1812 "Fire of Moscow." In 1880, Charles Garnier built his Panorama

Famously, the young Vincent van Gogh visited the Mesdag Panorama in 1881 and found, as he told his brother, that "it is a work that deserves all respect…its only fault is that it has no fault."[11]

Back to our visitor in the Passage de l'Opera, who, in search of a means of travel replacement, could also walk to one of the postcard sellers who, at some point in the nineteenth century, settled in the Passage des Panoramas and its continuation the Passage Jouffroy, and are still there today. There he might acquire a stereoscope and a few stereographs (pairs of black and white photographs that provided a three-dimensional view when seen through the stereoscope) and do what Oliver Wendell Holmes described in the *Atlantic Monthly* in 1859:

> I creep over the vast features of Rameses, on the face of his rockhewn Nubian temple; scale the huge mountain-crystal that calls itself the Pyramid of Cheops. I pace the length of three Titanic stones of the wall of Baalbec, mightiest masses of quarried rock that man has lifted into the air…I stroll through Rhenish vineyards, I sit under Roman arches, I walk the streets of once-buried cities, I look into the chasms of Alpine glaciers, and on the rush of wasteful cataracts. I pass, in a moment, from the banks of the Charles to the ford of the Jordan, and leave my outward frame in the arm-chair at my table, while in spirit I am looking down upon Jerusalem from the Mount of Olives.[12]

Like the panorama, and in striking contrast to the perception of contemporary commentators, the medium of the stereograph creates conditions markedly different from being in a particular location in person. Rosalind Krauss compared the view into the stereoscope with the experience of being in a cinema: "Both involve the isolation of the viewer with an image from which surrounding interference is masked out. In both, the image transports the viewer optically, while his body remains immobile. In both, the pleasure derives from the experience of the simulacrum: the appearance of reality from which any testing of the real-effect by actually, physically, moving through the scene is denied. And, in both the real-effect of the simulacrum is heightened by a temporal dilation."[13]

Film, of course, joined the media of the panorama and diorama shortly before the turn of the century and eventually replaced them entirely. Countless panorama buildings were taken down in the early years of the twentieth century to make room for movie theaters, signaling an astonishing shift in public viewing habits. Despite an abundance of shortcomings, the flickering, black-and-white moving image on a small bright rectangle, usually encountered in a noisy, smoke filled room, itself silent and fleeting, the length of its scenes determined by the director, was immediately more successful than the meticulously painted, colorful panorama that provided complete spatial immersion and could be viewed as long as one's heart desired. Was it the occasional movement of the camera that suggested the possibility of travel to the viewers, was it the potential for narrative that turned this new medium, inferior as it was in many aspects to its predecessor, into the quintessential art form of modernity?

The beginnings of cinema were also to be found in close proximity to the Passage de l'Opera. A short walk led to the basement room of the Grand Café on the Boulevard des Capucines, where, on December 28, 1895, the Lumière brothers showed the world's first projected movie to a paying audience. Their father had seen Thomas Edison's Kinetoscope in 1894 and described it to his sons, who developed a projection apparatus to accompany it. Soon, both Edison and the Lumière brothers were sending licensed cameramen to exotic locations all over the world. Georges Méliès, the great pioneer of fantastic cinema, soon joined in their enormous success. From his office in the Passage de l'Opera, he created films that transported his viewers into a different, magic realm in which the continuity of time and space was never certain.

In 1822, Quatremère de Quincy had already remarked that it was in fact the art of architecture that made the panorama possible. Indeed, architecture was complicit in the miraculous explosion of space that those willing to observe it experienced. The virtual space represented in panoramas far exceeded the limited actual space inside the rotunda. Architecture thus became the most accomplished tool for travel replacement.

Postcard shops in the Passage Jouffrey, ca. 1905. Period photograph.

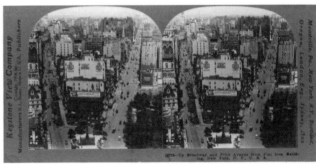

Broadway and Fifth Avenue as seen from the Flatiron Building, ca. 1904. Stereograph, Keystone View Company.

Rue du Caire, Exposition Universelle, Paris, 1889. Period photograph.

Panorama photograph of the Shinjuku business district, Tokyo, 2007. Image courtesy of Dietrich Neumann.

It is no coincidence that during the rise and widespread public success of the panorama, the phenomenon of historicism emerged in Western architecture, only to fade slowly when cinema arrived on the scene. Throughout the nineteenth century, and in particular in its second half, coinciding with an intense revival of panoramic viewing, public and private buildings created fully immersive environments which suggested that the visitor had been transported in time or space.

Neo-Gothic churches offered a medieval environment and a return to the time before Luther and Henry VIII, when Christianity was still, supposedly, peacefully unified. Neo-Renaissance palaces endowed their users and inhabitants with a transformation to the splendors of Italy and wealth and power of the Medici; Ludwig II, king of Bavaria, used the tropical garden with its Oriental architecture in the greenhouse atop the royal palace in Munich as a realm for his escapist dreams.

World's fairs often housed spectacular panoramas but also provided three-dimensional, open-air environments that convincingly transported the viewer into, for example, an "Oriental" street. At the Paris Exposition in 1889, the Rue du Caire, which was admired greatly by contemporary visitors for its realism and exactitude, consisted of buildings that had been demolished in Cairo to make room for a Haussmann-inspired boulevard. Kurt Forster has pointed out how Berlin's city planning under Karl Friedrich Schinkel, Germany's most important nineteenth-century architect and a former panorama painter, shifted toward an emphasis on viewpoints, visual connections, and overviews that suggested meaningful relationships among buildings through space, a predecessor of CinemaScope.[14]

As Louis Aragon makes clear in his description of the Passage de l'Opera, even spaces that were not historicist, but were decidedly utilitarian and free from references to other places or times, could turn into heterotopian spaces worthy of panoramic travel, if they were left alone long enough. The first chapter of *Le Paysan de Paris* of 1926 presents the passage as a place belonging to a different moment in time, bypassed by progress and modernity, an aquarium of relics of a past epoch. Walter Benjamin confessed to his friend Theodor Adorno in 1935 that reading this chapter made such an impression on him that "I could never read more than two or three

pages of this on going to bed, because my heart began beating so fast that I had to put it aside."[15]

The spaces of the panorama and of historicist architecture were soon complemented by the space of the bourgeois interior. It is no coincidence that the fashion for scenic wallpaper depicting continuous exotic landscapes on all four walls of a room began in France at the same moment in the late eighteenth century as the introduction of the panorama.[16] Xavier de Maistre published his famous *Voyage Around My Room* in 1794, just at the time when the panorama was invented, and, like it, provided a potential response to the love of travel. The author, sentenced to forty-two days of home confinement due to his unfortunate role in a duel, described his room in minute detail in the form of a travel journal that took his reader from the door to the armchair to the desk and further on to the bed, frequently interrupted by meditations on subjects such as color or philosophy. It was, de Maistre claimed humorously, "the new mode of traveling I introduce to the world." He pointed out to his readers that his journey had cost him nothing, that any traveler on this road would not need to fear "bleak winds or change of weather," and he assured the "cowards" that "they will be safe from pitfalls or quagmires."[17] The book was such a success that de Maistre published a sequel about a journey in his room at night in 1825.

In the second half of the nineteenth century, the interior assumed an important role in the discourse on travel and the panoramic experience. In his 1935 essay "Paris, the Capital of the Nineteenth Century," Walter Benjamin included short sections on the arcade, the panorama, and the interior. After the revolution, he argued, the role of the interior had changed and had become not unlike that of the panorama: "The private individual, who in the office has to deal with reality, needs the domestic interior to sustain him in his illusions." Benjamin excluded both commercial and social considerations from the interior. "From this arise the phantasmagorias of the interior—which, for the private man, represents the universe. In the interior, he brings together the far away and the long ago. His living room is a box in the theater of the world."[18] Much to Benjamin's chagrin, the young philosopher Dolf Sternberger adopted the concept of the panorama from Benjamin's essay and used it as a metaphor to access the complex social history of the nineteenth century. A long subsection of his 1938 book *Panorama: Views of the Nineteenth Century* treats the interior as a panoramic space, shut off from the world outside. Its screened-off windows and its "horror vacui" that had washed up countless pieces of art, gave access to the "inner Orient" of the inhabitants.[19] Shortly afterward, German philosopher Ernst Bloch picked up the thread of Benjamin and Sternberger's observations when he included an important chapter on the "Distance wish and historicizing room in the nineteenth century" in his seminal work *The Principle of Hope,* written while he was in exile in the United States between 1938 and 1947, and published after his return to Germany in the 1950s. Bloch wrote that the interior changed in the second half of the nineteenth century:

> A bourgeoisie that was becoming rich lay down in the bed of nobility, dreamed there after past styles, old-German, French, Italian, Oriental, pure souvenir. A constantly astonishing desire emerged to transform even No-Being into Appearing, to have their everyday apartment sailing under different colors. Travel substitute, indeed outdoing travel between their own four walls became the password, partly a historical, partly an exotic one.[20]

It is with a certain disappointment that Bloch notes how modern architecture has apparently relinquished its power to provide transfer to different lands, moods, and our "inner Orient." Instead of offering a travel replacement, "these days houses in many places look as if they are ready to leave. Although they are unadorned or for this very reason, they express departure. On the inside they are bright and bare like sick rooms, on the outside they seem like boxes on movable rods, but also like ships."[21]

Ceci tuera cela

The panorama existed as a prominent popular art form for roughly one hundred years before it was replaced by the cinema, which, through the novelty of movement, crosscutting, and close-ups offered a faster and more appealing version of travel replacement. At the same time, architecture, the extension of the panorama, gave up on its power to convincingly transport its inhabitants into other worlds. Now, one hundred years after the invention of film, the institution of cinema is challenged by a new proliferation of moving imagery, and by a profound redefinition of the medium of film through digital technology.

Today, films can easily be made and distributed by anyone, thanks to cheap video cameras and editing software. The experience of viewing moving imagery has long left the darkened cinema and has conquered the urban environment and created new fully immersive illusionary environments. The availability of bright LED lights has brought about urban screens which are no longer dependent on darkness. Critics have begun to ask about the impact of the urban screen on the experience of the city. "After the age of architecture-sculpture we are now in the time of cinematographic factitiousness… From now on architecture is only a movie…The city is no longer a theater (agora, forum) but the cinema of city lights," Paul Virilio wrote in 1991.[22] *Boston Globe* architecture critic Robert Campbell echoed his concerns

in 2006: "Now, the entire facade of a building, from sidewalk to roof, may be a digital screen that flashes ever-changing images. Is it a billboard? Is it architecture? Is it art? Who can say? Is this the world we're headed for? Will we even know anymore when we're in the real world and when we're in a media simulation? Will that cease to be a meaningful distinction?"[23]

Can it be a coincidence that just at this important moment, the old panoramic technique is being rediscovered? In Dresden and Leipzig, former gas tanks now house very successful new painted panoramas of Baroque Dresden and Ancient Rome.[24] At the same time, 360-degree digital panoramic photography has become highly popular and is fundamentally changing the way we record and teach buildings and their urban context. And architecture itself, accepting some help from new technologies, is rediscovering its ability to move, transport, and transform us.

1   Louis Aragon, *Paris Peasant* (Boston: Exact Change, 1994), 21. The first chapter of *Le Paysan de Paris,* from which this quote comes, was entitled "The Passage de l'Opera" and had appeared in four installments between June and September 1924 in the *Revue Européenne.*
2   Bernard Comment, *Das Panorama* (Berlin: Nicolai, 2000), 46.
3   For more information on panoramas see: Ralph Hyde, ed., *Panoramania!: The Art and Entertainment of the "All-Embracing" View* (London: Barbican Art Gallery, 1988); *Sehsucht: Das Panorama als Massenunterhaltung des 19. Jahrhunderts* (Bonn: Kunst- und Ausstellungshalle der Bundesrepublik Deutschland, 1993); Yvonne van Eekelen, ed., *The Magical Panorama* (The Hague: B. V. Panorama Mesdag / Waanders Publishers, 1996); Bernard Comment, *The Panorama* (London: Reaktion, 1999); Ton Rombout, ed., *The Panorama Phenomenon* (The Hague: B. V. Panorama Mesdag, 2006).
4   C. R. Leslie to Thomas J. Leslie (February 2, 1812), as quoted Hyde, *Panoramania!,* 28.
5   *Blackwood's Edinburgh Magazine* 15 (1824): 472–73, as quoted in Hyde, *Panoramania!,* 38.
6   *London Times* (December, 1861), as quoted in Hyde, *Panoramania!,* 38.
7   *Art Journal* 7 (1861), 319; as quoted in Hyde, *Panoramania!,* 38.
8   Roland Barthes, *The Eiffel Tower and Other Mythologies* (New York: Hill and Wang, 1979), 3–17.
9   For a list of existing panoramas see Rombout, ed., *The Panorama Phenomenon.*
10 Quatremère de Quincy, "Panorama," in *Dictionnaire historique d'architecture* (Paris: Librairie d'Adrien le Clere, 1832), as quoted in Odile Nouvel-Kammerer, ed., *French Scenic Wallpaper 1795–1865* (Paris: Musée des Arts Décoratifs, 1990), 168, 327.
11 Vincent van Gogh to Theo van Gogh, August/September 1881, http://webexhibits.org/vangogh/letter/10/149.htm. Regarding the Mesdag Panorama, see van Eekelen, ed., *The Magical Panorama.*
12 Oliver Wendell Holmes, "The Stereoscope and the Stereograph," *Atlantic Monthly* 3 (June 1859): 738–48.
13 Rosalind Krauss, "Photography's Discursive Spaces," in Richard Bolton, ed., *The Contest of Meaning: Critical Histories of Photography* (Cambridge, Mass.: MIT Press, 1989), 287–301; originally published in *Art Journal* 42 (Winter 1982).

14 Kurt W. Forster, "Schinkel's Panoramic Planning of Central Berlin," *Modulus* 16 (1983): 65ff.
15 Walter Benjamin to Theodor W. Adorno, May 31, 1931, in *Walter Benjamin: Selected Writings,* vol. 3 (Cambridge, Mass.: Harvard University Press, 2002), 51–53.
16 See Nouvel-Kammerer, *French Scenic Wallpaper 1795–1865.* Sandy Isenstadt has recently pointed out that this fashion saw a surprising revival with the advent of photomurals for interior decoration in the 1930s. See Sandy Isenstadt, *The Modern American House* (New York: Cambridge University Press, 2006), 230ff. See in particular the quoted essay, "Fantastic Screens become a Panorama of Travel," *Arts and Decoration* 46, no. 4 (June 1937): 18.
17 Xavier de Maistre, *Journey round my room* (1795; reprint, New York: Hurd and Houghton, 1871).
18 Walter Benjamin, "Paris, the Capital of the Nineteenth Century," in *Reflections: Essays, Aphorisms, Autobiographical Writings* (New York: Schocken Books, 1986), 154.
19 Dolf Sternberger, *Panorama oder Ansichten vom 19. Jahrhundert* (1938, reprint; Frankfurt: Suhrkamp Verlag, 1974), 166.
20 Ernst Bloch, *The Principle of Hope* (Cambridge, Mass.: MIT Press, 1986), 378.
21 Ibid., 733.
22 Paul Virilio, *Aesthetics of Disappearance* (New York: Semiotext(e), 1991), 65.
23 Robert Campbell, "WGBH Looks to Wrap New Headquarters in Digital Skin," *Boston Globe* (February 1, 2006).
24 See the work of the contemporary panorama painter Yadegar Asisi at http://www.asisi-factory.de/.

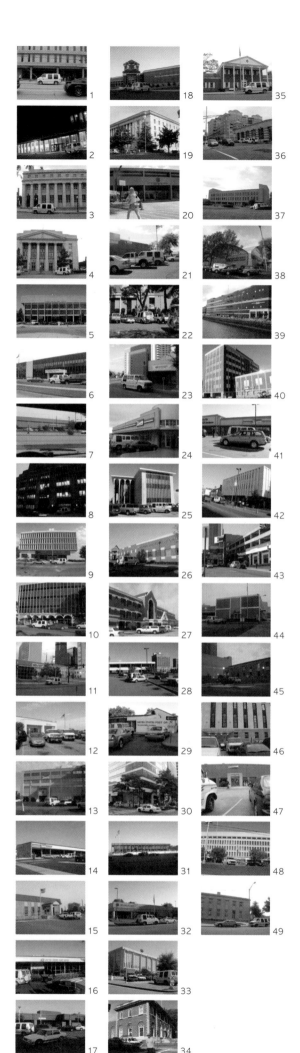

49 POST OFFICES

1   Indianapolis, IN (8/7/2006)
2   Springfield, IL (8/8)
3   Jefferson City, MO (8/10)
4   Topeka, KS (8/12)
5   Lincoln, NE (8/14)
6   Des Moines, IA (8/16)
7   Madison, WI (8/18)
8   St. Paul, MN (8/19)
9   Bismark, ND (8/21)
10 Pierre, SD (8/22)
11 Denver, CO (8/24)
12 Cheyenne, WY (8/25)
13 Salt Lake City, UT (8/26)
14 Boise, ID (8/28)
15 Helena, MT (8/30)
16 Olympia, WA (8/31)
17 Salem, OR (9/1)
18 Carson City, NV (9/5)
19 Sacramento, CA (9/6)
20 Honolulu, HI (9/6)
21 Phoenix, AZ (9/12)
22 Santa Fe, NM (9/14)
23 Oklahoma City, OK (9/14)
24 Austin, TX (9/18)
25 Baton Rouge, LA (9/19)
26 Little Rock, AR (9/21)
27 Jackson, MS (9/22)
28 Montgomery, AL (9/25)
29 Talahassee, FL (9/25)
30 Atlanta, GA (9/27)
31 Columbia, SC (9/28)
32 Raleigh, NC (9/30)
33 Richmond, VA (10/02)
34 Annapolis, MD (10/03)
35 Dover, DE (10/06)
36 Trenton, NJ (10/06)
37 Hartford, CT (10/10)
38 Providence, RI (10/11)
39 Boston, MA (10/12)
40 Augusta, ME (10/13)
41 Concord, NH (10/14)
42 Montpelier, VT (10/16)
43 Albany, NY (10/16)
44 Harrisburg, PA (10/17)
45 Charleston, WV (10/18)
46 Nashville, TN (10/19)
47 Frankfort, KY (10/20)
48 Columbus, OH (10/21)
49 Lansing, MI (10/23)

From:
Ramak Fazel
4201 N.Brooklawn Dr.
Ft. Wayne, IN. 46815.

7005 1450 0000 0242 4052

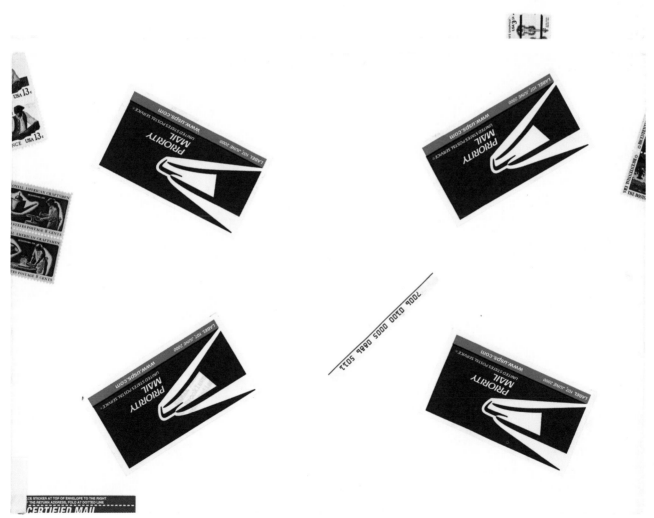

7006 0100 0000 0880 5011

RAMAK FAZEL
4201 BROOKLAWN DR.
FT. WAYNE, IN. 46815

RAMAK FAZEL
C/O GENERAL DELIVERY
AUGUSTA, ME
04330

INTERVIEW WITH RAMAK FAZEL

49 STATE CAPITOLS

Introduction: A Relationship with a Country through a Stamp Collection

In 1976, when I was eleven, my family brought me to the city of Fort Wayne, Indiana, in the United States of America, directly from Tehran, Iran. School proved easy but my free time options were limited by the fact that I didn't play football or baseball, and my father didn't hunt or fish. Having spent six years in Iran, I was more interested in math than girls. A family friend gave me a clutch of old stamps, and like millions of adolescents I was on my way to becoming a "stamp collector." Those were heady times for philatelic exploits in the U.S.: the 1976 bicentennial issues had stoked interest in the sleepy hobby, and the numerous USPS commemoratives served as a primer in American history. The subjects featured on the commemorative stamps seemed to buttress perfectly what we were being taught in grade school. Only later, as an adult, did I realize that the America I was learning about in school was in fact the narrow view of America commemorated through postage stamps.

The highlight of my stint as a collector came in 1979, when I convinced my father to drive me 550 miles to Washington, D.C., where I enthusiastically acquired stamps directly at the philatelic window of the main post office. The thrill of purchasing sheets of postage stamps at face value was heightened by the idea that my investment was bound to appreciate. (The lure of stamp collecting was in great part based on the idea of stamps as an investment vehicle!)

During those years, my family frequently exchanged letters with my grandparents in Tehran, and the postman's daily arrival was an especially exciting moment for my mother. In 1979, mail service was interrupted by the Islamic Revolution, and the costly and unreliable telephone link became our only connection to the family we had left behind. The following year, in 1980, I received my driver's license, and my relationship with stamp collecting came to an abrupt halt. All those stamps remained in my mother's house in Indiana until I rediscovered them in early 2006. My decision to release them as part of this project and use them for their intended purpose—mailing letters—allowed me to continue my education into the real meaning of America, the meaning that I could only discover by visiting all fifty states, the meaning that no commemorative issue has ever captured.—RF

P41

Your philatelically inspired road trip took you to all of the continental state capitals and the largest post office in each state. Can you describe the mechanics of the trip?

RF

I started in Indianapolis, Indiana. Before I left, I mapped out the shortest distance between the state capitals traveling only on interstate highways. That was the route I followed. In each city, I made a postcard using stamps from my collection and mailed it to myself in the next city care of General Delivery. When I arrived in a city, I went to the main post office to see if my postcard had arrived. Sometimes it had arrived and sometimes it hadn't—sometimes it took two or three days to arrive. But regardless, I made the next mailing and I waited. Once I picked up my postcard, I was free to go. I went to the capitol building, took the pictures, and drove on to the next town.

Sometimes I really had only fifteen minutes in a capital city. My postcard had arrived, I mailed the next one, and I needed to move on. So I'd go to the capitol building, do a quick tour, and then I'd leave. It was all about getting down and dirty and doing it quickly. I wanted to minimize my time. I didn't want to waste time. I didn't want to get sidetracked, even when there were other things to see. I only traveled on interstates; there were no winding side roads or scenic excursions. I never saw the Pacific Ocean, for example.

It was all business.

Exactly. In St. Louis, I was driving across the Mississippi River and there was the Gateway Arch. I hadn't been to St. Louis in years, I had friends there, and I would have liked to stop. But the best I could do was to take a couple of pictures with my digital camera as I drove by the arch.

You clearly had the logistics of your trip nailed down. Was there anything about being on the road that came as a surprise?

I hadn't planned on sleeping in Wal-Mart parking lots. I was driving and sleeping in an old conversion van and needed a place to park at night. I quickly realized that Wal-Mart was a safe haven, a place where I knew I would be secure as compared to public streets.

Really, they didn't bother you? Parking overnight in commercial areas seems to be such a taboo.

Not at all, Wal-Mart actually provides incentives for people to camp there. They want people spending the night because they shop, they become clients, and it shows goodwill to the public. So Wal-Marts were a kind of

For additional images of Ramak Fazel's postcards, see pages 176–179.

surprise. As soon as I'd get to the next parking lot I'd tell the security guard, "Hey, I'm sleeping in that white van over there," and they'd appreciate that. They'd keep an eye out for me.

Wal-Mart parking lots are one of the many American building typologies you encountered on your trip. The others are equally iconic types: state capitol buildings, state capital cities, and, of course, post offices. Let's start with the state capitals as cities. After all, what *is* a state capital? It's not the center of commerce, or culture, or anything, really, besides sometimes being the geographic center of a state.

Toward the end of the trip, I came to this realization. This may be a generalization, but in my mind I divided the capitals into two types of cities: the big capital cities and the little capital cities. The big capitals are cities like Boston, Massachusetts; Austin, Texas; Sacramento, California; Denver, Colorado; and Atlanta, Georgia. In those cities, the state had to compete with private interests in divvying up the land. In the small capitals, like Frankfort, Kentucky; Augusta, Maine; Montpelier, Vermont; and Jefferson City, Missouri, the state was the only game in town. In Pierre, South Dakota, they don't even have a bookstore. I was getting a haircut in a small strip mall, and I asked the woman cutting my hair about the local scene. She said, "Let's hope the state doesn't go out of business." Government jobs are just about the only opportunity that local people have for work in those cities. In Frankfort, Kentucky, I stumbled upon an Iranian restaurant. I went to have a meal, and the proprietor told me that things used to be much more active before the state opened a giant cafeteria. So by opening a giant cafeteria, the people working for the state agencies didn't have the incentive to go out anymore, to go eat on the street.

The small capitals sound like company towns for the government.

Right.

Let's talk about the capitol buildings. These buildings are all rather triumphant neoclassical structures which seem out of place in most American cities. On top of that, they're forced to accommodate lots of really prosaic, day-to-day stuff like someone's computer monitor, or someone's nine-to-five job. It seems that many of your photographs understand this and are not treating the capitols as noble stone edifices.

I was interested in intimate things that were happening. Little intimate moments with the backdrop of the capitol. I felt that the capitol buildings were theatrical backdrops to the real stuff that was going on, and could be anywhere. Because what's happening in those offices could be the same thing that's happening in any state office.

The period during which I visited these capitols, which was the beginning of August to the end of October, corresponded to the summer recess. So a lot of the function of government wasn't taking place. The places were really empty. The were almost haunted. And that was somehow favorable. It allowed me to work with these empty spaces with occasional things that happened.

Your pictures are not disrespectful, and they're not ironic, but they're certainly not celebratory either. How would you describe their tone?

When I first started on the trip, I wasn't thinking about the capitol building, I was thinking about all the things that might identify the capital city. So my first capital city was Indianapolis. I went to the Indy 500 track. I spent a whole day photographing the Indiana State Fair. Then on my way out of town, I stopped and visited a friend of mine who's a lawyer downtown, and who used to be a clerk to a state supreme court judge. His office is around the corner from the capitol building. And he said, "Ramak, why don't we go down to the capitol building, I'll show you around." We walked down there, I took a few pictures, and then I went on my way to Springfield, Illinois. When I got to Springfield, I went to the Lincoln tomb, I went to Lincoln's house, I went to the Lincoln presidential library. Then, as an afterthought, I went to the state capitol building and took a couple of pictures there. Then in the third city, Jefferson City, Missouri, the only thing going on was the capitol. I thought, wait a minute, I'm not going to find anything here. The only thing was this massive capitol complex in front of me, and around it just barren wasteland. And the same thing repeated itself in the fourth city, Topeka, Kansas. So that's when I really turned my attention to the capitol buildings.

As the capitol buildings became an organizing element of your trip, what did you notice about them as a building type?

I was struck by the over-restoration that was going on. If you had visited these buildings in the 1960s, you would have found something really fascinating. You would have seen double floors, retrofitted mezzanines, partition walls, and dropped ceilings. Today, all of that has been stripped out. The buildings have all been meticulously over-restored to their original state. So you don't see any of the layers of history.

The capitols, at least in the way you often photograph them, seem to be set apart from downtown, as if they are on a promontory. Is that true?

The capitols tend to have a lot of grounds around them. And I tried to photograph them in such a way that the architecture was prominent. The cupola was distinct. So that required stepping back from them, to see them from a distance.

But "prominent" isn't exactly the right word. The cupola is there as a repetitive element, but it's not the feature of the photograph. Especially with the way you used the flash. Often the focus is a car.

I didn't even realize how much the car kept coming up. It's hard to get away from the car, it really is. Friends of mine in Italy tell me, there's a saying in Italian, "Donne e motori." *Donne* is women, *motori* refers to everything with a motor. Automobile, motorcycle…those are the main areas of interest of Italian men.

Looking through all forty-nine post offices and capitol buildings, there is much more variation in the post office buildings than in the capitols. While the regional flair of the capitol might be a photograph of Maria Shriver and Arnold Schwarzenegger on the wall in California, or a lei around someone's neck in Hawaii, the architecture of the post office buildings varies from Quonset huts to the bases of skyscrapers.

That's true, in fact that's a good observation. The most impressive post offices, in my opinion, were the ones built immediately after the war. That was an era of civic pride and interest in modern architecture. Many of these post offices had elaborate lobbies with very high ceilings and long banks of counters. In the more recent post offices the architecture was far less distinguished. The post office in Concord, New Hampshire, was located in a strip mall. The main post office was in a really nondescript space between a Dollar General and an Ace Hardware.

Can you talk about the Postal Service and the role it played in your trip?

I had decided in the beginning to mail everything either with first class or with Priority Mail. I wanted to mail it with Priority because that required more postage. I wanted to use as many stamps as possible, but I didn't want to use more postage than was necessary. Even though on a couple of occasions I used a couple of cents more, because I couldn't round it off exactly. I used certified mail because that's proof that you mailed it. If you don't have the certified slip on it, you could go to the post office and just have them stamp it and not really put it in the postal system. Postal employees will do that for you, if you ask them.

That's another thing I realized. The postal employees are open to doing favors. Especially when they see that you're doing something philatelic, they get soft. Many of the older ones remembered some of those stamps. "Oh! I remember that one! Joanne, come take a look at this!" The postal employees were amazing. In Providence, Rhode Island, the clerk asked me if he could photocopy the postcard. The stamp I had used was a stamp that commemorated the post office in Providence, which was the first automated post office.

Your trip is based on the notion that it is valuable to travel around your home turf to better understand it, rather than seek out the exotic. There is an infallible grade-school straightforwardness about that.

The stamps were wonderful. I really felt like an adolescent again. The topics commemorated by stamps are very simple things. But they buttress perfectly what I was studying in grade school and what I remember of American history, which is all very superficial stuff.

It's as if you let your stamps drag you around the country, and you were just along for the ride. As architects we are a little envious of photographers. There are so many places that we want to go, but unless a trip is part of a project, there is a limit to what an architect can do while traveling. Maybe take some pictures, or make a sketch. As a photographer, you always have something to do: make a picture. Do you think you would have done this if it weren't for the pictures of the capitols?

That's a good question. Really, this trip, for me, would have been impossible if it weren't for the stamps. Because that gave me an excuse, almost, to stay away for three months. I had something to do, it was a ritual. I needed those kind of fixed things. I didn't have the company of anybody else.

To us your trip was more like *Walden* than *On the Road.* It was a solitary exercise, where you had your space and you had the parameters of your world really well defined. Is that right?

That's a nice analogy. It was more *Walden.* Even my finances, I was very careful about what I was spending, what I was eating. I would see things that I wanted to do but then I would realize that they were a little bit off the path. The constraints that I included in the project by design were compounded by the constraints imposed externally. While my scope didn't change, the postcard compositions and photographs of the capitols gradually started reflecting the shifting and, at times, deteriorating conditions under which I was working. Towards the end of the trip, I felt prepared for anything, and that's when I started feeling I was on the right track.

29   36   43

30   37   44

31   38   45

32   39   46

33   40   47

34   41   48

35   42   49

49 STATE CAPITOLS

1   Indianapolis, IN (8/7/2006)
2   Springfield, IL (8/8)
3   Jefferson City, MO (8/10)
4   Topeka, KS (8/12)
5   Lincoln, NE (8/14)
6   Des Moines, IA (8/16)
7   Madison, WI (8/18)
8   St. Paul, MN (8/19)
9   Bismark, ND (8/21)
10   Pierre, SD (8/22)
11   Denver, CO (8/24)
12   Cheyenne, WY (8/25)
13   Salt Lake City, UT (8/26)
14   Boise, ID (8/28)
15   Helena, MT (8/30)
16   Olympia, WA (8/31)
17   Salem, OR (9/1)
18   Carson City, NV (9/5)
19   Sacramento, CA (9/6)
20   Honolulu, HI (9/6)
21   Phoenix, AZ (9/12)
22   Santa Fe, NM (9/14)
23   Oklahoma City, OK (9/14)
24   Austin, TX (9/18)
25   Baton Rouge, LA (9/19)
26   Little Rock, AR (9/21)
27   Jackson, MS (9/22)
28   Montgomery, AL (9/25)
29   Talahassee, FL (9/25)
30   Atlanta, GA (9/27)
31   Columbia, SC (9/28)
32   Raleigh, NC (9/30)
33   Richmond, VA (10/02)
34   Annapolis, MD (10/03)
35   Dover, DE (10/06)
36   Trenton, NJ (10/06)
37   Hartford, CT (10/10)
38   Providence, RI (10/11)
39   Boston, MA (10/12)
40   Augusta, ME (10/13)
41   Concord, NH (10/14)
42   Montpelier, VT (10/16)
43   Albany, NY (10/16)
44   Harrisburg, PA (10/17)
45   Charleston, WV (10/18)
46   Nashville, TN (10/19)
47   Frankfort, KY (10/20)
48   Columbus, OH (10/21)
49   Lansing, MI (10/23)

Bowles's European Geographical Amusement, or Game of Geography; designed from the Grand Tour of Europe, by Dr. Nugent, 1795. Courtesy the James Marshall and Marie-Louise Osborn Collection, Beinecke Rare Book and Manuscript Library, Yale University.

This board game, one of several published by Carington Bowles, was designed to "introduce young Ladies and Gentlemen, by way of amusement, into the knowledge of geography." Each player, represented by a pillar, made their way across Europe on a route that mimicked the original Grand Tour. The first to arrive back in London was deemed "the best instructed and speediest traveller in Europe."

The tourists crossed the English Channel to Calais; proceeded through France, Spain, and Portugal en route to Italy; passed from Rome ("once mistress of the World, but now only capital of the Pope's dominions") to Greece and Turkey; continued through eastern Europe as far north as Russia and Norway; and made their way back to England via Germany, Holland, and Flanders. Along the way, they were imprisoned by the Inquisition in Madrid, drank claret in Bordeaux, learned Italian in Siena, and marveled at cabinets of curiosity in Dresden. A stop in Rotterdam was to be avoided: on landing there, the traveler was forced to return to Naples, "least his morals be corrupted by the smugglers of [that] place."

The game's tongue-in-cheek tone suggests the extent to which the Grand Tour permeated popular culture at the end of the eighteenth century. What was once an elite cultural experience had become an institutionalized itinerary so familiar to most Britons that it was ripe for caricature.

BOWLES's
EUROPEAN GEOGRAPHICAL
AMUSEMENT,
OR
GAME of GEOGRAPHY:

designed from the

GRAND TOUR of EUROPE.

By D: NUGENT.

Printed for the Proprietors BOWLES & CARVER.

N°. 69, S'. Pauls Church Yard.

LONDON.

DIRECTIONS for PLAYING.

Two or more Ladies or Gentlemen having agreed to make an excursion, or instructive tour of Europe, are to repeat the following Rules; and play the Game according to the following Rules.

Take the Totum and mark it on the sides from 1 to 8.

Every Traveller is to have one Pillar, and four Counters of the same colour.

Each Person is to spin the Totum once, observing who has the highest number; to him belongs the first spin. Begin to play by spinning the Totum; if it turns up 4, place your Pillar on that number, Oct. 6...

Where you are directed to stay one or more turns, lay down your Counters, as memorandums thereof, taking up one of them again every time you omit spinning, till they are all got back, and then spin again in your turn.

When you arrive at a button occupied by another, you are obliged to exchange places with him, and send him back to the place you came from...

Cuered at Stationers Hall.

---

1. CALAIS, the key of France, laid by the bigoted French.
2. ROUEN, capital of Normandy, where the famous Maid of Orleans was burnt in 1430.
3. PARIS, capital of France; *stay 2 turns to contemplate the Palace of the Tuilleries, the Louvre, Palais of Versailles, &c.*
4. ORLEANS, capital of the Orleanois; here the traveller will be shewn a brazen statue of the famous Maid of Orleans.
5. BLOIS, a pleasant town upon the Loire.
6. RENNES, the capital of Britany, in war time *stay two turns to fortify the town.*
7. ST. MALO, a sea-port town of Britany, famous for its privateers.
8. BREST, the principal sea-port of France; *stay one turn to view the fortifications and navy.*
9. NANTES, a sea-port town of Britany, famous for its brandy trade, and the edict of Henry IV. &c.
10. BOURDEAUX, capital of Guienne, where the traveller *stay one turn to regale himself with claret.*
11. BAYONNE, a sea-port town in Gascony, famous for its hams.
12. MARSAC, the capital of Old Castile.
13. MADRID, capital of Spain; *here you must contemplate the cabinet of curiosities, called King's Palace.*
14. GIBRALTAR, a strong fortified town in Spain, *before your arrival at this garrison, you are desired to view the fate of Charles XII. of Sweden, killed here, &c.*
15. SALAMANCA, a town in Spain, famous for its university.
16. OPORTO, a sea-port town in Portugal, noted for its wine trade.
17. LISBON, capital of Portugal; *here you are to talk with the inhabitants on the earthquake in 1755.*
18. SEVILLE, capital of Andalusia, noted for its commerce.
19. GRANADA, the capital of a province of that name.
20. CARTHAGENA, a sea-port town in Spain, famous for its wine trade.
21. MALAGA, a sea-port town in Spain, famous for its wine trade.
22. MINORCA, an island in the Mediterranean, famous for its excellent harbours, and fine honey.
23. MAJORCA, an island of the Mediterranean, subject to Spain.
24. NARBONNE, a city in Languedoc, *stay one turn to talk with the famous Fontaine.*
25. MONTPELLIER, a town of Languedoc.
26. MARSEILLES, a sea-port town of Provence, and one of the French trade to the Levant.
27. AIX, capital of Provence, famous for the mineral springs.
28. TOULON, a sea-port town of Provence; *stay two turns to view the famous harbour, &c.*
29. AVIGNON, a city in Provence, subject to the Pope.
30. DIJON, the capital of Burgundy, famous for its excellent wines.
31. BASIL, a town in Switzerland; *stay two turns to view the hospital, &c.*
32. GENEVA, the birth place and residence of the learned John Calvin.
33. TURIN, capital of the kingdom of Sardinia; *stay two turns to view the court, and country.*
34. MILAN, capital of the duchy of that name; famous for the church and library of St. Ambrose.
35. MANTUA, capital of the duchy of that name; *stay one turn to contemplate the birth-place of the celebrated poet Virgil.*
36. VENICE, capital of the republic of that name; *stay one turn to contemplate the famous carnival.*
37. FERRARA, a flourishing city, but greatly on the decline, formerly famous for their good wines.
38. FLORENCE, capital of Tuscany, one of the most beautiful, best built, and cleanest towns in Italy.
39. PADUA, capital of the duchy of that name, famed for the good wines.
40. ROME, the capital of the ecclesiastical state, and residence of the Pope.
41. NAPLES, capital of the kingdom of that name; famous for its good wines, &c.
42. GENOA, capital of the republic of the grand duchdom of Tuscany.
43. LEGHORN, a sea-port town in the Mediterranean, celebrated for an extensive commerce.
44. CORSICA, an island in the Mediterranean, subject to France; here sung Buonaparte.
45. SIENNA, a town in Tuscany; *stay two turns and here he spends three hours.*
46. VITERBO, a handsome town in the pope's territories, remarkable for the beauty of the women.
47. ROME... *stay one turn, and repeat all the dignitaries of the grand duke.*
48. ...

49. NAPLES, capital of the kingdom of that name, beware of the Lava of mount Vesuvius.
50. SCYLLA, a famous rock on the Calabrian shore, beware the traveller being shipwrecked, lose the chance of the game.
51. MESSINA, a sea-port town in Sicily, lately destroyed by an earthquake.
52. PALERMO, capital of the island of Sicily; on your way to Syracuse, for the famous volcano, mount Ætna.
53. SYRACUSE, a very ancient town, and once a flourishing state in Sicily; if it turns up 4, place your Pillar on that number, Oct. 6, and travel on to 10, Rochfort.
54. MALTA, a famous island, residence of the grand master of the knights of St. John of Jerusalem.
55. ATHENS, a town in Greece; *stay two turns to view the antiquities of this once celebrated seat of learning.*
56. CONSTANTINOPLE, the capital of the Turkish empire, and residence of the grand Seignior; *stay one turn to pay a visit to the English consul.*
57. BELGRADE, a town in Servia, subject to the Turks.
58. BUDA, capital of lower Hungary.
59. PRESBURG, capital of Hungary.
60. VIENNA, capital of Austria and residence of the emperor.
61. MUNICH, capital of Bavaria.
62. AUGSBURG, an imperial city in Swabia; *the protestant princes professed their confession of faith in 1530.*
63. NUREMBERG, an imperial city in Franconia; *stay one turn to see the regalia of the empire.*
64. PRAGUE, capital of Bohemia; *stay one turn to see the cathedral and fine bridge.*
65. CRACOW, capital of Silesia.
66. WARSAW, capital of Poland; *here the traveller must stay two turns and go back to Cadiz, 19, on account of the Pole, calling to the Turks, and perfecting the Diffidents.*
67. DANTZICK, a sea-port town of great trade in Poland.
68. KONIGSBERG, capital of the kingdom of Prussia.
69. STOCKHOLM, capital of Sweden.
70. FREDRICKSHAL, a town in Norway; *stay one turn to attend the fate of Charles XII. of Sweden, killed here.*
71. MOSCOW, second city in Russia.
72. ST. PETERSBURG, capital of Russia; *stay one turn to visit this city, founded by Peter the Great.*
73. ARCHANGEL, a sea-port town of Russia, on the White Sea.
74. ...

75. TORNEA, a town in Swedish Lapland, where the French Mathematicians measured a degree of the Arctic circle.
76. BERLIN, capital of the king of Prussia's German dominions.
77. DRESDEN, capital of the electorate of Saxony; *see the curiosities, cabinet of antiquities, called Kunst Kammer.*
78. LEIPSIC, a town in Saxony, famous for its annual fairs; *stay one turn to view the field of battle where...*
79. BERGEN, capital of the province of the same in Norway; *this being a Portuante number, the traveller will be removed to Bristol, 99.*
80. OSNABRICK, capital of a bishopric in Westphalia; *stay one turn to view the palace of his Royal Highness the Duke of York.*
81. HANOVER, capital of the electorate of that name.
82. FRANCFORT, an imperial city on the river Maine.
83. MENTZ, capital of the electorate of that name.
84. DUSSELDORF, a town in which is the electoral Palatine.
85. AMSTERDAM, capital of Holland; *stay three turns to view the curiosities of this great city, and return.*
86. STRELITZ; *stay two turns to view the duke's fine palace and gardens.*
87. ...
88. HAMBURG, an imperial city, famous for its extensive commerce.

91. ROTTERDAM, the second city in Holland; *the traveller must go back to Naples, 50, lost his morals here.*
92. MERTZ, capital of the electorate of that name, and bishopric of John Guttenberg, who invented the art of printing.
93. LONDON, capital of England, The Game.

JUST PUBLISHED,

Engraved and Printed in Colours, Bowles's Geography, at his Map and Print Warehouse, No. 69, St. Paul's Church Yard, London.

A new Geographical Cards, giving a View of the principal Cities of the known World.

from hence a packet boat goes to Dover.

VOYAGE TO THE OCCIDENT, CITY BREAK IN THE ORIENT

Ljiljana Blagojević

What happens to travel during times of war? Are there clear-cut boundaries between seemingly innocent Grand Tour itineraries and the trails of cultural wreckage? In other words, do war and tourism exclude each other? Or do these two massive contemporary enterprises intersect along global paths, or even happily coexist alongside one another? The situation in Europe in the late 1930s demonstrated that the awareness of war never stopped the strategic promotion of tourism, and that even when war was on the doorstep, traveling kept its allure.

The European War of 1939–41, which developed into the Second World War, was closing in on Belgrade, then a capital of the Kingdom of Yugoslavia, as the city's tourist organization was planning its most ambitious public promotion. After the success of its initial informational presentation, held at the Belgrade Fairground in the autumn of 1940, the Tourist Association of Belgrade decided to mount a large-scale exhibition of tourism for the 1941 fair season (fig. 1). A number of well-known artists, architects, and urbanists were commissioned to represent, by means of models and plans of tourist zones, the organization's strategy of "transition from tourism for the privileged and well-off, to mass tourism for all."[1]

For this event, the Tourist Association commissioned a "Study of Belgrade as a Tourist Historical-Cultural City," which included a radical plan for urban reconstruction that remains unique as a statement on the city's planning (fig. 2). Drawn up in the winter of 1940, just months before the war destroyed Belgrade, this plan proposed a surgical intervention in the historical center of the city. Following verbatim Le Corbusier's guidelines for the prevention of destruction in *la guerre aérienne,* it advocated the total demolition of Belgrade's central perimeter blocks, their replacement by open modern urban structures, and the proverbial death of the *rue corridor.* Intended to promote the city as a tourist destina-

tion in 1941, the plan paradoxically prefigured the city's devastation in the Luftwaffe bombardment of April 6, 1941, when the blitzkrieg overran Yugoslavia.

The plan's author was Milorad Pantović (1910–86), an uncompromising modern architect and an ardent traveler. As a modernist and a discerning traveler, Pantović was a perfect candidate for planning Belgrade as a city-break destination in the course of "mass tourism for all," but the war made travel impossible. To an astute urbanist, the context and timing of the plan would have been of crucial importance, as the invitation to produce the study followed soon after the exhibition of *Neue Deutsche Baukunst,* held at the German Pavilion of the Belgrade Fairground in October 1940. This exhibition included Albert Speer's models, plans, and visions for the reconstruction of Berlin, and, of particular interest for the local population, the plans for the Belgrade Olympic Stadium complex by Werner March, architect of the Olympic complex in Berlin.

For Pantović, the *Neue Deutsche Baukunst* exhibition in Belgrade must have represented an outright declaration of war against all that he stood for as an architect. I propose that Pantović expressly used a shockingly radical, modern urbanism to subvert the dominant politics of war and politically promoted cultural and architectural models. Pantović's plan does not show any trace of the Belgrade Fairground, though the only *raison d'être* of this plan was for it to be shown at the exhibition in this very complex. In his scheme, the whole territory of the left bank of the river Sava, where the complex was situated, was planned as a botanical garden with hardly any buildings. Pantović clearly crafted this design as a premonition of the impending war, not as a concrete proposal. The significance of this and other Pantović projects from the late 1930s becomes apparent when his work is investigated from its own center, against his influences that were outside the Belgrade architectural discourse of the period. For this task, I propose to focus on Pantović's sensibility as a traveler, which may have been the source of his very particular habit of mind.

Pantović undertook a four-year Grand Occidental Tour commencing in Berlin in 1935, months after he graduated from the architectural department at the University of Belgrade Technical Faculty.[2] From Berlin, he sent home a sketch for a "Cultural Center in steel and glass for Belgrade of the future," an unsolicited project published in the capital's daily newspaper *Politika*.[3] The related article, illustrated with the perspective drawing of the Cultural Center and a photograph of the architect, extensively quoted Pantović's description of the building and, more importantly, his position on the social significance of such a project. Pantović argued that 90 percent of the city's population, "a Belgradian small clerk, Belgradian worker or student, never spend holidays on the seaside or mountains," and therefore the city needed an institution for the "cultural upbringing of the working men, who are the skeleton of the State."[4] In other words, the strategy of attracting mass tourism at home formed the basis of the Cultural Center, which contained a 4,000-seat auditorium expandable into the vestibule/foyer space to a capacity of 10,000 spectators, a library and reading rooms, and an indoor swimming pool of Olympic dimensions surrounded by restaurants and galleries. Pantović believed that the financing of this ambitious scheme would be possible "if those burghers, whose names are carved in long lines of marble plaques in our churches as evidence of their generosity and care as for the heavenly settlement of their souls, would be as generous to this [earthly] home of culture."[5]

With his project for a Cultural Center for Belgrade masses, Pantović clearly responded to the metropolitan condition he found in Berlin, a city of 4.2 million inhabitants in 1935–36, nearing its population peak. He addressed the very notion of "collective mass," to use his term, even when Belgrade's population of 320,000 was a fraction of that of the major European metropolises. In Berlin, the masses, or rather Walter Benjamin's illusion of the masses *(Schein der Masse)*, were preparing to pack the spectacle of the 1936 Olympic Games. This event literally rekindled the flame as it resurrected the Olympic torch relay along the 3,422-kilometer route from Olympia to the Reichssportfeld in Berlin. As the torch was passed by 3,422 runners, it bound them and their regions to the Reich's spectacle. In its eight-day journey, the flame reflected the Reich's construction of cultural politics. More precisely, it marked the capitals on its itinerary—Athens, Sofia, Belgrade, Budapest, Vienna, Prague, and Berlin—as strategic points for the expansion of the Reich's discourse of realpolitik.

Welcomed by ovations from the city's masses, the Olympic torch paused in Belgrade for one hour on the morning of July 27, 1936, in order to light a flame on top of an "Olympic ceremonial altar," a temporary wooden construction erected in the very center of the city.[6] Belgrade's inclusion in the itinerary sparked ambitions for the internationalization of the city. The city's ultimate aim was to become a candidate for hosting the 1948 Olympic Games, as initiated during the Berlin Games by Svetomir Ðukić, the founder of the national Olympic movement and a member of the International Olympic Committee.

In an effort to further bind the city to an international network, city boosters decided to set in motion the long-postponed plan for the Belgrade Fairground. As a first step, they organized an architectural competition for the Fairground complex in 1936. The site chosen was situated on the grounds legally annexed to Belgrade the previous year, on the left bank of the Sava, next to the new suspension bridge (1932), and directly opposite the historical center of the city (fig. 3). The site was part of the empty marshy terrain between the historical cities of Belgrade and Zemun. It had served for centuries solely as a military territory, a no-man's-land between the shifting borders of divided and conflicting empires. The Sava had marked a geographical and political borderline from the time of the fourth-century division of the Roman Empire into the Eastern and Western Roman Empires until the mid-twentieth-century remapping of Europe by the Third Reich. In modern history, and up until the Berlin Congress of 1878, this territory between the Ottoman and the Hapsburg empires, and, thereafter (until World War I), between Austro-Hungary and Serbia, fulfilled the function of a *cordon sanitaire,* a zone observed and controlled as a disconnected breach between the Orient and the Occident.

Pantović addressed the site's very condition of disconnectedness in his competition entry for the Belgrade Fairground (fig. 4). If anything, his design centers on the planning of traffic, which acts as a binding coordinate system that creates a linear, open-ended construct of exhibition pavilions and pedestrian routes set into a lush park with lakes and ponds. Essentially urbanistic, the scheme makes the fairground a place of commerce, leisure, and recreation as well as a metropolitan thoroughfare. This dichotomy makes Pantović's proposal distinctive—it plans for the prospective growth and flexibility of the fairground complex itself, but also introduces the vision of a modern city on this terrain, anticipating the planning principles of the municipality of New Belgrade, which was constructed there in the postwar period. This vision of modern urbanism remained completely incomprehensible to the local eyes of Belgrade city officials because of "the lack of criteria for evaluating the advantages of the bold and interesting proposals from the technical, aesthetic, and economic aspects."[7]

Yet Pantović's proposal was rejected not only because of the lack of criteria for evaluation, but also because the plan's ethos diverged completely from the one binding the Yugoslav economy and politics to the route of the 1936 Olympic torch. The Belgrade Fairground constructed in 1937 clearly demonstrated this divergence (fig. 5).[8] In stark contrast to the functional linearity and nonhierarchical openness of Pantović's concept, the realized complex was one of axial symmetry and centrality, whose coordinate system originated in a dominating tower (fig. 6). As in the construction of the national pavilions of Italy, Hungary, Romania, and Czechoslovakia, Turkey, and Germany, the Belgrade Fairground complex reflected internationalization, fitting the dynamic of Axis economic expansion and its aim toward political domination (fig. 7).

Pantović's 1936 study tours of contemporary architecture in Denmark, Holland, Belgium, and Switzerland were bound to another Europe, the one he searched for upon leaving Berlin and moving to Paris. There, he found exactly what he was after: the most famous atelier of international modern architecture at 35, Rue de Sèvres. After a month of waiting for the atelier master to return from Brazil, Pantović finally met him for an interview in a tiny work cell. Le Corbusier, "[h]is face, framed by black spectacles, looking even paler, his slender silhouette making him look younger," took on this *"bon type Danubien"* to work in his "laboratory of experiments."[9] The *maître* recollected the itinerary of his own 1911 "Voyage to the Orient," on the eve of the Balkan Wars. He retraced the route along the Danube in Serbia: the towns Zaječar (where Pantović was born), Negotin, and Knjaževac set along the track of a "little Belgian railway, hanging precariously and vertiginously along the Bulgarian border…directly within the range of the Bulgarian guns."[10] He spoke of an earthenware jug with the Greek motif of Pegasus that he brought back from this region and held above his head when photographed in 1918 at his parents' home in La Chaux-de-Fonds. This same jug was published in his *L'Art décoratif d'aujourd'hui* (1925) with the caption noting the "story from the land of fine culture and imperishable art contain[ing] one of the most powerful lessons to be learnt today: evolution due to economics is inexorable and irresistible; regret is useless; poetry which seemed immortal is dead; everything begins again; that is what is fine and promises the joys of tomorrow."[11]

Pantović learned his most precious lesson in Paris laterally through collaboration with his colleagues in the Rue de Sèvres atelier. When they were working on the preparations for *L'Exposition Internationale des Arts et Techniques dans la Vie Moderne* (1937), Pantović invited his colleagues G. T. J. Kuiper, the Dutch architect from Rotterdam; Jean Bossu, the French architect and Le Corbusier's permanent collaborator; and Otto Clauss from Switzerland to participate in a competition for the regularization of Novi Sad in Serbia/Yugoslavia.[12] Teaming up after office hours in the studio they hired in the Boulevard Montparnasse, the international team produced a plan of Novi Sad (figs. 8, 9) as a functional city aiming "not to a geometric town plan, but a city which will be appropriate to human life, habits and psychology."[13]

In an article published after the competition, Pantović criticized not only the "sterile isolation" of the locally promoted and popular garden city concept and the "slavery of individualism" inherent in it, but also the concept supporting the abolition of private ownership. He wrote, "…those of a collectivist orientation, inspired by modern socio-economic and political movements… make citizens as if part of a huge military camp…a group disciplined and obedient in all manifestations of life, their circulation planned to a rhythm of calculation accurate to a minute…expecting the arrival of a purely material society which will provide housing and supply education and leisure with an almost commanding certainty."[14] Against these two poles, Pantović set the theoretical goals of the modern city, which "has to aim to save an individual from the processes of diminishing his intellectual, moral and psychological values…(and to) develop in an individual all his potential creative

activities, provide for his health…and to enliven the strength of personality in an individual."[15] This modern city, echoing Georg Simmel's metropolitan condition of individual freedom, was deemed "daring in its proposals and ideas," as noted by the competition jury,[16] and too daring, also, for the epoch in which, as Le Corbusier noted, "des forces immenses et occultes poussent à la guerre."[17]

Pantović and his colleagues brought their collaboration in line with Le Corbusier's *l'œuvre de paix,* which called for "Solidarité sur le plan de la vie."[18] The project in which he took part at the exhibition in the Pavilion des Temps Nouveaux yet again dealt with the masses. It was Le Corbusier's plan for the "National Center of Popular Entertainment for 100,000 Participants," a modernist complex including an Olympic stadium, theater, cinema, and "pyramide tronquée des fêtes a grand spectacle."[19] This project is preserved in Le Corbusier's archive and remains the only hard evidence of Pantović's work during his travels. All the competition plans, as well as the projects he exhibited in April 1936 in a gallery in the Rue du Faubourg Saint Honore as part of an exhibition of Yugoslav artists living in Paris, were lost.[20] Still, the traces point out that mass entertainment, spectacles, and model complexes—fairs and stadiums—were a constant in Pantović's work of this period. Even his last post, a letter from America mailed before returning home in 1939, reported on yet another mass spectacle: the World's Fair in New York. (In 1938, Pantović moved on to London, where he attended Amédée Ozenfant's Fine Arts School; when Ozenfant moved to New York, Pantović followed, extending his itinerary to the American continent.) He concluded his travels and his American letter by saying that the World's Fair was "a real document of a beginning of realization of a happier and a more beautiful world."[21]

However, the world was not finding happiness but war. When Pantović returned to Belgrade, it was at the city's fairground that the war had begun to form its narrative of terror. Constructed in 1937, the fairground spurred the first massive crossing of Belgrade citizens over the Sava. In the ten days of the 1st Autumn Fair in Belgrade (September 11–21, 1937), some 250,000 people visited. The numbers continued at the same level during the fairs held in 1938 and 1939, with record attendance noted in 1940, when around 290,000 people attended. For a city of 350,000 inhabitants, the fair was a mass event *par excellence,* and for the masses the fairground represented, to paraphrase Walter Benjamin, the city of the dreaming collective.[22]

With its exhibition of industry, the fair introduced a completely new mode of mass propaganda. But the glaring lights left the war industry's unrestricted movement into the exhibition space hidden in the shadows. State-of-the-art machines for agriculture or mining were combined with new models of antiaircraft machine guns, trench artillery, bombs, and gas masks. A demonstration of a simulated attack from the air alternated with a demonstration of a live television program. The fairgrounds imbued the seemingly innocent domain of fun with politics and became an operative mechanism of propaganda, preparing the masses for war, dragging them into the realpolitik of the Axis powers.

Fig. 1   Rajko Tatić, Milivoje Tričković, and Đorđe Lukić, Belgrade Fairground, 1937. Period postcard. Courtesy Miloš Jurišić.

2   Milorad Pantović, plan for the urban reconstruction of Belgrade, 1940. Negative from the architect's own documentation, as listed in his file in the Bibliography Department of the Serbian Academy of Sciences and Arts.

3   The site of the future Belgrade Fairground on the left bank of the river Sava, ca. 1920. Courtesy *Politika* Photography Archive.

4   Milorad Pantović, competition entry for the Belgrade Fairground, 1936. Courtesy Museum of the City of Belgrade.

5   The Belgrade Fairground. Period aerial photograph. Courtesy Museum of War Aviation, Surčin.

6   Aleksandar Sekulić, Central Tower at the Belgrade Fairground, 1937. Courtesy Miloš Jurišić.

7   German Pavilion at the Belgrade Fairground, 1939. Photograph from untitled period publication.

8   Milorad Pantović, G.T.J. Kuiper, Jean Bossu, and Otto Clauss, competition entry for the Regulation of Novi Sad, 1937. From *Arhitektura urbanizam* 38 (1966).

9   Milorad Pantović, G.T.J. Kuiper, Jean Bossu, and Otto Clauss, housing blocks units, Novi Sad. From *Savremena opština* 10–12 (1937).

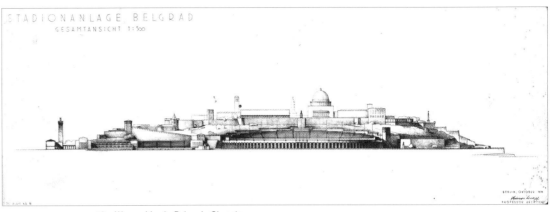

10   Werner March, Belgrade Olympic Stadium Complex at the site of the Belgrade fortress, 1939–40. Elevation. Courtesy Archive of Serbia and Montenegro.

11   Belgrade Fairground, 1937–41; *Juden-lager Semlin*, 1941–42; *Anhaltslager Semlin*, 1942–44. Courtesy Miloš Jurišić.

12   Camp internees at *Anhaltslager Semlin*,1942. (The Belgrade fortress site is in the background.) Courtesy Photography Archive of the Military Museum, Belgrade.

13   Milorad Pantović, Branko Žeželj, and Milan Krstić, New Belgrade Fair, 1957. Aerial photograph by M. Pavlović. From *Jugoslavija* 15 (1958).

14   Milorad Pantović and Branko Žeželj, Exhibition Hall 1 at the Belgrade Fair under construction, 1955–57. Photograph by M. Pavlović. From *Jugoslavija* 15 (1958).

15   The Belgrade Fair under construction, 1957. Photograph by M. Pavlović. From *Jugoslavija* 15 (1958).

16   Miodrag Popović (sculptor), Branislav Mitrović and Vasilije Milunović (architects), Memorial to the Victims of the Genocide 1941–45, Belgrade, 1995. Photograph by Milica Milojević.

These cultural politics culminated in the aforementioned exhibition *Neue Deutsche Baukunst,* opened on October 5, 1940, by the prince regent, with the prime minister of Yugoslavia, his entire cabinet, and the city's cultural elite in attendance. Special attention was given to the presentation of Werner March's plans, perspective drawings, and model for the Belgrade Olympic Complex (fig. 10). The development included the 55,000-seat Olympic Stadium, the 15,000-seat Swim Stadium, and the Academy of Physical Culture. The plans called for razing the ancient fortress of Belgrade, the city's *Stadtkrone,* and constructing a "Pantheon" in its place. The Pantheon's cupola, which dominated the city's skyline from both the Sava and Danube, was clearly evocative of Speer's Große Halle in Berlin.[23] In the forefront of the main perspective view, the left bank of the Sava, as viewed from the complex, is represented in its arcadian mythical state of nature. In reality, and concurrently with the exhibition, the actual European war brought into this state of nature a state of mass internment.

The site became a transit camp for the resettlement of 120,000 Germans from Bessarabia. As a period newspaper article read, it was a new colony on 27 hectares next to the fairground, "beautiful and modern," albeit temporary, but hygienic and well-lit by electric street lamps.[24] Six months later, in April 1941, after the capitulation of Yugoslavia, the Sava became a state border between the two asymmetrically and violently created nation states: German-occupied Serbia and the puppet Independent State of Croatia. On October 28, 1941, the decision was made to transform what had been the Belgrade Fairground, now an abandoned place on territory belonging to the Independent State of Croatia, into a concentration camp run by the Gestapo (fig. 11).

The camp was officially designated a *"Judenlager Semlin,"* being the center of the "Final Solution of the Jewish Question in Serbia." In December 1941, some 600 Roma and some 6,400 women, children, and elderly Jewish citizens of Serbia were interned in the camp. From March to May 1942, the Jewish camp inmates were taken to their deaths in groups of 80 to 100 by a gas chamber truck brought over from the Eastern front. With the Final Solution in Serbia reported to Berlin as the first carried out in its entirety in Europe in May 1942, the camp was repopulated as an *"Anhaltslager Semlin."* It was a reception/transit camp for the internment of dissident citizens of Serbia, patriots, partisan fighters from Croatia and Bosnia, communists, and prisoners from other Croatian camps who were strong enough to be relocated to work camps in Germany and Norway (fig. 12). By the time that the camp was finally disbanded in 1942, with most of the original buildings demolished in the Allied bombardment, some 10,000 of a total of 32,000 prisoners lost their lives at the Belgrade Fairground.[25]

Back in 1940, when Pantović planned Belgrade as a modern tourist city for the exhibition at the fairground, its geopolitical position was but a transit stop on the itinerary of European resettlements. Six months later, in a state of war, the fairground itself became the destination of terror and death. Pantović's plan of a modern city reflected the tension of Europe going to war, and as such represented a unique antiwar statement. Unfortunately,

this statement fell on deaf ears, quite like Le Corbusier's paradigmatic cry "Des canons, des munitions? Merci! Des Logis…S. V. P."[26] Pantović's plan was of no consequence. Its significance, as well as that of the competition projects for the Belgrade Fairground and Novi Sad, is evident only in the profound changes to the planning paradigm in the postwar period, long after the original plans were forgotten.

In his postwar career, Pantović received major awards for his work and was honored as an elected member of the Serbian Academy of Sciences and Arts. In his official biography as an academician, his projects from the late 1930s are duly listed, yet there is no record of them in the Academy's archive or in its bibliographical department. With the original plans lost, all that remains of Pantović's groundbreaking work is the complex for the new Belgrade Fair, his most acclaimed achievement, completed in 1957 (fig. 13).

Constructed under the new sociopolitical conditions of socialist Yugoslavia, the fair had a new location on the right bank of the Sava. Pantović won the competition in 1954, with a concept loosely resembling the one from 1935.[27] But the project was drastically altered in the ensuing development phase. Once again, travel was the catalyst for change. Together with the project engineers, Branko Žeželj and Milan Krstić, Pantović undertook a study tour of Europe's fairs in Hannover, Munich, Paris, Brussels, and Milan. The resulting design reflects Pantović's impressions from this trip, especially from the encounters with new engineering of shallow concrete domes. Illustrative of this inspiration is the design of the dome of Hall 1, with its radiating ribs measuring 107 meters in diameter, making it one of the largest domes constructed in Europe (fig. 14). But what makes this project of special significance, apart from its masterly engineering, is the overall rationale of this new urban space, noted by a period commentator as a "social center…[where] the strong pulse of the capital will beat."[28] As one of the most important architectural undertakings of the socialist Yugoslavia, the fairground, once more, became a model of internationalization. This time, however, it was a model of open invitation, showing no preference for any particular international network and reflecting the political positioning of Yugoslavia between the cold war factions of West and East.

In the first weeks of its opening, the new Belgrade Fair attracted some 1,100,000 people. By virtue of its planning and design, it became, as Pantović noted, "a new city center…a new urban organism which would be used all year round as a cultural and recreational center of the city."[29] It is no accident that Pantović planned this place with an open and democratic ethos, as if his travels had found their ideal destination, finally a place of individual freedom in a metropolis (fig. 15). It was a destination, however, that offered all too brief a respite. The end of the cold war brought the Yugoslav wars of the 1990s and what can only be described as "the condition of mere Nature, and of war of every one against his neighbor," to use Hobbes's famous line. As Giorgio Agamben writes, "At issue in the former Yugoslavia is… an incurable rupture of the old *nomos* and a dislocation of populations and human lives along entirely new lines of flight."[30]

If war redefines travel as the exit route of an emigrant, a refugee, a displaced or a stateless person, its destination is ever the camp, "which is now securely logged within the city's interior,"[31] as pointed out by Agamben. And if travel follows a war trail backtracked by reporters and international crisis mediators, its destination is often a luxurious touch-base for the go-betweens. The Hyatt Regency Belgrade, which opened on the eve of the wars in 1990, was such a destination. Its interiors imported a design philosophy of "creating a sense of place—a well-designed and integrated package of fantasy, drama, and creature comfort...[a] unique and sensitive response to location, architecture, and client vision."[32] Ironically, the Hyatt hotel sits on a block that backs onto the original Belgrade Fairground site, a former camp now firmly lodged within the inner city, inhabited by the poor and destitute.

Since the end of the Second World War, the fairground site has served as a transient habitation space, its temporary residents constantly awaiting relocation. In 1987, "The Old Fairground—Gestapo Camp" was listed as a cultural monument, but what remained of the complex had been neglected and left to decay. A modest plaque was put up on the site by a local organization of partisan war veterans, and in 1995 the "Memorial to the Victims of the Genocide 1941–45" was constructed outside the camp site on the Sava riverfront (fig. 16). If Pantović's visionary fairground competition plan were laid over the current situation, the hotel and the monument would mark its longitudinal end points. The area in between, however, remains a blind spot, its reconstruction conditional on the resettlement of its inhabitants, the site foreshadowing the perpetual dislocation of individuals and funds which both war and tourism generate into a permanent economy of travel.

1   R. St., "U okviru ovogodišnjih Beogradskih sajmova održaće se velika turistička izložba," *Politika* (February 25, 1941): 12.
2   A year spent in Berlin was intensive for the young architect working as an assistant on the Siemensstadt project; thereafter on various projects for industrial building for Siemens and Zeiss at the architectural office Siemens-Bauabteilug, in the group led by Hans Hertlein; and attending town-planning courses taught by Hermann Jansen at the Technischen Hochschule Berlin-Charlottenburg. All biographical details are from the Archive of the Serbian Academy of Sciences and Arts, Belgrade, file on Milorad Pantović.
3   V. L., "Dom kulture, u gvožđu i staklu, za Beograd budućnosti," *Politika* (May 6, 1935): 8.
4   Ibid.
5   Ibid.
6   "Uz oduševljene ovacije građanstva olimpijska buktinja proneta je kroz Beograd," *Politika* (July 28, 1936): 14.
7   Editorial comment in Milorad Pantović, "Jesu li dosadašnji urbanski sistemi negativni: ako jesu, da li postoji mogućnost primene jednog novog sistema?", *Savremena opština* 10–12 (1937): 253.
8   Belgrade Fairground was eventually constructed by architects Milivoje Tričković, Đorđe Lukić, and Rajko Tatić in 1937.
9   Milorad Pantović, "Atelje L. C.—Rue de Sèvres 35," *Arhitektura urbanizam* 35–36 (1965): 80–81.
10   Le Corbusier, *Journey to the East*, edited

and annotated by Ivan Žaknić, trans. Ivan Žaknić in collaboration with Nicole Pertuiset (Cambridge, Mass.: MIT Press, 1989), 44.
11   Le Corbusier, *The Decorative Art of Today*, trans. James I. Dunnett (1925, reprint; Cambridge, Mass.: MIT Press, 1987), 35.
12   G. T. J. Kuiper, "Stage te Parijs," *De 8 en OPBOUW* 4 (February 26, 1938): 38–39.
13   Pantović, "Jesu li dosadašnji," 255.
14   Ibid., 254.
15   Ibid., 260.
16   Editorial comment in Pantović, "Jesu li dosadašnji," 254.
17   "Immense, and hidden forces are pushing into war." Le Corbusier, *Des canons, des munitions? Merci! Des logis…S. V. P.* (Paris: L'Architecture d'aujourdhui, 1937), 143.
18   Ibid.
19   Ibid., 98–103.
20   As reported by the architect, the exhibition included eighteen artists and presentations of architectural projects by himself and his colleagues from Le Corbusier's atelier, Ksenija Grisogono and Ernst Weissmann, as well as by Krsto Filipović. M. P., "Pismo iz Pariza: Osamnaest jugoslovenskih slikara i četiri arhitekta izlažu u Parizu," *Politika* (April 10, 1937): 7.
21   M. P., "Pismo iz Amerike: Svetska izložba 1939 godine u Njujorku," *Politika* (January 15, 1939): 8.
22   See Walter Benjamin, *The Arcades Project,* translated by Howard Eiland, and Kevin McLaughlin, (Cambridge, Mass.: The Belknap Press of Harvard University Press, 1999),

108 [D3,7], 388–404 [K1,1–K9a,1].
23   See Thomas Schmidt, *Werner March: Architekt des Olympia-Stadions, 1894–1976* (Basel: Birkhäuser Verlag), 97–98.
24   "Na levoj obali Save, prekoputa Beograda, podiže se logor koji će primiti Nemce iz Besarabije na njihovom putu za Nemačku," *Politika* (September 7, 1940): 11.
25   Milan Koljanin, *Nemački logor na Beogradskom sajmištu 1941–1944* (Belgrade: Institut za savremenu istoriju, 1992).
26   Title of book by Le Corbusier cited above, see note 17.
27   The coauthor of the competition project was Vladeta Maksimović, but he did not take part in the further development of the project.
28   Oliver Minić, "The Belgrade Fair," *Jugoslavija* 15 (1958): 122.
29   Milorad Pantović, "Novo Beogradsko sajmište," *Godišnjak Muzeja grada Beograda* 4 (1957): 599.
30   Giorgio Agamben, *Homo Sacer: Sovereign Power and Bare Life,* trans. Daniel Heller-Roazen (Stanford University Press, 1998), 176.
31   Ibid.
32   Interior design by Hirsch Bedner Associates. Citation taken from the firm's Web site: www.hbadesign.com.

Edward Burtynsky,
Oil Fields No. 23,
Cold Lake Production
Area, Cold Lake,
Alberta 2001.

For an interview with Edward
Burtynsky and additional photos
by Burtynsky, see pages 153–161.

The Wrong Story

Keller Easterling

An inverted travelogue does not trek into the epic territory of heroic adventure, but rather wanders in the opposite direction toward the wrong events in the wrong story. One finds here an expansive field of information unconstrained by aplomb, heroism, exoticism, or authenticity. There is no host. There is no first person. The trajectory only occasionally attaches itself to the wrong travelers for some temporary momentum through the looking glass. This is not the story of the friend who rented a motor boat to buzz around Loch Ness and then spent the rest of the day reading the autobiography of David Niven. One does not find the famous woman who draws the blinds to read the Jane Austen novel for the fourteenth time while in Trieste. Indeed.

Watching DVDs in a darkened hotel room in Eastern Europe at 3:30 in the afternoon on a sunny day does not portray the same languorous, unexpected cool. This is something closer to being wrong. The engines of the inverted travelogue are the travelers...

Detective stories need murders; travel stories need adventures and dangers. Weakling characters are not typically protagonists in these tales. While they are occasionally granted a deviant literature, alternative characters are funny because of their buffoonery, their inability to be adventurous enough to face the standard dangers. Buffoons of travel reify titans of travel. Domestic travel stories, road trips back home, or picaresque journeys may travel into time or into culture to expose and lampoon social constructs. Frothy shipboard romances and farces are travel stories exploring the elitism of place by identifying the obvious tourists who do not belong. Yet in an overwhelming number of travel narratives, an elitism of physical risk or exertion also appears. Even interior psychological narratives, typically regarding a young man's loves and strivings, routinely script themselves as worthy of the scale of adventurous or dangerous global travel. Often only the pageants of war and resistance are deemed to be commensurate with his inner struggle.

Indeed, foreign wars and epic combat haunt the narratives of international travel, whether in the context of national military campaigns or polarized political orthodoxies, meeting either on the battleground or at the barricade. Armed franchise of the queen, geographic conquest, righteous revolution, or wartime intrigues all associate travel with militarized violence or oppositional stances. Many citizens of the last century encountered foreign lands as soldiers in patriotic service to national defense. Travel, consistently in the shadow of these conflicts, makes the traveler, whether tourist or novelist, comparable in some ways to the soldier or foreign correspondent. Even the Peace Corps, although not militarized, was certainly a nationalized component of cold war competition. On other political fronts, independent political troops have also righteously marched into the deepest darkest realms of the world's poverty to expose another sort of enemy—the inequities of market capital. There they often find the violence of economies and wars intertwined. Though the settings may change from pirate ships to colonial outposts, from CIA-style Hilton hotels to militant economic revolution, from battlegrounds to refugee camps, or from James Michener to John Le Carré, the traveler does combat with the world. He exposes himself to dangers.

At the end of the cold war the battle lines of travel

narratives have shifted, yet both political theories and tales of travel often still adopt the most accustomed competitive or combative dispositions. The Grand Strategist would say that nations, in their own collective anarchy, now fight against terrorism. Some would, in Huntington fashion, formulate a "clash of civilizations" between of the "West and the rest." Conventional nation-to-nation war and pervasive military presence is the only answer. For others, capital, now a transnational force, remains to become the new superpower enemy. Occasionally, with little structural alteration to the organization of war and espionage, the international corporation is merely substituted as the menacing enemy or villain in disguise. The global intrigue jump-cuts from country to country fighting an entity with varying degrees of subtlety from the James Bond cartoon to a chilly, faceless corporation. The structure of anticorporate movies like *The Constant Gardener* is strikingly similar to those of cold war spy stories. The corporation is sometimes even treated with a limited repertoire of aggression—resistance in the streets takes the form of a binary face-off as in the "battle of Seattle." In Hardt and Negri's *Empire,* the ur-force is treated with an expanded global repertoire while still maintaining an Empire–Counter Empire binary resistance. Total War, rendered, not by Clausewitz or Ludendorff, but by the left, continues to track the way militarization pervades almost every aspect of culture and industry. If infrastructure is an apparatus of military logistics, the means of delivering the home country to the troops abroad, then it naturally follows, for thinkers like Paul Virilio and others (e.g., James Der Derian, Manuel DeLanda) that urbanism is also a military apparatus. For Virilio, war replaces political economy and is indistinct from civil society.[1] Miraculously, in these arguments that, like Debord's spectacle, construct a tragic totalizing global force, some innocents are still both part of but also persecuted by and resistant to the *über* force. In these impossibly dramatic (and even aggrandizing) formulations, monisms and binaries prevail to structure information.

The engines of the inverted travelogue are the travelers who…point out, with false modesty, the simplest direction of travel to a group that has already long since begun to move in a different direction. These are the ones feigning decisive leadership while others must insert their fare into turnstiles and brush the crumbs off their coat; the ones who wander away from an adventure or a fight;

the ones who are wondering how any live experience might compare to watching TV; the ones who, just at the moment when others begin to speak, are thinking about when they will stop speaking.

On the threshold of the wrong story following the wrong traveler toward the wrong events, is a quest for…

Whatever the epic profile of the adventure traveler in novels and other narratives, in a contemporary economy, this character now possesses a very different kind of power. Supposedly, the travel buffoon stays safe and avoids issues at the quick of culture. The character of questionable taste on a cruise ship or the international business drone are subjects of sport for their adherence to the logistics of spatial projects, corporate schedules, and frequent flyer miles. This traveler joins the glamorous globetrotter and the cool denizens of generic first-class interiors and is the author of a great deal of global infrastructure. The supposed buffoon is now a central modern subject commanding vast economies, described, very durably, by the likes of Dean MacCannell, as a popular social scientist or a consumer/ethnographer. Still, from Zygmunt Bauman's rendering, he is the "alter ego" of the vagabond who stands for all of the other transient forces in the contemporary world. Spurred on by desires of all sorts, these tourists consume everything from experience economy luxuries to offerings from the global sex trade. Many travelers are then not entirely different from any underworld character in a network with their own rules. The tourist presents some of the same dangers and etiologies of the most powerful global corporations or terrorist forces who wander the world and only shelter in the state.

Yet, what can be learned when the trajectory of this traveler is still portrayed in tragic narrative structures? Michel Houellebecq's novel *Platform* provides a service here. In one sense Houellebecq ventures into new political territories around the world: club resorts as repeatable spatial products meet sex tourism in southeast Asia meet the terrorist targeting of tourism. In another sense, the book provides the final ejaculatory apotheosis to novels of nationalized internationalism. Here the middle-aged soft porn of Robin Moore or Tom Clancy is more like normal porn. Now the violence of terrorism is suitable to accompany the interior monologue of narcissistic self-deprecation. Impotence (all evidence to the contrary) is a deliberate component of this self-loathing/self-loving heroism, if it is to maintain the familiar zero hour structure of an interior narrative. After *Platform's* final terrorist explosion of the resort in which the protagonist's ideal sexual partner is perhaps conveniently killed, the novel must end. What else would the protagonist do, with the partner or with the world? What else can be done after epic self-loathing, in the story's relatively conventional, tragic denouement? The rendering of familiar narrative structures as ineffectual offers either an attractive anesthetizing narcotic, a conventional vessel in which to look at writing by itself, or, perhaps, one rehearsal for peeking around the limits of these narrative structures.

On the threshold of the wrong story following the wrong traveler toward the **wrong events, is a quest for... consequential things that were not supposed to happen. From the nearest ordinary** threshold, gliding past cues to the pageants of adventure...

Since so much knowledge has been and could rightly continue to be arranged within the epistemes of war and resistance, the occasional exhaustion of war's narrative templates is useful. How much would one know about the world after consistently marching in that direction, arranging our events in terms of symmetrical binary structures of combat and opposition? Wars and conflicts press themselves into our view. Yet telling are those moments when they seem increasingly to lack information. For instance, the resistance marshaled to stop incomprehensible wars finds itself displaced or pushing on a nonexistent door. Voting can be systematically displaced from participatory democracy. These are our political phantoms or events that do not behave according to orthodoxies or cannot be taxonomized by the left or the right. The architecture of global relations is not, of course, arranged as a series of symmetrical face-offs or head-to-head battlegrounds. Militarization does not now, nor has it ever, penetrated the whole of our society in keeping with the sentiments of total war. New technologies and inventions do not always flow from military funding. Far from being a world with sides and causes, there is ample evidence of overlapping networks of influence and allegiance. It is neither easy to declare the prevailing dominance of the nation state nor its fabled death in the face of internationalism. Indeed, both these theories possess, in their structure of argumentation, the very combative, this-kills-that habit of mind that often organizes historical events and political phenomena in terms of successive rather than coexistent and recurring events.

It is much more likely that state and nonstate forces reinforce each other, providing each other camouflage and cover during advantageous moments. Nations pursue what Stephen Krasner has called "hypocritical sovereignty." State and nonstate actors in an ancient mutually sustaining partnership often rely on the lubrication

of transnational proxies to reinforce the power of the state while war is often the national pageant to cover for a wide array of nonstate activities that like to remain under the radar and outside of political jurisdictions. For every forthright gesture there is a duplicitous one. For every rational economic game, there is cheating and caprice. When somewhere at the other end of a thousand cool and indirect ricochets we find intensely primitive violence or terrorism, we sometimes concoct continuums between the ecumenical and the tribal; we fuel the engines of regular war, fight harder, yell louder, strengthen the left or strengthen the right. Yet the chemistry of righteous mimicry and competition only has the power to further escalate those tensions that do inflame the world. Our exhausted forms of tragic or combative narratives often then square up to an illusive enemy in regular wars aimed at the wrong violence.

This "extrastatecraft," which has the ability to use conventional statecraft and war as its camouflage, can alternatively serve as the material for resourceful political leverage. Extrastatecraft may not conform to political orthodoxies or recognized economic logics, and it remains extrinsic to and in excess of proper political channels. Yet it is, nevertheless, often responsible for major political and cultural changes. The advent of inventions, persuasions, technologies, and networks can be either insidiously collusive with or independent of the most well rehearsed forms of global conflict. A third thing that does not take sides in a symmetrical fight is often an effective distraction to break the deadlock of escalating symmetrical tensions. These are the silent under-the-table deals that suddenly change a political complexion without military maneuvers or any of the other official political instruments of statecraft. If there is the possibility of false logics in the pervasive application of military epistemes and tragic combative structures of reasoning, then are there not vast pastures of nonconforming information that lie outside the boundaries of this bracket— territory within which events are cast in a different register to "brush against the grain of history"? Multiple forces, assembling and shape-shifting, replace the fantasy Goliath of monolithic capital or corporate culture with even more insidious moving targets. There are few narrative templates for recording these events that are not "supposed" to happen, the untheorized phantoms of politics proper.

From the nearest ordinary threshold, gliding past cues to the pageants of adventure... **we step off into another species of global infrastructure. The trajectory moves between** fluorescent-lit board rooms where one changes from shoes to slippers...

Some of the most radical changes to the globalizing world are not being written in the language of law or diplomacy but in the language of architecture and urbanism. Architecture operates in the realm of extrastatecraft, and its position outside of proper political events makes it potentially even more effective.

Yet many architects are shielded from all of this global reconnaissance by the plush insulation of oblivion. Many traveling architects do not know anything but enthusiasm for looking at buildings and cities. Alternatives are returned with a blank stare, untroubled by a lack of comprehension. When in range of a building one has not seen, there is no choice but to briskly scout it out and look at it for a long time. Nothing about this is perceived to be tedious. Instead, these are moments of ardor for architects. Officious and persistent with the unwitting staff of the building, the architect swarms and scurries, entitled, as an architect know-it-all, to see details that should, by rights, be unavailable to the layman. (Occasionally, the architect can even match the elitism of place and disdain for the tourist perfected by selected continental philosophers of the left.) One should also have access to a storehouse of amusing, even accurate, historical anecdotes, comparative detail, and creative connoisseurship. The character who would lie about seeing a building, or be satisfied to see it from a speeding cab, would, with the proper tip-off, be seen as rip-roaringly funny.

Other architects and urbanists cast themselves as international warriors against architecture's pact with capital. There are architects crafting creative new forms of practice at the world's border crossings, battlegrounds, and barrios, researching, exposing, and mediating between the various scales of power in operation between global finance and informal economies. The clichés of travel, danger, and exertion sometimes accompany this direction, when poverty and trouble stand as a form of exoticism or an ontological aesthetic of despair within which they perpetuate the perfection of either innocence or guilt.

Perhaps one crucial threshold onto the spatial events that are not supposed to happen can be found by looking incorrectly at the very spaces that are often understood to be most closely linked to statecraft and nation-building, namely infrastructure. Infrastructure networks are already the vehicles of travel, the means by which soldiers, spies, and ordinary tourists propel themselves into the world. Infrastructure can be seen as a vehicle of the militarization that clearly pervades so much of culture—the means by which military technologies, both innovations and remainders, infiltrate civil society and markets. An inverted travelogue starts at alternative moments in history and opens onto the wrong adventures: business histories, histories of the gradually spreading networks of transportation and communica-tion as well as the networks of migration and propagating spatial products of global development. The wrong narrative would focus on ways in which the systems and networks in place might not always act like an extension of war, but rather like an extension of international banking, corporate governance, or global consultancies with aversions to war. If war is infrastructure speeded up, the wrong narrative would dwell on the protracted stalemates, the polite burnishing of stability, and the confidence games of corruption between state and non-state forces.

For instance, Armand Mattelart positions his research on communication at the moment in the last quarter of the nineteenth century when increasingly global infrastructures, international organizations, and multinational corporations began to grow new global communication networks like transatlantic cable and radio while just on the brink of becoming pawns of the intensely nationalized international ambition *(Realpolitik* to *Weltpolitik).* For Mattelart, then as now, "historical research is manifested mainly in the form of a return to national histories while the international is still left by the wayside." Indeed, Mattelart describes this history as a "field that is still young and uncharted."[2] Perhaps because Mattelart argues that communication infrastructure "serves first to make war," the managerial controls on which he also dilates at length somehow remain in the register of the phantasm, and yet these are perhaps the primary subjects of this story. The business histories of, for instance, John Dunning and Mira Wilkins read with the encyclopedic enthusiasm of lepidopterists, collecting evidence of an abundant history of seeming precocious global connections in a history that we only thought we knew. Alfred D. Chandler Jr.'s *The Visible Hand: The Managerial Revolution in American Business* presents a historical episode that serves as a place from which to push off against the grain of history with his description of the American railroad conglomerates of the late nineteenth century that were larger than any public enterprise, had no origin in the military, employed more men than the military, and had capital assets to rival those of the U. S. Treasury.[3] These little cracks and toeholds in history are perhaps antecedents to our contemporary political phantoms.

Weaning attention away from the pageant (or camouflage) of war and even from the crusading righteousness of resistance that assumes the same structure, alternative tours of the world may explore other dispositions of aggression within organizations and networks and other forms of violence breaking on different fronts all around the world. *Architecture may contribute many such untheorized events to relieve the default forms of combative argumentation.* We find architecture's politics in places other than borders and battlegrounds, and we search for ties to new forms of violence that do not respond to our blunt forms of aggressive statecraft. An alternative tour tracks the violence that the State Department did not start and therefore has no idea how to address. These are sites perhaps considered impure by the left, sites that are not the aftermath and proof of the injustices of capital. These are stories tainted with business and banking practices that can be told by the journals of the right. A tight focus on the authenticity of place or the authentically situated bottom-up *perruque* might quarantine issues from the other scale in an associative network. The portrayal of these spaces as "non-places" of repetitive anonymity bearing down on the psyche of the traveler is a melodrama inappropriate to the exploration. Similarly, the euphoria of connectivity between many global registers is not the fascination. This is not the stuff of either melodramatic tragedy or one-world hype, but rather the stuff of ingenuity. The unabashed trek into false consciousness is propelled through a cross-graining index of events outlying our favored political explanations. This index constitutes crucial points in outline of a wilderness—fulcrums and trap doors that seesaw into another world or opportunity with perhaps unfamiliar powers of leverage. The ingenuity of the long con feeds on these moments when, smiling, nodding, and bowing, the bait and switch bears scale and consequence.

The trajectory moves between fluorescent-lit board rooms where one changes from shoes to slippers…a Western Union center in the Philippines, a distracted comparison of McKinsey white papers, a slowly moving field of automated container vehicles, an export processing zone in Mauritius, the traces of information in the corporate PowerPoint, or a detangling of submarine cable.

Again, there is no frictionless continuity, no exhilaration of connectivity but rather…

Many narratives keep company with this inverted travelogue. Picaresque rather than epic structures provide some company. Daniel Defoe, Henry Fielding, and Rabelais travel to geographic locations while also journeying into the conventions of society. Jonathan Swift and Lewis Carroll can travel not only in time but other dimensions of perception and imagination. In that sense, Rachel Carson's *Silent Spring,* as an exploration of an unexplored region in a different scale, also serves as a model. Allan Sekula's *Fish Story* was a geographic jour-

ney, but those foreign locations were not its destination. Sekula rode massive vessels of containerized shipping to discover the jagged shapes and peculiar economies of global trade networks. Haruki Murakami's easy narratives travel to geographic locations while also exploring a suspended territory in which Colonel Sanders can drift in and out. Benton MacKaye's book *The New Exploration,* overtly cast as travel, regarded Peary and Amundsen's expeditions to the North and South Poles to be the final episodes in the earth's territorial exploration. The new exploration he described was a journey to discover the landscape of sociotechnical systems that had been installed in the terrestrial surface for the previous hundred years. This "iron wilderness" was a constructed landscape that, despite being a man-made component of the very spaces we habit, was as foreign as a more exotic landscape. Like his colleague Stuart Chase's "Coals to Newcastle," it was a journey into the seemingly perverse logics of infrastructures—the unpredictable events that required a revision of expectations and analysis. MacKaye's eccentric, sentimental prose described a journey into a physical, material landscape as well as a journey into the other side of a dominant cultural preconception.

Again, there is no frictionless continuity, no exhilaration of connectivity but rather…a Brownian bounce off of discontinuities. An adventure in correlative thinking about things that don't make sense, this travel follows the coals to Newcastle or the tax-funded Halliburtons to tax-free Dubai, laws that restrict tobacco use but protect the sales of guns, the collapse of rail in the United States, or the strange protracted movements of goods through jagged quotas and trajectories around the world.

Having replaced shoes with slippers, already, the suspense that fuels adventure does not begin to mount. One will sometimes need to go to war but this journey…

There is no host. There is no first person. The wrong traveler only occasionally keeps the narrative going down the wrong path. Travel to a foreign location does not lend a badge of authenticity to the narrative. Travel is neither necessarily safe nor necessarily dangerous. The growing networks themselves are the subjects of travel. Multiple authors and trajectories save the narrative from the archaic ego. Their story need not spin around the moments of head-to-head contact with the thorny world, but rather orbits around something on TV, in the monotony of other media messages and Web chatter, in the foibles, manners, and dispositions that sustain attention without the exertions of heroic stories and privileged narrators. Besides, while the narrative may seem to be temporarily following Michael K. or the travel buffoon, it is often Melville's confidence man who, dressed in white, turns around, offering one of his many profiles. Indeed these passages are often propelled by confidence games and tricks that evaporate in environments of righteousness. The stories follow the "unreasonable man" and his contagious details or persuasions that finally rule the world. They travel to the volatile moments—reversals of iron-clad values or trajectories presumed to be progressive. Travel operates in those strata where it is possible to see *what people will trade*—to see what global forces can be taken for.

Having replaced shoes with slippers, already, the suspense that fuels adventure does not begin to mount. One will sometimes need to go to war but this journey…does not start with muddy boots walking through the streets of Kinshasa. It perhaps begins in stocking feet, in a 1970s interior suspended within the last fifty years. In one of thousands of such thresholds the slippers printed with the insignia of the JR, or Japan Railway Company, because this would clearly be the wrong story. Japanese trains were not supposed to happen within the economic and political logics of their time. Postwar Japan used rail as the means by which to travel away from war, using technologies that the cold war world would abandon for visions of automobile and aerospace advancement. This is not the railroad which, in the infamous quote of Cecil Rhodes, serves as an "instrument of pacification which costs less than the cannon and carries farther."[4] It is more akin to the late-nineteenth-century U.S. railroad of Chandler's description in that it is not solely the result of militarization. Finally, the wrong technology has proven to be one of the few not to be based on problematic logics regarding speed, safety, or environment. In the inner sanctums of corporate pride and scientific testing of high-speed, gigantic rooms test wind effects in millimeters. Carnivalesque machines, soberly outfitted to reproduce the precise environment of the train, test any possible discomforts to the passenger at high speed. Hurtling down the tracks at 110 miles per hour, all attention goes to the white-gloved hand of the train conductor sometimes resting on a throttle, sometimes raising an index finger in the air to mark the precise coincidence between the passage of the train and the tic on a stopwatch mounted nearby. The thrill of powerful destruction seems distracted by precision and pride.

Nobody really cares what happened to a narrator on that train. The novelist's default self-pity about repetitive anomic interiors of alienation do not propel the narrative of trains now, not only in Japan, but in Germany, France, Taiwan, or China. There are too many fulcrums into too many other worlds of curiosity, some of them in a historical register, others not yet even appearing in the news.

Some threads of story return to the Shinkansen debut in 1964, coincident with the Tokyo Olympics and an example of one of the first World Bank projects. Other threads follow the changing corporate structures and partnerships of Hitachi, Kawasaki, and Mitsubishi as their various personal and PowerPoint presentations target areas of the world suitable to the Shinkansen formula. Not conspiracy theories but rather simpler fascinations and curiosity fuel interest in the staggering number of global affiliates.

One extreme trap door between these boardrooms

lands surprisingly in the Middle East, at the epicenter of oil. The Dubai Metro, an enterprise between Japanese companies and the emirate, which will travel the length of the Sheikh Zayed Road and eventually run parallel to a high-speed rail ringing the gulf and connecting with the Saudi land bridge between the Red Sea and the Gulf, will make possible travel from Dubai to Damascus.

Here in the haunts of petro-dollars and the tedium of development hype, curiosities follow techniques and investing patterns of Islamic banking to a ramifying set of networks around the world. Now the influences are pervasively atomized, with information moving in sources that are far from public. The narrative travels not to astonishing enclaves and glittering man-made islands. Fulcrums that launch the story through a somewhat larger scale differential, taking the story to the wrong conclusion, such as one that opens onto the Alsunut development, a 1,660-acre business enclave at the confluence of the White and Blue Nile in Khartoum. Here a nexus of Chinese companies and development expertise from the UAE are signaling free-zone, world-city fluency, while excluding those Sudanese without the correct racial profile and connections to the Arab world. Only a special sort of travel, the wrong sort of travel, does not die in this special vein of corporate nondisclosure and censorship associated with kingdoms. That closed door, like the peripatetic moves of petrodollars, is itself a wilderness that explores far more powerful information than anything one might find on the ground, in supposedly authentic contact with actual sites of expenditure.

If the narrative makes a glancing bounce back to China or the UAE, it might find itself again in East Africa, perhaps even in another free zone. At the Athi River zone, on the road between Nairobi and Mombasa, cotton makes just such a bounce. The raw crop is processed in a few of the zone buildings, then bought by China, made into cloth, and sold back to a garment company in the same zone, just a few doors down, where a Kenyan company can make cloth more cheaply than China. That nothing about the story seems likely or believable is a good indication that the narrative is opening onto territory previously obscured by the wrong expectations.

The narrative is also not supposed to stumble on the zone at the Athi River because it does not conform to one of the chief critiques of the zone: that it is abusive to labor. The Athi River, as a zone directed by the government, is the place where unionized labor is perhaps most easily able to organize.

And on the road from Nairobi to Mombasa, the network of things that are not supposed to happen might even cross back over a previous thread in these particular strands of narrative. Somewhere on the wayside of this road, a German executive of Kenya Data Networks has buried the fiber-optic cable that is already being used to increase data and telephony capacity beyond that of the Intelsat-era satellite beams that are still the only link to international communication networks. The tiny strand of cable somewhere in the dirt anticipates a connection in Mombasa to international submarine cable.

It was not supposed to happen that some places in the world would remain unattached to international fiber-optic cable, especially a country that had been well served during the colonial period with generations of submarine cable delivering telegraphy and telephony. In MacKaye's terms, the fiber and microwave wilderness is still unfamiliar. Indeed, that cable, somewhere in the dirt, parallels the British East Africa Company's railroad from Mombasa to Nairobi, which was a segment in Cecil Rhodes's railway dream to outdo the German and other European colonial interests. The anteroom to the government minister's office in Nairobi, with its inexpensive dark paneling, red carpet, and a deadbolt lately installed on the door, gets pretty good CNN reception. From that room, where World Bank consultants wait with everyone else, broadband might cost ten times what it is supposed to cost and what it costs everywhere else in the world. The cell phone network that was supposed to make political process more transparent has been used to organize some of the horrific violence out on the road between Mombasa and Nairobi, and there is no State Department to help because this is not violence understood with the sovereign rules and interests of nations.

Heavy suspension buses travel on roads like the ones between Mombasa and Nairobi or Sarajevo and Belgrade because there is no better way to travel. The bus moves past self-organized forms of illegal building that seem as perfectly contagious in this landscape as they do in Guadalajara and Venezuela…

END

All images courtesy of Rustam Mehta

1   Paul Virilio and Sylvère Lotringer, *Pure War* (New York: Semiotext(e), 1983 and 1997), 14, 17.

2   Armand Mattelart, *Mapping World Communication: War, Progress, Culture* (London: University of Minnesota Press, 1994), 243.
3   Alfred D. Chandler Jr., *The Visible Hand: The Managerial Revolution in American Business* (Cambridge, Mass.: Harvard University Press, 1977), 204–5.
4   Mattelart, *Mapping World Communication*, 20.

ERICH MENDELSOHN AT WAR[1]

Enrique Ramirez

But in order to reeducate the people at large, beautiful per se, to that beautiful end, to rebuild their towns and dwellings—the visible expression, the broad acre of their social and civic consciousness—the people themselves must first experience the fight for existence, experience personal danger and common sacrifice, the turmoil of mechanized battles, the mental preparedness for being blotted out at a second's notice.
Erich Mendelsohn, April 22, 1942

Lecture Circuits

April 1942. A noticeable, foggy chill still envelops the campus at the University of California at Berkeley. Smallish clumps of midday Pacific layer fog are caught in the campus's vast greenery. Students, in various stages of scholarship, travel back and forth among the paved walkways. Undergraduates decked in thin, tropical wool sweaters, necks bundled in merino swaths (or, if women, in thigh-length A-line skirts), protect themselves against the late afternoon chill. Some are even wearing military uniforms. All types of ranks, branches of service are represented in the collegiate walk. Naval ensigns wear white, wide-flared pants and cartoonish sailor's caps rakishly tilted toward the back of their heads. While NCOs and lower-ranked officers wear their well-known tropical khaki, their Army and Marine counterparts flaunt their chocolate-brown field tunics.

Very little here, on this day, hides the fact that this has been indeed a difficult year for the American war effort. In the Pacific, the navy's surprising victory at Midway has provided something to keep American minds off what has been a series of setbacks: the army's surrender to Japanese forces in the Philippines, the near loss of the Aleutian islands of Attu and Kiska to the Imperial Japanese Navy. The staggering, Herculean task of mobilizing for the European theater of operations is just beginning. Rumors abound. Will there be a European invasion? A North African offensive? Yet the mood here is cheerful. There is a sense of excitement as people fill in the auditorium at the School of Architecture.

This evening, Erich Mendelsohn will deliver the last of his "Lectures on Architecture." The architect, by now famous for his various projects in Germany and England, has generated a remarkable following in the United States. The lectures coincide with an exhibition of Mendelsohn's projects at the San Francisco Museum of Art. There, for the first time, audiences were able to see a comprehensive portfolio of the architect's work: the organic, sweeping, winglike forms of the Einsteinturm at Potsdam; the graceful, curved facade of the Schocken Department Store at Chemnitz; the staid, white planar surfaces of the De La Warr Pavilion at Bexhill-on-Sea, England (a difficult project borne from a difficult relationship with Serge Chermayeff); the monumental white *brises-soleil* and geometrical solids of his Palestine projects, such as the Hebrew University Medical Center at Mt. Scopus in Jerusalem, as well as the Government Hospital at Haifa. There were even photographs of Mendelsohn's Leningrad textile factory.

The retrospective was a living document, a testament to Erich Mendelsohn's worldview. The photographs show many of the architect's guises: beguiling expressionist, dedicated socialist, scientific positivist, and devout Jew. When mapped out, the photographs explain Mendelsohn's own personal geographies and travel itineraries. Yet these gelatin prints can only suggest the personal, professional, and political struggles which the architect had to endure. Suggest, for Mendelsohn completed many of these works when he was a refugee. And "refugee" is a loaded term, an idea whose complexity is exemplified by Mendelsohn's work and travel during this period—not only was he an artistic iconoclast (his work was not featured in the 1927 *Weissenhofsiedlung* at Stuttgart) but also a political and religious outcast on the run from the burgeoning Nazi regime.

The three Berkeley lectures mirror the latest episode in Mendelsohn's travels. The first two lectures, titled "Architecture in a World Crisis" and "Architecture Today," feature a distinct emphasis on European works. Both begin with thoughtful exegeses on the Gallery of Machines at the Paris Exhibition of 1889. The building, a canopy of networked steel and glass, is, for Mendelsohn, emblematic of a "first true realization of the structural revolution,"[2] as well as a testament to construction as a "*creative* achievement" and "visionary formative capacity."[3] Yet in his third lecture, "Architecture in a Rebuilt

World," he discredits recent architecture and planning projects as "mere intellectual exercises," opting instead for a highly rational, technical, scientific approach. Mendelsohn continues, providing the audience with a vision of the architectural profession in the foreseeable postwar climate. He states:

> We see the town plan itself as a symphonic composition *conducted* by an impulsive force—a powerful shock absorber—by a man entirely devoted to *our* age, to a spirited and ever-renewed organic world. We see this symphonic composition *performed* by a team of idealists, each highly trained and shrewd in his craft, each directing his part of the plan and watching with authority the work to be done.[4]

Mendelsohn sees examples of this in a variety of instances. Interspersed with images of war materiel and implements of long-distance travel—artillery shells, battleships, seaplanes—Mendelsohn focuses on images of infrastructural projects and residential developments throughout the United States. These are evidence not only of a fascination with America, but something greater. Concentrating on an image of the Grand Canyon, Mendelsohn states:

> Indeed, the complex world of contemporary architecture and town planning…is the primal sign of a society again on unity of mind and matter. Building has transcended its special field to a common conception of scientific facts—world control—and of technological scale—world order—a conception on which, ultimately, the future society will have to function, on which it must work and shape its existence.[5]

This moment is poignant for several reasons. First, it affirms architectural modernism's rationalist imprimatur. It also links this rationalism with a decidedly scientific slant. It confirms the idea of the architect as a type of specialist or consultant, not just a promulgator of aesthetic viewpoints.

Yet the moment is important for another more important reason. At this moment, in the Berkeley lecture hall, the sum total of Mendelsohn's travels reaches an apotheosis. From his battlefield sketches on the Russian front in 1918, to travels by train and steamship to various points in Central and Eastern Europe, to more travel to England and Palestine, as well as passage by airplane and train in the western United States, here, in the hallowed halls of American academia, Mendelsohn finally finds a place where he can let his architectural thinking unfurl to its greatest potential.

Travels and Voyages

Travel has long been a paradigm for architectural education and practice. For the architect, travel did have certain romantic associations. One immediately thinks of no less than John Soane or Karl Friedrich Schinkel, with respective sketchbooks in hand, traveling to various ports of call and destinations in Europe. It is classic ur-*flânerie:* the wandering architect indeed a kaleidoscope equipped with vision, taking stock of architectural inventories throughout the world. Following this wholly Benjaminian itinerary, then, the traveling architect is a type of collector as well. Put another way, architecture's objects were objects of connoisseurship. Thus, for example, in March of 1818, Jeffrey Wyatt, an

English architect whose main client was King George IV, collected a vast array of architectural fragments lifted from Leptis Magna, an archaeological excavation site on the Libyan coast of North Africa. Wyatt reassembled the pieces, consisting of "22 granite columns, 15 marble columns, 10 capitals, 25 pedestals, 7 loose slabs, 10 pieces of cornice, 5 inscribed slabs, and various fragments of sculptured figures," at Windsor Great Park in 1826.[6]

The architectural voyage thus implied dual discoveries. Not only did travel afford the novice architect an education, but it also provided a way for new knowledge to be disseminated. The architect was the vessel for this knowledge, a propagator of new forms and curator of ancient heritage. This type of model certainly persists to this day.

For Erich Mendelsohn, however, travel implied much more than just the passage between two ports of call. It was an intellectual trajectory. In 1924, the architect made his first voyage to America on board the *Deutschland.* Fritz Lang, the famous film director, was his companion for this voyage, an experience that would prove formative for both of them. Aboard the *Deutschland's* deck, Fritz Lang would have seen a massing of medium-height buildings crowning the very spit of land forming Manhattan's own prow, with the Brooklyn Bridge's iron tendrils reaching across the gray waters for nearby land. Lang's first visit to New York resulted in a series of photographs that inspired those dystopian urban visions forever associated with *Metropolis* (1927). In one of these, a night scene on Broadway, lighted Coca-Cola and Dairylea billboards leave incandescent traces across the celluloid. It is as if Lang were momentarily disoriented, moving too rapidly, avoiding the onslaught of artificial light while keeping the camera aperture open. This light inscribes everything as a double image, anticipating the scene in *Metropolis* when the technocrat Joh Fredersen stares outside his own office at the frenzied city lights flickering faster and faster: a vision of a city in disrepair.

Lang's photograph would eventually make its way onto the pages of Erich Mendelsohn's *Amerika: Bilderbuch eines Architekten* (1926). Mendelsohn, who was not only a fellow passenger aboard the *Deutschland* but also toured New York with Lang, processed his own ideas about the American metropolis differently. Whereas Lang found inspiration in this trip for his upcoming films, Mendelsohn was overtly caustic in his appraisals. He did admire much of the industrial architecture he saw during his travels in the United States, but was nevertheless struck by the abject moral bankruptcy that such buildings represented.

The text accompanying the photographs in *Amerika* is pithy and biting. Indeed, in the very opening chapter to the book, called "Typical American Traits,"[7] a picture of Manhattan from the sea inspired Mendelsohn to describe the city as the "Port of the world. Announcer of the new country, of liberty and the unmeasurable wealth behind it."[8] Such ire is tempered with cautious optimism in Mendelsohn's caption for Lang's nighttime photograph of Broadway:

> Uncanny. The contours of the building are erased.
> But in one's consciousness they still rise, chase one another, trample one another.

This is the foil for the flaming scripts, the rocket fire of moving illuminating ads, emerging and submerging, disappearing and breaking out again over the thousands of autos and the maelstrom of pleasure-seeking people.

Still disordered, because exaggerated, but all the same full of imaginative beauty, which will one day be complete.[9]

This first visit to the United States had a powerful impact on Mendelsohn's subsequent work. The photographs of skyscrapers, industrial structures, and city streets gracing the pages of *Amerika* are portentous. If, for Le Corbusier, the aerial view is totalizing in its ability to indict urbanism's own failures, then for Mendelsohn the Sheeler-like views from below opt for something else. In the preface to *Amerika,* the architect declares that "America demands nothing of our love, but wants to be treated by us as unemotionally as we are treated by her. In architecture this country supplies everything: the worst of Europe's refuse, deformed offspring of civilization, but she also gives hope of a new world."[10]

Mendelsohn's own captions reinforce this totalizing conception of architecture, its ability to encapsulate *everything.* In the introduction to *Amerika,* Mendelsohn noted, "For what we generally characterize today as 'typically American' is a caricature of the European mother countries of Americans."[11] Yet Mendelsohn finessed the idea of typicality by suggesting that a single American city was a synecdoche for a larger swath of European cities. Describing New York to his wife, Louise, in a 1924 letter, Mendelsohn declares that the towering spires of the Woolworth Building stand for something else, something greater: "That is not a city in the European sense, that is the whole world, in a pot."[12]

Eighteen years later, with several retrospectives and travels completed, Mendelsohn gave no indication that he had changed his views. Standing in front of a rapt audience at Berkeley in April 1942, an image of Moses King's futuristic New York hovering on the screen behind him, Mendelsohn declared, "In 1889, the year, you will remember, of the Gallery of Machines in Paris, the dream of New York's Piranesi—and I take New York as being for us the nearest example of metropolitan centers all over the world—simply accepted the then-prevailing town planning and traffic dilettantism as the cherished idol of things to come."[13] Fortunately, the current war provided plenty of opportunities to rid the world of such architectural pretension. War necessitated travel of a different sort.

Wars of Information

The Second World War featured various types of conflict. There is, of course, the obvious type—modern, mechanized war. This type of war is known through its various implements and devices. In modern war, tanks move like ironclad crustaceans across bombed-out landscapes. Columns of weary soldiers march along country roads, their destination marked by lightning flashes of artillery rounds in the far distance. The drumlike report of machine-gun fire echoes in city streets. Gray-hulled armadas plow whitecaps, patrolling for enemy submarines lurking in the icy depths. Dive bombers swoop in hell-bound angles, engines screaming as their target be-

comes larger and larger in a pilot's fixed bombsight. The thunderous, earth-moving concussions grind granite to cinders as waves of bombers unleash their deadly freight on cities, miles below.

War also involved a certain type of mischief. Battlefield commanders and intelligence officers initiated operations designed to fool or distract their opponents. *Partizan* units in Nazi-occupied countries would complete small missions. Snipping telegraph wires, stealing gasoline, adjusting the gauge of railroad tracks—such small diversions could, in the aggregate, seriously interrupt enemy operations. Such operations undoubtedly relied on accurate, consistent intelligence. Reprisals would certainly result—whole villages would be decimated, conspirators garroted and hung from lampposts—a testament to the deadly business of information exchange.

Information was the war's greatest commodity, the "only real medium of exchange."[14] Information was also a distributed medium, its parcels proliferating through a vast network of subtle and invisible conduits. Indeed, this is the world of Graham Greene and Eric Ambler's novels, as well as of Carroll Reed's films. These artists' works reincarnate the informational infrastructures undergirding the landscape of military operations during the Second World War. In this shadowy world, the nodes of information exchange are familiar. Cities become the stage set for this *pas de deux* of intelligence and counterintelligence. In the penumbras of Liverpool Street Station, darkened alleyways of various Parisian arrondissements, or in the wolfram mines outside Lisbon, unknown wars of information were waged.

Here, then, was travel of a different sort. Whether affiliated with MI6, OSS, OVRA,[15] Gestapo, whatever one's shade of insurgency and counterinsurgency, espionage necessitated travel. There were, of course, technological advances that allowed operatives to listen to their enemies far away from the warring fronts. Yet the bulk of intelligence operations relied on the familiar implements of transportation networks: night trains, steamships, passenger airplanes, military transport, cars, trucks, horses, mules. Each destination contained information, and it was the operative's task to gather such information. The operative's métier was reading cities and landscapes. Of course, some information's value was directly proportional to the amount of deceit needed to propagate it, or to the number of lives lost to obtain it. Other forms of information were everywhere, in furtive glances, casual conversations, even in books and newspapers. The operative's role was to decode such information, to unravel the spin and report the facts.

Architectures of Intelligence

A bustling metropolis of thirty souls, Clover was the largest settlement in Tooele County, Utah, during the opening moments of World War II. The meteorologist and folklorist Ronald L. Ives even acknowledged that everyone else in the United States viewed Tooele County as the "center of depopulation."[16] Not to be excluded from this group was Secretary of War Henry Stimson, who urged President Franklin Roosevelt to consider parts of Tooele County as a potential site for wartime testing. At this time, the Chemical Warfare Service (CWS), a branch of the United States Army involved in

13.	April 1, 1943	Foundations for German Structures completed.
14.	April 5, 1943	Brickwork for German Structures started.
15.	April 12, 1943	Final drawings issued.
16.	April 16, 1943	First truck of millwork arrived for Japanese Structures.
17.	May 11, 1943	Construction completed by contractor and accepted by architect-engineer.
18.	May 14, 1943	All test furnishings received.
19.	May 15, 1943	All mats received and installed. Structure inspected by U. S. District Engineer. Structure ready for tests.
20.	May 17, 1943	Penetration tests started.

V. ACKNOWLEDGMENTS

The expeditious handling of this project and the ability to reproduce structural details is largely due to the cooperation and capable assistance received from the following:

U. S. District Engineer	- Col. E.G. Thomas & staff
Office of Chief of Engineers	- Mr. O.F. Sieder & staff
Area Engineer	- Capt. J. R. Hamblen
CWS-Technical	- Lt. Col. W.G. Wilson
Contractor	- Ford J. Twaits Company
Sub-contractor	- Pemberton Lumber&Millwork Co.
Sub-contractor	- Union-National Co. Inc.
Sub-contractor	- Allen Industries
Consultant & Architect	- Antonin Raymond
Consultant	- Eric Mendelssohn
Consultant	- Dr. Wachsman
Consultant	- Dr. Paul Zucker
Consultant	- Mr. Hans Knoll
Consultant	- Mr. George Hartmueller
Consultant	- RKO Studios (Authenticity Division)
Consultant	- Mr. Phillip Sawyer
Consultant	- Mr. Alfred Gemperle

NFM)GS
WTK)BCS
HAR)

C O N F I D E N T I A L

Masthead from the 1943 Standard Oil Development Report to the Chemical Warfare Service Technical Division. This document lists the various persons working on the Dugway project, including Mendelsohn, Raymond, and "Doctor" Wachsmann. The list also includes Hans Knoll, who had started his furniture company in the United States in New York, and Paul Zucker, the art historian who would go on to moderate the symposium "New Architecture and City Planning," in 1944, and coauthor "The Human Scale in City Planning" with Josep Lluis Sert, also in 1944. From an untitled publication issued by the National Defense Research Committee.

First declassified image of the Dugway project. Although the article is about Antonin Raymond, note the image of Mendelsohn and Wachsmann's "German Village" at the top. *Architectural Forum* (January 1946).

German Village, interior view of roof framing in attic, looking south. Courtesy Library of Congress, Historic American Engineering Record, Historic American Building Survey.

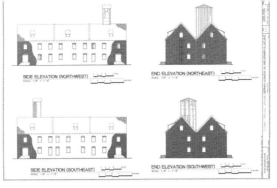

Elevations of German Village. Courtesy Library of Congress, Historic American Engineering Record, Historic American Building Survey.

View of southwest end of German Village looking northeast. Courtesy Library of Congress, Historic American Engineering Record, Historic American Building Survey.

View of German Village. Courtesy Library of Congress, Historic American Engineering Record, Historic American Building Survey.

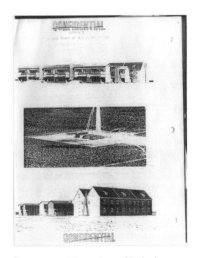

The uppermost image is used in the January 1946 *Architectural Forum* article. Also note the pristine condition of the test structures in the lowest image. From an untitled publication issued by the National Defense Research Committee.

German village, interior view of newel post at south stairwell, looking north. Courtesy Library of Congress, Historic American Engineering Record, Historic American Building Survey.
Examples of typical German furniture construction. From an untitled publication issued by the National Defense Research Committee.

chemical weapons testing, pressed the War Department for facilities to supplement the crammed and outdated facilities at Edgewood Technical Arsenal in Maryland and Eglin Field on the Florida panhandle. On February 6, 1942, President Roosevelt signed a bill to withdraw 126,720 acres of land from the public domain for use by the CWS. Named after the myriad wagon tracks—or "dugways"—carved into the open terrain, construction of Dugway Proving Ground began in earnest in March 1942. Unlike the Edgewood Technical Arsenal, whose proximity to major population centers made large-scale testing of biological and chemical weapons undesirable, Dugway Proving Ground was favored for its remoteness and lack of population. More importantly, a 1948 publication by former CWS officers and scientists identified the true allure of Dugway Proving Ground. The report stated that the cold, hot, and occasionally humid climate permitted laboratory and field-testing under variable combat conditions.

Under the command of Major John R. Burns, Dugway Proving Ground started as a group of portable structures occupied by army, navy, and National Defense Research Committee (NDRC) personnel. As American involvement increased in Europe and the Pacific, Dugway Proving Ground became the primary facility for the testing of countless toxic agents, flamethrowers, chemical spray systems, and biological warfare weapons.[17] Among the many physicists and chemists at Dugway Proving Ground were a handful of meteorologists who used wind and temperature data to measure the dispersal of phosgene, cyanogen chloride, and hydrogen cyanide bombs "ranging in size from 100 to 4000 pounds."[18] Ronald L. Ives was one of these meteorologists. Although the exact nature of his involvement in these testing programs is lost to history, he illustrates the dangerous and ominous nature of Dugway Proving Ground, reminiscing about an advertisement in *The Sandblast,* the weekly newsletter at the facility:

THIS SUMMER
SEND YOUR BOY TO DUGWAY
HEALTHY, INSTRUCTIVE, DIFFERENT
4300 FEET ABOVE SEA LEVEL
HIKING, MOTOR TRIPS, MANUAL TRAINING
SELECTED CLIENTELE—HAS PRESIDENTIAL APPROVAL
SPECIALLY TRAINED LEADERS, EXCELLENT HOSPITAL
AND MORGUE FACILITIES

Boys at Dugway are asked to do little tasks about the camp to prepare them for life. Military atmosphere. No idle moments. Applicants screened by Army Intelligence.
Other camps under the same management at Kiska, Bizerte, and Guadacanal.[19]

Pictures of wartime structures at Dugway Proving Ground do not immediately inspire a similar sense of dread. In a 1943 photograph, Dog Area, the central CWS test installation at Dugway Proving Ground, looks almost ordinary, like a small town in the middle of a desert landscape. Low, squat wooden houses sit among laboratories with brick facades. Above-ground power and telephone lines weave an aerial grid mirroring the orthogonal arrangements of unpaved streets and sidewalks. Occasional smatterings of succulents dot the horizon, and far in the distance, scrub brush gathers across

the flats reaching far to Granite Peak. An aerial photograph of Dog Area reveals the extent of the wooden and brick structures. From the air, more streets can be seen intersecting at right angles. Toward the bottom of the picture, a Boeing B-17 heavy bomber and an assortment of medium and dive bombers sit on the tarmac in front of a hangar at Michael Army Air Field, the only airstrip at Dugway Proving Ground. Other pictures of Dog Area begin to reveal networks of pipes and cold-storage facilities. Those pictures taken in 1944 give a sense of further developments at Dugway Proving Ground. In June of that year, a separate research station was constructed for testing biological weapons. Located 30 miles west of Dog Area, the Granite Peak Installation, or GPI-2, eventually became *the* center of biological weapons research during World War II.[20] Because of its isolation, the research station required its own utilities, living quarters, laboratories, and medical facilities, including a pump house and "underground igloo-storage building."[21]

Over forty years later, a map published by the United States Department of Interior hints at the extent of work completed at Dugway Proving Ground. An area once known for occasional silver mining, the map contains a series of cryptic titles. An "Aerial Spray Grid" sits next to a "Downwind Grid Array." Michael Army Air Field sits on Stark Road, in between Cedar Mountain Range and Camel Back Mountain. In the North, the "CDA Grid" rests by a dot labeled "CBR Gun Position." Further west, on Goodyear Road, far beyond Granite Peak and GPI-2, sits the "Radar Calibration course" and the mysterious "drop zone."

Starting at GPI-2, if one traces a finger east across the map of Dugway Proving Ground, he or she will inevitably run into another part of the facility called Peter Area. There, marked as a little square slightly south of Stark Road, sits "German Village," or Building 8100. From May 17, 1943, to September 1, 1943, Building 8100 and a series of adjacent "Japanese" villages were bombed again and again by aircraft taking off from Michael Army Air Field.[22] No idle moments indeed, for the building represents a forgotten moment in Erich Mendelsohn's career. Working out of offices in Croton-on-Hudson, New York, as well as out of War Department meetings, Mendelsohn provided the United States Army Air Force with some very important information—architecture intelligence, so to speak.

The Operation
In 1943, Dugway Proving Ground was a figurative hell on earth. A famous line from Canto III of Dante's *Inferno* even graced one wall of the military police gatehouse on Stark Road: "abandon hope, all ye who enter here."[23] Enlisted men working for the Chemical Warfare Service expressed no love for the temporary wooden houses and laboratories, often referring to the secret outpost in Tooele County as "Oblivion Junction" or "Limbo."[24] Their station was one of total, unquestioned devotion to the war effort. And in 1943, this meant testing the M69 incendiary on a series of "Experimental foreign villages... designed to make more 'good Nazis' and 'ancestors.'"[25]

On March 12, 1943, following the successful napalm tests at Harvard University and Edgewood Technical Arsenal, the CWS Technical Division sent "Request

SPCWT 161" to the board of directors of the Standard Oil Development Company. The U. S. Army not only hired this branch of Standard Oil for the development and testing of different types of plastics, synthetic oils, and fuels, but also as the sole manufacturer and processor of napalm. The contract thus requested the "research and design" and construction of facilities for the testing of incendiaries at Dugway Proving Ground. The CWS Technical Division and the Standard Oil Development Company officially entered into a contract for the creation of "Typical German and Japanese Test Structures" on March 18, 1943.[26] Documents reveal that the "structures" were really accurate replicas of German and Japanese housing, designed to test the effects of the M69 napalm bomb.[27]

Representatives of the CWS's Technical and Industrial Divisions, along with NDRC and Standard Oil Development Company staff, met in Elizabeth, New Jersey, on March 19, 1943, to finalize plans for the design and construction of the test structures. A May 1943 Standard Oil Development Company document, the official record of CWS "Request SPCWT 161," also notes that "several consultants" were present at this meeting.[28] Among these "consultants" were architects Erich Mendelsohn, Konrad Wachsmann, and Antonin Raymond.[29]

The term "consultant" is interesting for its contradictory associations. It is a confirmation of Mendelsohn's views that the architect is a type of specialist deploying highly rational and scientific tools at his disposal. However, the term rings of military intelligence. Indeed, these architects' charge was to provide the War Department with vital information about German and Japanese architecture. How these architectures were built or how they looked was not as important as how they burned. The scope of the Dugway project created a different spectrum for architectural practice—the erstwhile giver of form has suddenly become the destroyer of worlds. Mendelsohn, Wachsmann, and Raymond's full-scale models of German and Japanese housing depict the horrible shift from habitation to incineration.

The three architects attended the March 19, 1943, meeting with the CWS Technical Division, Standard Oil Development Company, and the NDRC to present findings on the state of housing in Germany and Japan. The findings would be used to evaluate the potential of German and Japanese cities as targets of incendiary bombing attacks. Each architect had a specific role in the project.[30] Mendelsohn provided the CWS and Standard Oil Development Company with information about the characteristics of German industrial structures.[31] More specifically, Mendelsohn provided specific data about the amount of roof coverage in Augsburg, Berlin and its surroundings, Breslau, Danzig, Dresden and its surroundings, Duisburg, Frankfurt am Main, Halle, Hannover and its surroundings, Königsberg, Leipzig and its surroundings, Magdeburg, Mannheim, Munich, Nürnberg, and Stuttgart.[32]

The CWS and Standard Oil Development Company authorized this specific type of survey because it was interested in the flammability of roofs in major German cities. The idea here was that in a typical air attack, M69 incendiary clusters would be dropped on the densest urban areas of Germany. Louis H. Fieser's tests at Harvard and Edgewood Technical Arsenal revealed that a wooden test house bombed with "raw gasoline was merely singed" while another bombed with napalm "burned to the ground."[33] These results were surely on the mind of CWS officers when they consulted with Mendelsohn to determine the extent of wooden roof construction in Germany.

The construction of German Village began on March 29, 1943. A local building contractor, the Ford J. Twaits Company, handled the site construction, with John F. Brandt as the project architect.[34] German Village actually consisted of six "typical" German dwellings, each built with two apartments, for a total of twelve residences. The structure was separated by 40-foot fire-breaks that allowed firefighters access and that prevented the total destruction of the structure. Six apartments, three on the first floor and three on the second, imitated Rhineland construction, while another six replicated Central German construction in the same pattern. A common party wall separated the Rhineland and Central German apartment blocks, reflecting how each block would actually have interfaced with its urban neighbors. Although Central German and Rhineland apartment blocks were never found in such close proximity as they were at Dugway Proving Ground, the structure was nevertheless accurate, as the test structure "closely adhered to the authentic German construction, including framing, outer masonry and inner firewall construction, flooring, mortise and tenon joinery, and roof sheathing."[35] The CWS and Standard Oil Development Company originally considered the construction of a third, eastern-German type of housing block, but determined that the Central German block could be used for this purpose as well. They also made efforts to carefully study the brick exterior and interior walls. In particular, they reasoned that the targeted German urban industrial housing, both stone and brick, contained a very high number of masonry fire divisions between blocks and rooms. Since the German test structure was erected to accommodate aerial bombing from as high as 20,000 feet, and since the German structures sat on the desert floor, Standard Oil added a broadly painted, vertical stripe on one end of the southern block for use as a high-altitude targeting indicator. Bombers had to drop a large number of small incendiaries so that individual rooms within apartment blocks were set ablaze through the attic floor, thus not allowing a fire to be contained by multiple firewalls. A reinforced concrete bunker, also referred to as a bomb shelter, was erected east of the test structure with the requirement that it be able to withstand the impact of a 500-pound incendiary dropped from 20,000 feet.[36]

"The Unchangeable Message of War and Revolution!"

Upon a first glance, German Village looks rather unremarkable. Nestled among unpaved access roads, the building is eerily devoid of context. The southwest brick facade is split into three equal sections, each representing a residential unit, each lacking detailing or ornamentation. Nine windows puncture the second (top) story. The bottom floor contains four windows, with three single doors and two double doors. A series of drainage pipes divides the roof into thirds, each containing a prominent dormer window facing northwest. The northwest section of German Village tells more about the organization of the building. In fact, the previous structure is repeated, with the windows, dormers, and doors also facing southeast. The only difference between this part of German Village and the former is that this one features a tall, windowless roofed promontory jutting upward.

German Village is incomparable in the sense that it defies any type of serious scrutiny. Is it sham architecture? A distraction in an otherwise brilliant career? Although the building lacks the architect's signature expressionistic élan, it represents the end point of Mendelsohn's wartime travels.

Travels of this type are, to a certain extent, familiar. The first half of the twentieth century could very well be considered a type of design diaspora. Much has already been written about how architects and designers were displaced by authoritarian, nationalist, and antidemocratic regimes. We know about the Bauhaus exodus, for example. The United States became a fertile ground for the likes of Herbert Bayer, Mies van der Rohe, and Walter Gropius. The same could be said for England, where designers like Arthur Korn and Ernö Goldfinger became influential figures within expatriate design communities. Lesser-known artists, such as the Catalan anti-Franco graphic designer Josep Renau, are slowly becoming the subject of proper historical treatment. However tragic the individual stories may be, these designers' predicaments are known.

But we come to understand Mendelsohn's involvement in the Dugway project as something different. It is true that the exigent demands of global war required extraordinary commitments from everyone, including established designers. Hoyt C. Hottel, the MIT chemist responsible for bringing Mendelsohn to the CWS's attention, remarked in a 1984 lecture on the nature of the commitment required by the Dugway project. He writes, "Wartime research turns up more than a few participants whose actions show a strong self-interest, many participants who work diligently and selflessly with the sole motivation of winning the war quickly, and a very few whose consciences are troubled when they think of the consequences, in human suffering, of their effort."[37] Mendelsohn's Berkeley lectures exhibit all of these three aspects. But perhaps it is the last category, that of the wartime researcher who is so absorbed by the project that he shows little remorse for the consequences of an action, that holds our attention here.

In particular, we look to one example of the results achieved by the Dugway project. On the night of March 9, 1945, three hundred B-29 Superfortress bombers from the 73rd and 313th Bombardment Wings flew to Tokyo from bases in the Northern Mariana Islands in the Pacific. Stripped of radar equipment and armament, their bomb bays bloated with tons of M69 incendiary bombs, these aircraft started one of the largest fires in history. The fire engulfed 16 square miles of the densest part of Tokyo. Over 80,000 Japanese civilians died on that night. Not all were burned to ash. Some asphyxiated to death, as the conflagration literally sucked all the oxygen out of the air. This process caused typhoons of fire that traveled near the speed of sound. The destruction of Tokyo was not sudden. After watching their neighborhoods burn, some hapless victims decided to jump in rivers or to hide in makeshift bomb shelters. They literally boiled or cooked in those places in which they tried to avoid the destruction. Neither Mendelsohn, Wachsmann, nor Raymond acknowledged the human toll of their project. In processing the extent of this devastation, could we, even for a moment, consider it remarkable that it began with a series of voyages made by a German refugee?

This was a different type of architecture voyage, for the Dugway project demanded that architectural information be used for a new, terrifying purpose: the systematic razing of cities in Europe and Asia. The smoldering ruins of German and Japanese cities provided the necessary tabula rasa Mendelsohn envisioned for his vision of architecture practice in the postwar world, a vision he clearly defined in 1942, just as he was preparing for the Dugway project:

The total earthquake of this revolution, the great fire of this war leaves us no time to hesitate or to postpone decisions. We must prepare now for what this country, the whole world, demands and expects of us: guidance on the road to a new era; it is the longing for life, when death is omnipresent; the devotion to truth, when truth is on trial; the courage of action, when values become stagnant, that remold the spirit and redirect the march of man.[38]

1   This paper is based on research completed at the Yale School of Architecture from 2005 to 2006, as well as on papers presented at the University of Virginia in September 2006 and Harvard University in February 2007. This paper was also inspired by my MED thesis, completed in May 2007, titled *Built to Destroy: Erich Mendelsohn's, Konrad Wachsmann's, and Antonin Raymond's "Typical German and Japanese Test Structures" at Dugway Proving Ground, Utah.*

2   Erich Mendelsohn, "Architecture in a World Crisis," in *Three Lectures on Architecture* (Berkeley: University of California Press, 1944), 7. This lecture was delivered on April 16, 1942.

3   Mendelsohn, "Architecture Today," in ibid., 22. This lecture was delivered on April 22, 1942.

4   Ibid., 41.

5   Ibid., 47.

6   Sophie Thomas, "Assembling History: Fragments and Ruins," *European Romantic Review* 14 (2003): 177–86.

7   "Das Typisch Amerikanische."

8   Erich Mendelsohn, "Hafen der Welt. Verkünder des neuen Landes, der Freiheit und des hinter ihr liegenden unermeßlichen Reichturms," in *Amerika: Bilderbuch eines Architekten* (Berlin: Rudolf Mosse Verlag, 1928), 12. Compare a more recent version of the book, where the same passage is translated as, "Port of the world. Announcer of the new country, of liberty and what lies behind it: measureless wealth, the most reckless exploitation, gold seekers and world domination." Stanley Appelbaum, trans., *Erich Mendelsohn's "Amerika": 82 Photographs* (New York: Dover Publications, 1993), 1.

9   Ibid., 52. The original caption reads:

Unheimlich. Die Konturen der Häuser sind aus gewischt. Aber in Bewußtsein steigen sie noch, laufen einander nach, überennen sich.

Das ist die Folie für die Flammenschriften, das Raketenfeuer der beweglichen Lichtreklame, auf- und untertauchend, verschwindend und ausbrechend über den Tausenden von Autos und dem Lustwirbel der Menschen.

Noch ungeordnet, weil übersteigert, aber doch schon voll von phantastischer Schönheit, die einmal vollendet sein wird.

Mendelsohn, *Amerika,* 130.

10   Louise Mendelsohn to Bruno Zevi, in Zevi, *Erich Mendelsohn: The Complete Works* (Boston: Birkhäuser Verlag, 1997), 80–81.

11   Appelbaum, trans., *Erich Mendelsohn's "America",* xi.

12   "Das ist keine Stadt im europäischen Sinn, das ist die Welt, ganz, in einem Topf." Erich Mendelsohn to Louise Mendelsohn, October 16, 1924, in Oskar Beyer, ed., *Erich Mendelsohn: Breife eines Architekten* (Munich: Prestel Verlag, 1961), 61.

13   Mendelsohn, "Architecture in a Rebuilt World," 35.

14   Thomas Pynchon, *Gravity's Rainbow* (New York: Viking, 1972), 258.

15   Organizzazione per la Vigilanza e la Repressione dell'Antifascismo, the Italian secret police under Victor Emmanuel III and Benito Mussolini's reigns.

16   Ronald L. Ives, "Dugway Tales," *Western Folklore* 6, no. 1 (January 1947): 53.

17   Historic American Engineering Record, National Park Service, Department of the Interior, "Dugway Proving Ground, Dugway, Tooele County, Utah: Written Historical and Descriptive Data," HAER No. UT-35 (1984), 15 (hereafter cited as HAER).

18   Chemical Corps Association, *The Chemical Warfare Service in World War II: A Report of Accomplishments* (New York: Reinhold, 1948), 36.

19   Ives, 58.

20   HAER, 24.

21   Ibid.

22   Ibid.

23   Ives, 53.

24   Ibid., 55.

25   Ibid. For more information about the design and development of the M69 incendiary bomb, see Louis F. Fieser, *The Scientific Method: A Personal Account of Unusual Projects in War and in Peace* (New York: Reinhold, 1964); Chemical Corps Association, *The Chemical Warfare Service in World War II: A Report of Accomplishments* (New York: Reinhold, 1948); and Charles Sterling Popple, *Standard Oil Company (New Jersey) in World War II* (New Jersey: Standard Oil Company of New Jersey, 1952). Materials regarding the results of the M69 trials at Dugway Proving Ground are located at the National Archives, ETF 550 E-2844, Military Intelligence Division, Great Britain, "Dropping Trials of Incendiary Bombs against Representative Structures at Dugway, USA, October 12, 1943," *Edgewood Arsenal Technical Files Relating to Foreign Chemical, Radiological, and Biological Warfare Retired to the Defense Intelligence Agency for Reference Purposes* (Entry 1-B), Records of the Defense Intelligence Agency (Record Group 373); and ETF 550 E-2844, Military Intelligence Division, Great Britain, IBTP/Report/128, "Comparison of the Japanese Targets and Test Results at the Building Research Station, Edgewood Arsenal and Dugway Proving Ground, H. M. Llewellyn, M. A. London," Report No. R3583-45, June 29, 1945, *Edgewood Arsenal Technical Files Relating to Foreign Chemical, Radiological, and Biological Warfare Retired to the Defense Intelligence Agency for Reference Purposes* (Entry 1-B), Records of the Defense Intelligence Agency (Record Group 373).

26   Standard Oil Development Company, "Design and Construction of Typical German and Japanese Structures at Dugway Proving Grounds, Utah," SOD Project 30601, SP-CWT 161 (May 27, 1943), 15.

27   See HAER, "Dugway Proving Ground, German-Japanese Village, German Village: Photographs, Written Historical and Descriptive Data, Reduced Copies of Measured Drawings," HAER UT-92-A, UT0568 (April 2, 2001).

28   Ibid.

29   Ibid.

30   Documents indicate that the Chemical Warfare Service had been interested in consulting with the "Gropius group at Harvard" for this project. Ibid., 3.

31   Ibid.

32   The exact methodology of this is unclear. Although the 2001 HAER report indicates that there is some dispute as to whether Mendelsohn actually authored this survey, the 1943 Standard Oil Development Company Report notes that the survey "was made by one of Germany's former leading architects." See Standard Oil Development Company, 3. Because the Chemical Warfare Service relied on Wachsmann's knowledge of wood construction for the project, the 1943 document suggests that Mendelsohn was the likely author of the survey.

33   Chemical Corps Association, 69.

34   Although Brandt's initials are on all the drawings, the exact nature of his involvement is unknown.

35   Ibid.

36   Ibid., 6.

37   Hoyt C. Hottel, "Simulation of Fire Research in the United States after 1940 (A Historical Account)," *Combustion Science and Technology* 39, no.1 (January 1984): 5.

38   Mendelsohn, "Architecture In a Rebuilt World," 48.

View of Soane's Model Room on the second floor of 13 Lincoln's Inn Fields, C.J. Richardson, c. 1834–35. © The British Library Board.

This watercolor shows Soane's Model Room, upon its completion in 1834, and was engraved for publication in Soane's *Description of the House and Museum* of 1835. It is taken from the window looking across the room at the large two-tier model stand, which was made for Soane when he bought the large cork model of Pompeii displayed on the lower tier. The stand was designed to allow for the display of additional cork and plaster models in an imaginative "architectural composition" around the outside of both upper and lower levels. These included cork models of the Temple of Vesta at Tivoli (in the foreground at the corner of the lower tier) and the Greek Doric temples at Paestum; a collection of twenty plaster of Paris models by Francois Fouquet of conjectural reconstructions of antique buildings (Fouquet's model of the Pantheon can be seen in a glass case at the corner of the upper level); and models of Soane's own projects (on the bottom of the stand, to left of the cupboard doors, is a model of his famous Bank Stock Office for the Bank of England). The model stand incorporated a plan chest in the base, which contained collections of drawings by English architects including William Kent and Soane's near-contemporaries Sir William Chambers and James Wyatt. Thus, Soane's model stand served as a microcosm of the history of architecture that focused on worthy buildings from the past but also included his own work and that of his contemporaries.—*Helen Dorey*

For more on Sir John Soane, see page 46. For additional images from Sir John Soane's Model Room, see pages 26 and 170–171.

Plaster model of the "restored" Temple of Vesta at Tivoli, made by Francois Fouquet (fl. 1792–1835). Photograph by Geremy Butler. Courtesy the Trustees of Sir John Soane's Museum.

This model is one of twenty "restorations" of ancient Greek and Roman buildings made by the Parisian model maker Francois Fouquet, and purchased by Soane in 1834 from the architect Edward Cresy for one hundred pounds. Fouquet worked with his father, Jean-Pierre Fouquet (1752–1829), producing models for architects and collectors from the 1790s until the 1830s. Francois Fouquet's models tend to be smaller and more finely detailed than those of his father. It is thought that they were made by building up the plaster over a framework of thin internal metal armatures and then carving the extraordinarily fine capitals and entablatures by hand. The Fouquets produced models for the École Polytechnique as well as for the model gallery of the artist and collector Louis-Francois Cassas (1756–1827). Soane may have seen this collection when he visited Paris in 1814 during the "Hundred Days of Peace" before the Battle of Waterloo. The Fouquets' exquisite models were well known to architect-collectors in England, and John Nash and Robert Smirke also owned examples of their work.

The evidence for Fouquet's reconstructions probably came from a variety of published sources, and perhaps also from Cassas's own drawings of antique ruins. The measurements used for this model were probably based on those published by Antoine Desgodetz in *Les édifices antiques de Rome dessinés et mesurés très exactement* (1779). Desgodetz shows an entablature with two ox heads in each intercolumniation and one over each column, as used by Fouquet. Desgodetz does not reconstruct a dome, but other possible sources, such as Palladio and Serlio, show a stepped dome

similar to the Pantheon. Fouquet seems to have modeled his dome on that of Durand, published in *Recueil et parallèle des édifices de tout genre* (1800), but he uses two rather than three steps at the base and adds the pineapple finial. The circular stepped platform below the temple may have come entirely from Fouquet's imagination. —*H. D.*

Cork model of the Temple of Vesta at Tivoli, near Rome, made by Giovanni Altieri (fl. 1767–90), 1770s. Photograph by Hugh Kelly. Courtesy the Trustees of Sir John Soane's Museum.

The temple of Vesta, dating from the early first century B.C. and set dramatically on the edge of a precipice, was Soane's favorite antique building. He was probably introduced to it by his earliest teacher, George Dance the Younger, and he sketched and took careful measurements of it as a student in Italy in 1778–79. The temple remained a powerful source of inspiration throughout his career, its distinctive order appearing in some of Soane's most famous works, such as the Tivoli Corner at the Bank of England. Soane even created a "Tivoli Recess" at Lincoln's Inn Fields in tribute to the temple. In later life, his pupil John Sanders referred to the temple in a letter as "your darling Tivoli."

The model was first displayed in Soane's Dome area at the back of the Museum, perched on top of a teetering pile of architectural fragments. It was then a prominent exhibit in Soane's first Model Room, created in 1828 in the attic of Lincoln's Inn Fields. In Soane's second Model Room, the model is shown on the central stand. Curiously, it was not displayed next to the plaster model by Fouquet of the same building, although both were in the Model Room, and Soane surely used the contrast between the cork ruins and the plaster reconstructions for didactic purposes. —*H. D.*

A Tour of the Monuments of the Great American Void

SALT LAKE CITY, GREAT SALT LAKE, GREAT SALT LAKE DESERT...

Matthew Coolidge

A tour of the Monuments of the Great American Void begins at the crossroads of the old west and the new, in Salt Lake City, Utah. The route travels counterclockwise, around the Great Salt Lake, past ruins of old railway towns and fortresses of the current imperial regime. It connects to the cosmos through rocket plants and astronomical land art, and to the future past, through buried by-products of the national industry-scape, interred for millennia in this most away place in the country.

The amount of time the tour could take ranges from a lifetime to two days (starting in Salt Lake City and over-nighting in Wendover), or the amount of time it takes you to read this.

Voyagers should begin at Salt Lake City's point of origin: Temple Square.

Find your way there, near the intersection of Interstate 80 (San Francisco/New York) and Interstate 15 (San Diego/Alberta). All the numbered roads in Salt Lake City originate, and radiate, from Temple Square. After listening to the silence of the Tabernacle, get in your car and head west on North Temple Street, north on West 300 Street, west on North 600 Street, to the on-ramp of Interstate 15, heading north.

Part One: The Perceptual Void

From the interstate, the Great Salt Lake is often on the edge of perceptibility. It is elusive, vague, and mysterious, at times almost impossible to look at. The water and sky merge to create a silvery, perceptual chasm. It is down this hole, into this perceptual drain, that we are headed. Robert Smithson's precedent (especially his essay "A Tour of the Monuments of Passaic") sets the trajectory from which to launch into an experiential miasmic odyssey.

Like Smithson's *Spiral Jetty* itself, the journey is a counterclockwise spiral inward, around the lake, and into the void. To follow along the path of least resistance, like captives of the great hemispheric Coriolis effect, is to go down the drain of the Great Basin. But this is where the metaphor stops, as there is no away. This basin does not drain anywhere. There is no connection with the rest of the continental landscape, no sedimentary streams of erosion carrying the powdered mountains out to the sea. What happens in the Basin stays in the Basin. The drain is plugged, and the backed up flood is the Great Salt Lake.

In the age of the glaciers, Pleistocene ancestors of the Great Salt Lake once covered much of the state. Even the high ground, where Temple Square is today, was once submerged. Then a great rupture occurred in the north, ending Utah's terrestrial baptism, when the lake broke through its natural dam and spilled across southern Idaho. As this cataclysmic inundation dissipated and the lake shrank, a new age took hold. Now it is evaporation that rules this landscape.

In the Great Salt Lake basin it rains as little as 4 inches per year, while the evaporation rate can be as high as 6 feet per year. Snow-melt coming down the slopes of the Wasatch keep the lake in a fluctuating equilibrium. Over the past forty years, the lake surface elevation has changed within a range of 20 feet, and, along with its gradual shoreline, this resulted in a doubling, and halving, in size.

In 1986, the lake was at the highest it had been in a hundred years. Railways and real estate were being flooded, so the state built a battery of pumps at the edge of the lake to spread the lake out into the western salt flats. Twenty years later the lake was near its lowest level again, a foot and a half lower than when the *Spiral Jetty* was constructed in 1970. Today, in March 2008, the lake level is exactly where it was when the *Spiral Jetty* was made.

To get to the *Spiral Jetty* take exit 368 off Interstate 15 at Brigham City

and head west. Go past the last gas station you will see for a while, in the town of Corinne (once, nearly, the Gentile capital of Utah.) Continue west on Highway 83 for another 20 miles to the left turn toward Promontory. After 8 miles the paved road ends at the visitor center for the Golden Spike National Historic Site. It was here in 1869 that the last part of the first transcontinental railway was completed, joining the two halves of the country together. Many years ago the tracks were abandoned and torn out. There used to be a big pyramid-shaped monument at the site where the tracks were joined. Over time, a segment of the tracks came back, just enough to run two restored locomotives toward each other to reenact the event. A visitor center was built by the National Park Service, and then the monument was relocated to the front of the building.

The *Spiral Jetty* is another 12 miles past the visitor center, down dirt roads that get worse for the last 3 miles. Five and a half miles from the Golden Spike Visitor Center, there is a fork: go left. After another mile, turn right just before the corral. Stay on this road all the way to the edge of the Great Salt Lake. First you will see the oil jetty, sometimes mistaken for the *Spiral Jetty*. This was the site of the first productive oil well in the state of Utah. It is now a ruin. Go half a mile further along the shore and you will be at the *Spiral Jetty*.

Bob Phillips is the contractor who built the *Spiral Jetty* for Smithson. When he meets visitors he tells them how his rocky relationship with Smithson became one of mutual appreciation as the *Spiral Jetty* grew, and how the nine-day construction period was extended another five days when Smithson hired him again to change the form of the tip of the jetty to what we see today. Two other employees of the Whitaker Construction Company worked on the *Spiral Jetty*, driving the dozer and loader, and backing the dump truck out further and further on the emerging spiral to deposit its load of rock on the mud. Phillips was experienced at this sort of work, as he had built miles of dikes in the lake for the evaporation ponds of the Great Salt Lake Minerals Corporation.

You are on Rozel Point, the view is westward across the lake. Gunnison Island is visible in the distance, one of several uninhabited islands in the lake. Beyond it is Lakeside, where the Lucin Cutoff, a filled-in railway causeway 22 miles long that divides the lake in two, makes landfall on the west shore. Beyond that are the mothballed lake pumps at Hogup, and the bombing targets of the Utah Test and Training Range. Beyond that, far out of sight, are the *Sun Tunnels,* the next stop. But to get there you have to drive for three hours over the top of the lake.

Though it is possible to drive on the old railway roadbed to the other side of the lake, the road is neglected, remote, and, they say, full of leftover railway spikes. Back out the way you came, past the Golden Spike, back to Highway 83, and take a left, northbound. On your right is the sprawling ATK rocket plant, a several-dozen-square-mile complex of explosives production and storage facilities. It was put here to be away from everything. ATK made the boosters that blew up the space shuttle at this plant. They also made many of the nation's intercontinental ballistic missile engines here, some of which are still deployed on submarines and in the silos of the Great Plains, pointed who knows where. Note the metal buildings with the emergency evacuation slides, for getting out in a hurry, and the wide swath of bulldozed earth around the whole plant that serves as a firebreak.

Take a left near the end of the plant to stay on Highway 83, and soon you will join Interstate 84, northbound. Exit 7, Snowville, is home to the last gas and business of any kind you will pass for the next 170 miles. At the next exit, exit 5, head west on Highway 42/30, a straight line running parallel to the Idaho state line, a couple of miles to the north. After 17 miles, bear left, staying on Highway 30, and heading southwest. Finally some buildings come into view: the Asian American Meditation Center, surrounded by trailers and goats. This is ranching country, and the lake is barely in sight to the south. The road passes through two small towns, Park Valley and Rosette, neither with any services except a highway department yard, a Mormon church, a school, and a telephone relay station.

Forty miles past Rosette is Grouse Creek Junction, where there are no buildings, just a sign where a dirt road heads south 12 miles to Lucin. A small rail town, Lucin was a place where steam trains were filled with water from a pipe that connected to a spring up in the Pilot Range. This is where the Lucin Cutoff hit the ground after crossing the mudflats in a perfectly straight line for over 50 miles from Lakeside (east of Lakeside the cutoff divides the Great Salt Lake in two, and makes landfall at Promontory Point, south of the *Spiral Jetty*). At Lucin a rectangular pond, shaded by trees, and a root cellar are all that remain of the community that was once here. Freight trains still come through but do not stop.

Sun Tunnels are just a few miles from of the town of Lucin. Head south from the pond for two miles, then bear left. After 2.2 miles, bear right. *Sun Tunnels* emerge from the flat plain as a distant gray dot that slowly grows into a cluster of four 18-foot-long concrete tubes. The tubes lie on their sides in an open x configuration. Each pair of tubes is lined up with the sun on the horizon on either the summer or winter solstices. They were constructed by the artist Nancy Holt, who visited the region often with her husband, Robert Smithson. It is tempting to make comparisons between the two famous land art sites of the Great Salt Lake desert: one a feminine, circular, astrological axis mundi, the other a peninsular, quarried rock pile, but it is best to just let them be to become much more on their own.

This remote spot is a terrestrial and cosmic crossroads. Dirt bikers love the *Sun Tunnels* as much as anyone. It is an enigmatic destination, an oasis, providing tubular shade in the sun-drenched plains of northwest Utah. Sun worshipers appear on the solstices to witness the alignment of the tubes with the rising and the setting of the sun. You might meet people here, and, if you do, they are no doubt from far away too.

Head back to the north/south dirt road you were on two miles back and go south. This dirt road continues for 50 miles, along the mudflats known as the Barren Desert on one side and the Pilot Range on the other. The pointed summit at the southern end of the range is Pilot Peak, used as a navigational aid by emigrants crossing the flats from the east, including the Donner Reed party that passed just south of Pilot Peak on their way toward their fate in the snows of the Sierras.

After over an hour, pavement appears near the end, and the road passes over Leppy Pass, revealing the salt flats and Interstate 80 below. The Salt Flat Cafe provides Mexican food and gas just before the interstate. One exit to the west is the town of Wendover, which calls itself a town "On the Edge," and it is. It is located where the Basin and Range of Nevada spills into the Salt Flats of Utah. Bisected by the state line, the town also claims to have "Too much fun for just one state." It is also where the Enola Gay practiced for a few months before heading to Tinian and Hiroshima.

The Center for Land Use Interpretation has a number of exhibit buildings at the old airbase, some of which are open to the public 24/7/365, others by appointment only. Visitors are free to explore wherever there are no "no trespassing" signs. There are several casinos in town, and entertainment nightly. Though we are 120 miles from Salt Lake City, the tour is only at the halfway point.

Part Two: The Material Void

Many of the monuments along the south shore of the lake are related to the removal or placement of material in the region, the material void. One of the emptiest places in America, this region draws material into it like a vacuum. Conversely, much of the material that is native to this place is extracted and dispersed across the world.

Take Interstate 80, a continental Main Street, heading eastbound out of Wendover. You'll pass Danger Cave, an archaeological site that was worked by Dr. Robert Heizer, father of the earthworks artist Michael Heizer, friend/enemy of Robert Smithson. Danger Cave is one of the oldest sites of continuous occupation in the country, though no Indians live there anymore. It is gated to keep intruders out (though vandals use car jacks to pry the bars apart).

The first exit after Wendover is the Bonneville Speedway access road. It is a four-mile peninsula of asphalt that ends at the salt flats. This road is the great American road to nowhere—the asphalt abruptly stops at a rounded cul-du-sac type bulb, surrounded on all sides by a sea of white salt. The end of the road marks the beginning of a roadless 2-D void, the landscape tabula rasa, the limits of imagination. Like an unwound *Spiral Jetty*, this road is a point of embarkation to another terrestrial realm.

Left on the flats, people tend to wander around aimlessly, wallowing in directionlessness. For once, there is no reason to go anywhere in particular. Despite their featurelessness, the salt flats are among the most energizing places in the country. Because there is so little to look at, anything that is placed on the ground stands out, and has meaning. Like a giant white museum wall, tipped over and extending

for miles, anything you put on the salt flats looks good. Commercial photography and film production crews are frequent visitors.

Back on 80, heading east, at the midpoint of the longest stretch of interstate without an exit (38 miles), across from a new cell tower, the third of the great trilogy of site specific artwork around the Lake looms: *Metaphor: The Tree of Utah*. This construction is the work of an Iranian-Swedish artist, Karl Momen, who made it because he felt that the salt flats were just too empty. A mix of Surrealism, Russian Constructivism, and pragmatism, the 87-foot-tall tree is a true manifestation of the void.

As further testament to the "emptiness" of this stretch of highway, large yellow highway signs east of the *Tree* warn drowsy drivers to pull over in this land so empty and boring that it induces sleep. South of this point, in 2004, the Genesis space probe crashed into Dugway Proving Ground, like a saucer on an alien planet, which this may in fact be.

The road is perfectly straight and flat, skimming the surface of a deep sea of mud. At Knolls, the first exit after the Bonneville Salt Flats (exit 41), a gas station is no longer there. Northward off the frontage road, a road leads to the gate of the Grassy Mountain hazardous waste site where ashes, dust, and filtercake from toxic industries across the nation are buried with asbestos and PCBs. Behind this is a bunker from an early medium range missile test site. Beyond that, northbound, is a target zone of the Utah Test and Training Range.

The next exit east on 80, exit 49, is Clive, where a closed hazardous waste incinerator is seemingly abandoned, its gates thrown open. Nearby at the radioactive waste burial site known as Envirocare, pieces of the DOE plant at Oak Ridge, Tennessee, are visible on top of the mound, being broken up by men in white suits for permanent entombment below, along with parts of other radioactive places across America, a veritable nuke site museum/midden mound.

The next exit eastbound on the 80, though it says "no services," leads to the Aptus incinerator at Aragonite, a chemical waste disposal facility accepting waste from across the country. It is operated by Clean Harbors, a company from Braintree, Massachusetts, with its origins in the toxic sludge of Boston harbor.

A little further, the Aragonite Rest Area is the only rest area in the state of Utah with a residence for its keepers, as it is considered too remote a commute from anywhere people live. The rest area offers a good view of the haz-

ardous waste incinerator, and though the interpretive plaques speak of wild horses, they are nowhere to be seen.

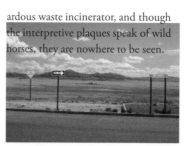

Eastbound again, the interstate leaves the salty mudflats of the Great Salt Lake Desert and heads over a pass. At the top of the pass is exit 62, with a paved road that heads north for 15 miles to the gate of the Air Force's Utah Test and Training Range's north area base, a place called Oasis. Within the fenced military area are several target areas for weapons testing, conducted mostly out of Edwards Air Force Base in California, or Hill Air Force Base north of Salt Lake City. Bearing right, before approaching the gate, the road through the range is public, though signs are posted warning travelers to not leave the roadway. After a few miles, on the right, a sign labels a gate as the "TTU," the "Thermal Treatment Unit," where ICBM rocket motors are disposed of explosively and other bombs and obsolete munitions are burned.

Continuing north, the road ends after descending into the former rail town of Lakeside, where nobody lives, but where a quarry for ballast rock for

the railway is still active. Lakeside is a peninsula, with the Great Salt Lake on one side, and the mudflats of the Great Salt Lake Desert on the other. To the east the Lucin Cutoff makes its journey across the lake, and the two lakes created by the cutoff are visibly distinct, with the saltier water of the north visibly red (due to microorganisms that grow in very salty water) and the bluer water on the south side of the cutoff (where more fresh water comes in from the mountains). Westward from Lakeside are the mudflats, crossed by the cutoff to Lucin, 50 miles away in a straight line. A few miles out, next to the tracks, are the pump house and canal for the Great Salt Lake pumping project.

Past exit 62, the interstate drops into the Skull Valley, where there is a haze of chlorine gas originating from the only magnesium plant in the U.S. The gas sometimes spreads south toward the Goshute Indian Reservation, where tribal leaders are trying to build a home for spent fuel rods from Midwestern nuclear power plants. The Skull Valley Goshute Reservation is immediately downwind of Dugway Proving Ground, the nation's biological and chemical weapons proving ground.

The next exit, number 70, is the town of Delle, still posted as "for sale" after more than ten years. At exit 77, a photogenic abandoned gas station that has been used in several films is now flattened, scattered debris. To the north you can see the stack of the magnesium plant, 12 miles distant, at the end of a dead-end road. There, five hundred people work to extract magnesium from the concentrated brine of the Great Salt Lake. South of this exit is Highway 196, the main road into the Skull Valley. The road passes the town of Iosepa, where Polynesian settlers came in the mid-1800s to be closer to the Mormon church. The dry valley proved difficult to farm, quite different from their lush tropical homeland, and they eventually died or left. Further south you pass an abandoned rocket test site, with Russian signage left from the START treaty verification process, before getting to the main gate at Dugway.

Onward, east on Interstate 80—the home stretch of the tour. The Great Salt Lake is now fully visible to the north, though first in the form of artificial ponds constructed to evaporate water to extract salt. Cargill and Morton salt plants are both visible next to the road (exits 77 and 84, respectively). At the exit for Tooele, massive munitions storage igloo fields are visible from the highway, as well as the chemical weapons incinerator further south.

Where the Oquirrh Mountains hit the lake is the largest smokestack in America, at the Kennecott Copper Smelter. At 1,215 feet tall, it is just 35 feet shorter than the Empire State building. The smelter building is part of a chain of plants that process ore from the Bingham Copper Pit, 12 miles south. The Bingham Copper Pit is accessed by exiting the interstate at the smelter (exit 102), then heading east on Highway 201 for 2 miles, then south on Highway 111 for 10 miles, until you see the sign for the pit. They charge a small entry fee at the gate and

direct you to the visitor center, located on the rim.

The Bingham Pit may or may not be "the biggest hole on earth" (it depends how you define "big"), but it really doesn't matter. It is 2.5 miles wide and ¾-miles deep. Looking into it is like looking into space. It is the ultimate man-made landscape void. When the pit first began operation, in 1907, it was the first large-scale open pit operation in the U.S. Moving enough material to process this much low-grade ore had never been done. The bold plan that was implemented used a railway with movable tracks to transport tremendous amounts of blasted rock. The train spiraled into the mountain on tracks built on the ledges of the sides. The effect was like a giant screw drill.

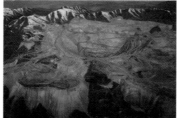

Funding for the project came from the Guggenheim family, who later built a museum bearing their name in New York City with the profits made from investments in industry across the country, like the Bingham Pit. The museum is a kind of cultural ingot extracted and refined from the raw material of the earth. And the museum, curiously, has a multistory open space in the middle, surrounded by a long spiral ramp. Before he died, in 1973, Smithson proposed building a four-part spiral sculpture at the bottom of the Bingham Pit. The proposal was never seriously considered by the company. But the plan looks remarkably like it might be a drain—a drain for the bottom of the Great Basin.

Back on the interstate, heading east, is the last stop on the tour, the Saltair III pavilion (exit 104). This is a shoreline building constructed as a gateway to the lake. The cavernous, echoing, vacant Saltair III has had the feeling of a future ruin since the day it was built (construction was halted for a few years in the late 1980s, as the lake was so high that waves were breaking through the partially constructed main hall). Though open to the public, usually the only life inside is the attendant at a sparse souvenir shop. Out the back door, a white expanse of muddy sand leads, eventually (depending on the lake level), and anticlimactically, to the water's edge. Ambivalence toward the Great Salt Lake is measurable.

Saltair III is a smaller re-creation of a grand Moorish pavilion that once existed nearby. A hundred years ago there were several Victorian pavilions on the southern shore of the lake, and people swam and frolicked in the salty water. As times changed (and silt piled up and began to stink), all of these buildings were torn down, burned, or collapsed, including the largest and grandest of them all, the original Saltair II.

At the site of Saltair II, a few miles east on the shoreline road, some old passenger railcars decay, and the partially submerged jetty that led to the pavilion can be seen stretching out into the emptiness of the Great Salt Lake. Saltair II was still there in the 1960s, a teetering spooky ruin. At that time it was used as a filming location for *Carnival of Souls,* a film that seems to have been written for the picturesque relic. In the movie, the protagonist, a young organist at a church, gazes out at the fenced ruin, which seems to be drawing her toward it. Her companion, a minister, asks her, "What attraction could there be for you, out there?" She replies, "I'm not sure. I'm a reasonable person, I don't know…Maybe I want to satisfy myself that the place is nothing more than it appears to be." "Shall we go along now?" the minister says, disapprovingly, as he guides her back to the car. They leave, but she says wistfully to herself, "Maybe I can come back some other time."

Head back on Interstate 80, at exit 111 (South 7200 West Street). The prefab building surrounded by the piles of dirt is a closed-down visitor information center.

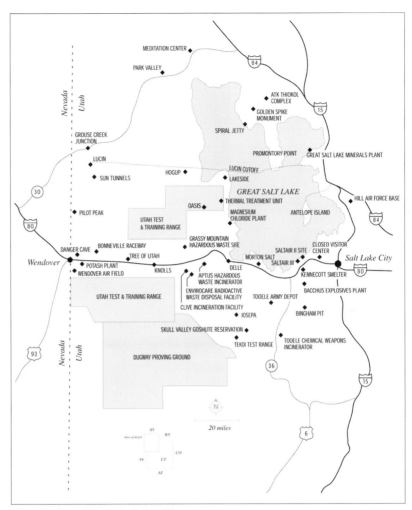

Images courtesy of The Center for Land Use Interpretation (CLUI) photo archive. Map by CLUI.

A

B

C

D

Re-drawing Hadrian's Villa
Re-writing Caochangdi Urban Village

Robert Mangurian and Mary-Ann Ray

In the late twentieth century, we established the Atelier Italia and embarked upon a decade-long project to document Hadrian's Villa through a photographic record of every existing surface of its structures and by producing a detailed measured plan of the entire site at an accuracy of about 1 centimeter. In the early twenty-first century, the research branch of our practice established B. A. S. E. (Beijing Architecture Studio Enterprise), or Ji Di, which has turned its attention upon Caochangdi Village in Beijing. The Village has undergone a series of extreme changes since its beginnings as a wild grassland and its subsequent subjection to the forces at play during the imperial and cultural revolution eras, and now it has become a mix of entrepreneurial farmers and world class artists and galleries. The documentation of Caochangdi Village takes the form of mappings, interviews, and digital photographs. Caochangdi provides a particular and detailed story of change, one that in a broader sense helps to understand the forces and human consequences behind rapid change in urbanizing Asia. And finally, the late-twentieth-century project at Hadrian's Villa is revisited and updated. Work is currently underway to produce an online GIS-based interactive digital archive of the plan and photographic documentation in collaboration with the Institute of Advanced Technology in the Humanities at the University of Virginia.

In both projects, there is a clear desire to "assay its spade in ever-new places, and in the old ones delve to ever-deeper depths." (Lars Lerup once referred to our work with this Walter Benjamin quote.) As travelers, we tend to get stuck in places, and even move in—we now have studios and houses adjacent to Hadrian's Villa and in Caochangdi Village, as well as our home base at Studioworks in Los Angeles.

At Hadrian's Villa (or Villa Adriana), we were interested in this postmodern icon of architecture and plan making, and interested in it not just as a plan graphic but as a living, spatial complex. Our work over the ten years allowed us to "spatialize," in de Certeau's sense, the Villa on a daily basis. It was not a relic of the past, but a site of active production. From a straightforward and practical point of view, we were surprised to find that the best plan of the Villa we could muster up was the crude reprinted tourist map found in Edmund Bacon's *Design of Cities*. We later found Piranesi's surprisingly comprehensive plan, and while it was tremendously accurate, as we eventually discovered and confirmed, it did not carry the level of detail we were craving.

In Caochangdi, we have been amazed to watch change occur before our eyes, and then to learn that this change has been ongoing since it was wilderness and hunting grounds to the northeast of the city of Beijing up to its current status as one of the globe's hottest art zones (as described in *Vanity Fair,* the *New York Times, Condé Nast Traveler,* etc.). Having been disappointed by many superficial readings of the phenomenon of rapid change in urbanizing Asia, Caochangdi seemed to hold an opportunity to unfold a particular story of this in depth, and in a way that might describe the causes and effects of change in economic, spatial, social, political, architectural, and human ways.

Villa Adriana, Atelier Italia, Summers, 1985–95

Robert Mangurian (RM) received a phone call from Anina Nosei[1] in the early 1980s introducing him to her friend Paola Igliori.[2] Paola had an exquisite country villa in Ronciglione, just north of Rome,[3] and was interested in renting part of it, called Villa Lina, for the summer. Both RM and Mary-Ann Ray (MAR) had spent time at the American Academy in Rome, and RM had taken UCLA students to Rome using studio space at the American Academy. Paola sent photographs of Villa Lina, and RM on two occasions again took UCLA students to Rome, these times using the fantastic buildings of Villa Lina within the hazelnut trees of Paola's property. On the third occasion, MAR joined in but this time with a mix of SCI-Arc and UCLA students. With two cooks and five cars, thirty minutes from Rome, ten minutes from Caprarola, twenty minutes from Villa Lante, and postmodernism well under way, what could have been better for the student of architecture? We invented a kind of studio project sited on the archaeological site just outside modern Tarquinia and let the students run free within what seemed like the birthplace of conscious architecture and a kind of museum of these artifacts.

It was during that summer of 1985 that (on a lark) we made a group visit to Villa Adriana. It was our belief that being the architectural tourist with camera in hand wasn't quite right. The ease of passing by the historical artifacts and "taking them," we felt, had the effect of placing these buildings easily in the past, and in fact placing some distance between the viewer and the things viewed. Some action was necessary, and the more engaging the better. The sketchbook was OK, but finally also a little too easy. We came up with a plan, naively, to

All images courtesy of Studioworks.

A The New Socialist Village Central Party Projects adding new separated storm and sanitary sewer lines, water supply lines, and gas lines in a massive hand-dug trench. All of this occurs along a little-used road leading out of the Village toward the hulk of the new National Film Museum at the end of a dysfunctional axis.

B Villa Adriana, early-twentieth-century view.
C Villa Adriana, aerial view showing approximately one quarter of the Villa.
D Caochangdi Village. Aerial photograph. Airport Expressway at upper left and 5th Ring Road upper right to bottom left.

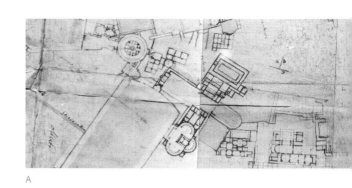

A

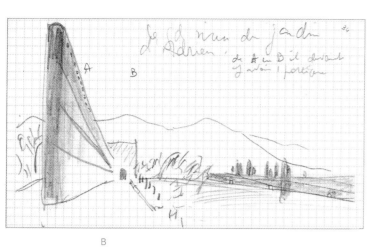

B

C

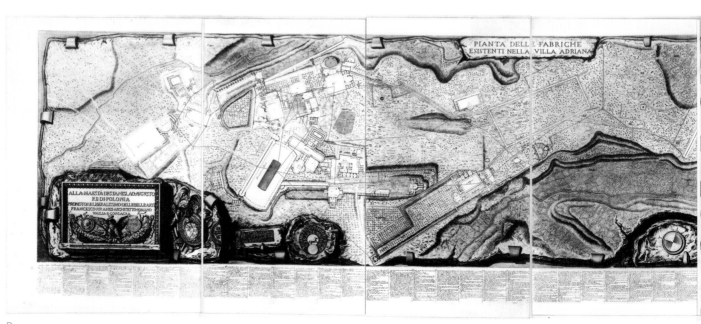

D

measure the entirety of the known Villa Adriana—not in detail, but enough to produce a plan. The existing plans that we knew of were simply not useful (we were unaware of Piranesi's plan), and the act of "crawling" over a building through measuring would have the effect of "consuming" more of the content. And clearly, the production of the plans and sections would allow an analysis and close reading not available through the "drive-by shooting" approach.

We arrived in three vintage Fiats at the Villa early one morning in late July of 1985, armed with simple measuring tapes and clipboards and with no official *permesso*[4] to do measuring. After the overall tour of the Villa (with sketchbooks in hand and cameras with film), and lunch brought from Villa Lina, we started in at two buildings that looked relatively simple to tackle—the Triclinio and the Ospitale. Our techniques during that session, and during a subsequent session, were crude and naive.[5] We tried to save time by measuring only half of symmetrical spaces and we took no diagonals (necessary, we were to learn later to carefully control the orthogonal geometry).

Back at Villa Lina that next day, we made our first drawings of Villa Adriana (without utilizing the required diagonals) and "discovered" to our astonishment that the both the Triclinio and the Ospitale utilized the root two and golden section proportions in addition to the simple square. It was during the remeasuring of the Ospitale for diagonals and corrections two years later that we discovered that swinging the diagonals with the measuring tapes replicated the very act of laying out the spaces in the first place during construction. The easiest way to control rectangular space was to utilize one of these two proportioning systems. In today's terms, this is the equivalent of laying out our complex geometries/spaces utilizing the same software that is used to design these geometries/spaces.

During that fall of 1985, through discussions with William MacDonald, who was at the Getty Center conducting research on a book he and John Pinto were writing on Hadrian's Villa,[6] we became hooked and resolved to continue our work. Bill pointed out that the last thorough overall plan of the complete Villa was

measured and drawn by Piranesi and published by his son Francesco in 1781. During the ensuing year we began to acquire the existing documentation of the Villa (both texts and drawings), and in the summer of 1986 we began the serious "assault" on the Villa, with the first of ten groups of fifteen Atelier members each. That summer we did our first real measuring and photo documentation. We developed the careful measuring techniques that were perfected in subsequent years to achieve highly accurate modern archaeological standards. Our routine, backed up by the five cars and two cooks—the magnificent Claudia and Peppa—consisted of three trips to the Villa each week starting at 5:30 A.M. at Villa Lina and ending with a fantastic meal at 8:30 P.M. under the trellis back at Villa Lina. The next day or two was spent drawing up the work from the measurements and noting the necessary corrections.[7] This routine continued from mid-June to late August each year, with a break for about five days mid-summer for some serious Italian travel and architecture viewing.

Hadrian's Villa is clearly one of the most important and influential works within architecture. Hadrian, Roman emperor from 117 to 138 A.D., was a kind of architect (equivalent to our own Thomas Jefferson, but with greater resources). He built extensively within Rome and throughout the Empire at a time when Roman architecture was at the height of its creative production. The Villa was Hadrian's "experimental ground," allowing him to pursue ideas within the developing discipline:

…and he built up the Tiber villa wonderfully, in such a way that he could apply it to the names of provinces and places most renowned and could call (parts of it), for example, the Lycaeum, the Academy, the Prytany, the Canopus, the Poecile, the Tempe. And so that he might omit nothing, he even fashioned a Hades.
—*Scriptores Historiae Augustae* HA, Hadr. 26.5[8]

The villa Hadrian developed is extensive, played out over its 2½-mile-long by ½-mile-wide site involving over fifty significant building elements.

The Villa was rediscovered in the early Renaissance and has been a source of inspiration for architects ever since. The Canopus can be seen in Bramante's Belvedere, and several water elements from the Villa influenced parts of Ligorio's Villa d'Este. Ligorio wrote extensively about the Villa and measured and drew parts.[9] In modern times both Le Corbusier[10] and Kahn spent considerable time at the Villa and were strongly influenced by the planning, form, and construction of the architecture.

A Giovanni Battista Piranesi, plan cartoon of the Villa Adriana. 1777.
B Le Corbusier's sketch of the Pecile Wall from *Carnet V, Voyage d'Orient, October 20–26, 1911*.
C Atelier Italia general survey at the Pecile Wall.
D Giovanni Battista Piranesi, plan of Villa Adriana. Published by F. Piranesi (1781). Giovanni Battista Piranesi spent (according to his signature) thirty-five years intermittently recording both the plan and views of Villa Adriana. After his death, his son published the plan. G. B. Piranesi finished the cartoon of the plan in 1777, one year before his death. The overall plan shown here includes an overlay of the Atelier Italia general instrument survey (shown in red lines). The offset circles indicate the surprisingly minor inaccuracies of the Piranesi plan, obtained through massive clearing and utilizing careful on-site observations and 3-4-5 chains for triangulation.

A

B

C

Ghicciaia Sotto Terra—Underground "Ice Storage"
July, August 1990

The underground "Ice Storage" (sometimes we called it "Snow Storage") was cleared by Team Mercury in late July 1990. This was our first really clear look at it. The southernmost length was opened up by shoving to both sides rubble from the collapsed skylight, and, after inching through on our sides, we found that this stretch did not have side legs like the northern stretch did. The acoustics were incredible, and we made use of the almost endless reverberations by performing our version of a Gregorian chant with a chorus of atonal drones under the necessary candlelight. In the time-consuming preparations for measuring, a stand line—an arbitrary but straight line established between two clear corners of a room—was pulled through the entire length of both the northern and southern main chamber, and points were plumbed and marked on the ceiling with delicate graphite crosshairs. In other parts of the villa, we used red and blue lumber crayons, but the flawless and intact casein-like skin—waterproofed with an animal protein such as egg or milk—seemed too sacred for marking. Corrections were made to Piranesi's crude and inaccurate plan, and to Salza Prina Ricotti's recent plan: sixteen-sided leg rooms rather than the Piranesi's centipede affair, and the southern length without any rooms at all. Judging from the stand line, the plan is nearly straight—not serpentine as depicted by Ricotti's plan and Piranesi's. We also saw a small rectangular room just to the north of the ice rooms. It may have been the big, gashed opening where excavated earth could have been pulled out easily, since its ceiling—unlike the entirely carved out space of the storage itself—consisted of a continuous concrete vault. The measuring activity was quite difficult—all by candlelight and flashlights to set zero end, read the tape, and note the measurement on the measurement sheet. The photo documentation was all done with candle light. Added to this were the strange flying spiders. Clearly, the ice came from the headwaters of the five aqueducts that originate many miles to the east of Tivoli.

A Photograph of the underground Ice Storage main vault showing the insulated surfaces (using volcanic pumice) waterproofed with a protein based paint. Because of the complete lack of light, Tri-X film was pushed to 1600 ASA and candles were lit while three members of the Atelier moved around the space washing the walls with flashlights in order to capture the image in five-minute exposures.
B Photograph of the side vault.

C Atelier Italia plan of the Ice Storage.
D Giovanni Battista Piranesi, plan detail showing Ice Storage underground structure at Villa Adriana. 1781.
E Measurement sheet of Ice Storage recorded by Atelier Italia on July 21 and July 26, 1990.
F Plan of Serapeum-Saqqara. An eighteenth-dynasty underground tomb associated with the cult of the Apis Bulls, this structure and the Canopus, near Alexandria, were known by Hadrian.

G Piranesi signature, located in western criptoportico. It reads, "G. B. Piranesi restudied these ruins to discover and draw the plan…an almost impossible task because of the great exertion and suffering it entailed."
H Photo log recording the camera positions and angles of the documentation of every surface of the structure.

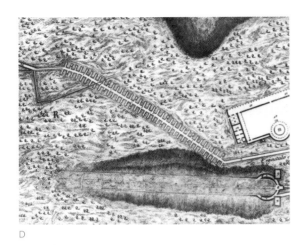

D

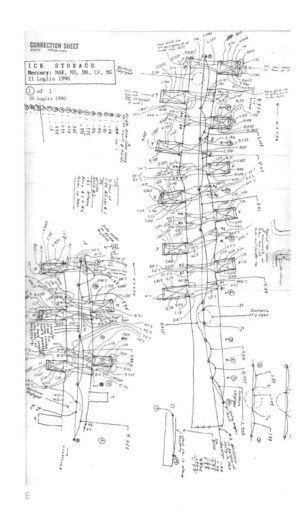

E

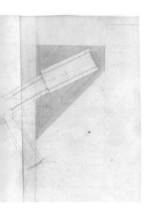

F

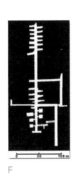

G

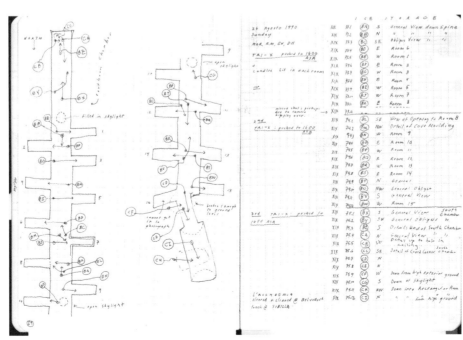

H

In very recent times, the Villa has served as an iconic reference for the postmodern era, and was featured as an example within Colin Rowe's *Collage City,* and Bacon's *Design of Cities.*

Our work consisted of hand measuring each building along with the associated retaining walls and odd structures that comprise the Villa. We have not measured the few buildings that have been carefully measured by others since the 1950s, starting with Friederich Rakob's work at the northern end of the Piazza d'Oro. The work includes all structures and constructions on both the government land and the privately owned land. The work is carried out according to current archaeological standards and is conducted with the official permission and approval of the Soprintendenza Archaeologica per il Lazio. Bill MacDonald, John Pinto, Friederich Rakob, Eugenia Salza Prina Ricotti, C. F. Giuliani, P. Verduchi, Zaccaria Mari—the active archaeologists and historians involved at the Villa—have all been consulted regularly through the course of the work and have provided invaluable assistance. The field measurements of each building (and associated walls, outbuildings, etc.) have resulted in a series of plan, section, and elevation drawings. In addition to the measured drawings, we have undertaken extensive photo documentation of each building. Every building surface and many details are recorded through 2¼-inch black-and-white photography. Our archive now consists of over 8,000 catalogued photographs. The Getty Center has purchased about half of the current collection. Our field work—hand measuring, drawing, and photographing individual buildings and elements—is about 95 percent complete. Throughout the course of the field work, the Atelier has also discovered about forty new brick stamps previously unknown, and some of these have revised the dating of several buildings or building complexes. In the 1990s we began our general survey utilizing state-of-the-art electronic surveying equipment. The general survey has allowed us to connect each of the buildings and building elements to develop the general plan.

Our formal work on the Villa ceased after the summer of 1995. During that summer and the one before, we were finding that we were remeasuring certain buildings to bring some of the early "measures" up to current standards. In addition, we found that we were often spending much time clearing blackberry bushes only to find the odd retaining wall (seen on Piranesi's plan). This kind of work was of interest to RM and MAR, but the Atelier group was losing patience. After that summer of 1995, we realized that there was nothing else to measure.[11] Our interest turned elsewhere, but afraid of losing touch with Villa Adriana, we acquired a small plot of land above the southernmost part of the Villa. Now known as Villa Peggy,[12] the land contains about eighty olive trees and a small "day house" (that has expanded miraculously). It turns out that the olive trees contained olives. (In all our years measuring and documenting at Villa Adriana, we never once noticed an olive on the many trees within the confines of the Villa.) The olives from Villa Peggy, and from the groves of the Lolli and Bulgarini families, become very fine olive oil. But we continue to involve ourselves with Villa Adriana. We are not willing to cede the Villa to the archaeologists and the architectural historians.

Through our work at Villa Adriana, we have come to see architectural history in a very different way, and the emphasis in placing buildings in historical order and preferencing their description as to be understood within the "historical" context seems to us now all wrong. The "historical" record of Villa Adriana is enlightening. Yes, work on the Villa, since the time of the "first sighting" by Pius II through our work and others' at present can be seen as flushing out the understanding of the villa in the traditional historical sense. More information available on the Villa allows the historical reading to be more accurate. This is of course true. But this misses what seems to be really going on. The string of architects and recorders operating and acting upon the Villa in the past 350 years (known accounts and mostly "silent" accounts)[13] has internalized the Villa for each generation. The work undertaken at the Villa by these architects was more to bring the Villa into the present of their generation than to historicize the Villa. Thus, their work on the Villa, and ours as well, intends to bring observation, commentary, insight, and action through works of architecture so that Villa Adriana, clearly still there and always in the present, remains in the discourse of built and theoretical work.

We have come to feel that it is one of the works of the architect to take on some of the "buildings from the past" and bring them into the present so that the understanding and consciousness of these buildings matches the position that is in the present. Only those buildings destroyed or decayed beyond useful recognition can be relegated only to architectural history. The work by each generation can allow the "architectures of note"[14] to be brought into the present to match their actual existence in the present, both in general and clearly within the discipline. This allows for a kind of "genetic suturing" that keeps the work alive and connected. In the present age of the new and the spectacle, attempting to operate freely and without the "string attached," this is the work of seeing the historical not mainly as that but rather in the present and still very much alive.

A Criptoportico looking east.
B Detail of Sala di Pilastri Dorici looking up at column/lintel (with Roman iron concrete reinforcement).
C Atelier Italia plan of Sala di Pilastri Dorici drawn from hand measurements and triangulations.
D Composite of Sala di Pilastri Dorici looking southeast.

A

B

C

D

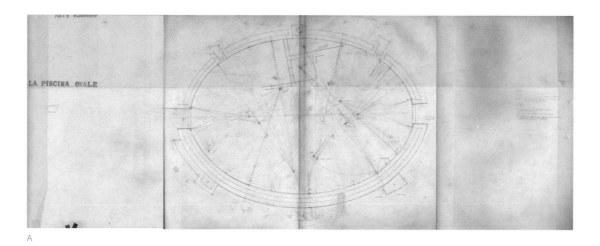

A

Alloggienenti de Liberti— Quarters of the Liberti

July, August 1988

(The following are notes describing some of the work on a building adjacent to La Piscina Ovale, located just to the south.)

The Quarters of the Liberti, just to the east of the south end of the Piazza d'Oro and adjacent to La Piscina Ovale, was our second difficult building of July 1988. The building sits at the same level as the Piazza d'Oro quadrangle, but the land falls off sharply at the edge on the east side. Both Contini and Piranesi show the building—Contini shows the plan of the top of the building, while Piranesi shows the underground part. The French arrived on the scene in the late seventeenth century and did a serious excavation (or participated in the nineteenth-century excavations). No one else seems to have fussed with this building since 1885. MAR had climbed over the fence from the Piazza d'Oro in the summer of 1987 and had struggled through many bushes and other growths covering "something."

On Thursday, July 21, we arrive to do the clearing. We were allowed to drive directly to the building (I think that day we arrived by the metal gate just to the east of the Pretorio). This was our first full-scale drive into the Villa, facilitated by Adriano d'Offizi, Villa Adriana's *capo de servizio*. We had talked to Adriano earlier in the summer and had asked him to have his people clear the area of the Quarters of the Liberti and the lower Piscina Ovale. When we arrived, of course, we found the same enormous pile of seemingly hundred-year-old growths (although they were probably really not much more than twenty-five years old). At first there appeared to be nothing on the top side. There was a clear series of tall retaining walls below with rooms inside at the northeast side of the building. We started at the top platform, which was completely covered with brush. Our strategy was to clear only where we found walls and thus save effort. The problem was that there weren't many walls visible. Soon, evidence of walls appeared and we cleared and dug along these walls. We followed walls perpendicular to each other and dug down (about a half meter) and found corners. After we had been on the site for a good part of the morning (again only clearing where it was absolutely necessary), I looked up to discover that we had cleared everything except for a perfectly gridded grove of olive trees. These trees appeared to have been planted after the French left.

We spent the entire day clearing and digging. We uncovered much of what the French had excavated and began to discover more detail. We finished the day as usual at Bar Belli (operated by the poet G. G. Belli's grandchildren—two brothers), licking our wounds over Peronis and peanuts.

We returned to the Quarters of the Liberti on Monday, July 25. We did more clearing and digging, and finally began measuring. We carefully set up a large rectangle with diagonals and a smaller rectangular within using triangulation, and connected the two sets of four points. This was done quite carefully to establish a control structure for all of the subsequent points, walls, etc. We were to return to this area many times for corrections until we finally discovered that one of our "control" points was incorrectly measured (it seemed like it took the good part of August to find this mistake).

A Atelier Italia plan of La Piscina Ovale, a small gladitorial amphitheater, drawn from hand measurements and triangulations.
B Log book for La Piscina Ovale from July 15, 1989.
C West side of La Piscina Ovale showing substructure of seating.

D Measurement sheet of La Piscina Ovale recorded by Atelier Italia on July 15, 1990.

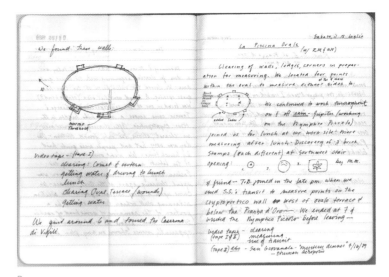

B

C

D

Re-drawing Hadrian's Villa   111

A

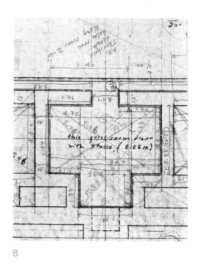

B

C

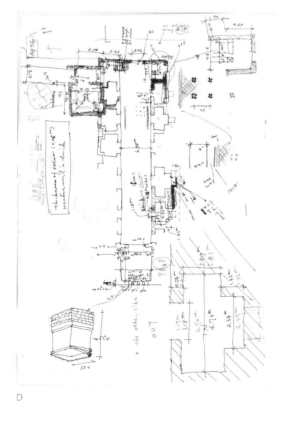

D

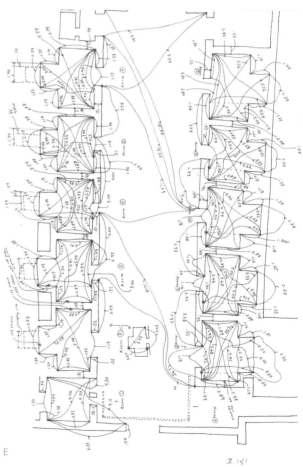

E

F

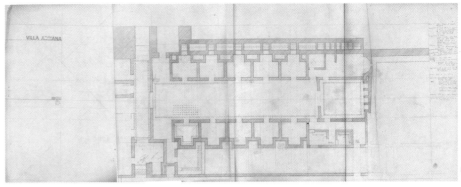

G

H

I

A View of a single room in the Ospitale.
B Correction sheet (partial) showing secrets of geometries.
C Atelier Italia, 1991. Left to right: Carol Lowry, Leslie Sydnor, Jacqueline Freedman (not visible), Peter Arnold (not visible), Jody Alpert (not visible), Alexander Kitchen (not visible), Nina Welch, Hadley Soutter, George Newburn (collaborator), Claudia Capaldi (cook), Peppa Contiani (cook), Elizabeth Martin, Dara Schaefer, Larry Tighe, Sheila Wolf, Eric Thompson, Beth Gibb, Robert Mangurian (Studioworks), Mary-Ann Ray (Studioworks photographer).
D Measurement sheet, 1985.
E Measurement sheet, 1987.
F View of the Ospitale looking north.
G Atelier Italia plan of the Ospitale drawn from hand measurements and triangulations.
H View of Roccabruna Tower at summer solstice. This small upper window on the northwest facade lets in a slit of light on the opposite interior wall exactly at the time of the sun setting.
I Atelier Italia, 1992. Left to right: Robert Mangurian (Studioworks), Heather Donaghy, Kirsten Gottschalk, David Hecht, Hope Mitnick, Ben Wilkes, Jennifer Conron, Greg Roth, Jackson Butler, John Barone, Kok Yang Ng, Michael Samra, Karin Schou, Jennifer Kim, Mako Otaki, Brian Allaire, Carol Lowry, George Newburn (collaborator), Mary-Ann Ray (Studioworks).

During the ten years of Atelier Italia's work at Villa Adriana, over 150 graduate and undergraduate students participated from universities throughout North America. Many are now involved in teaching, operating their own firms, or operating within significant firms. Several have gone on to win the Rome Prize and other traveling fellowships. Robert Mangurian and Mary-Ann Ray are indebted to their rigorous and intense involvement during the ten weeks each summer, and their dedication (often after the summer's work) to the work of documenting Villa Adriana. We owe a special thanks to collaborator George Newburn, who participated for over half of the years at Villa Adriana, and to David Hecht, Alexander Kitchin, Eric Vogel, Kai Uwe-Bergman, and Tomaso Bradshaw for providing leadership as assistants. And a very special thanks to Paola Igliori for providing the spectacular living and working quarters in Ronciglione (just to the north of Rome), and a very, very special thanks to our cooks, who provided the gastronomic and spiritual cohesion for each summer's work.

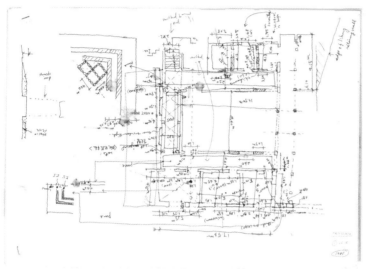

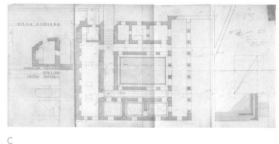

Triclinio: First Measuring
Summer 1985

For some reason, this was the first space to attract us when we visited the Villa. Our intention was to quickly construct a plan over the next few weeks, as a kind of sideline to the studio we were teaching in Ronciglione for SCI-Arc and UCLA students. We naively surveyed half the space with a series of linear measurements, then doubled the plan to plot the symmetry, and recorded the patterns of the black-and-white floor mosaic and some of the details of the column bases. We measured a few other spaces that same day using these simple techniques.

Making the drawings back in our studio was extraordinary as we discovered the unexpected underlying geometries and proportions built into the space. The central room of the Triclinio was proportioned using the diagonal of a square rotated (what we call the root two proportion common to the A system of European paper), easily laid out during the construction of the space. The following autumn, in Los Angeles, we met Bill MacDonald. He pointed us to the Piranesi plan and advised us to take diagonals—to triangulate the spaces we measured and carefully record all the subtle features and details we saw. His work with Michael Boyle at the Villa's Small Baths was our first example of good archaeological measuring, and we studied it closely. The Piranesi plan impressed us, and we realized we were following his lead. Eventually, we returned to triangulate the Triclinio rooms.

Canopus: Measuring and Living
July–August, 1990

The Canopus, located at the southernmost area of main sections of the Villa, required two months of our attention. Le Corbusier's sketches and comments on the extended apse clearly lead to Ronchamp. This strange vaulted apse behind the spectacular Triclinium features a backlit condition achieved through the absence of the completion of the vault. Above is a small aqueduct that feeds water to the large semicircular dome of the Canopus, including a water curtain that has the ability through controlling devices above to appear—thereby revealing the entire backlit depth of the apse—and to disappear, by blocking the water. During the measuring—and at other times—we made use of the dining area, which faced north and was always cool in the summer. And at the end of each summer's work, after dining on top of the Rocca Bruna Tower, we always ended up in this space for candlelit dessert.

A   Composite view of the Triclinio looking south from the edge of the Palazzo Imperiale.
B   Penetralia Apse of the Canopus.
C   Atelier Italia plan of the Triclinio drawn from hand measurements and triangulations.

D   Canopus Triclinio.
E   View from the Canopus Triclinio to the reflecting pool to the north.
F   Measurement sheets of the Canopus recorded in 1990.
G   Atelier Italia plan of the Canopus drawn from hand measurements and triangulations.
H   Measurement sheet of the Triclinio.
I   Sketch by Le Corbusier: Canopus deep apse (1910).

D

E

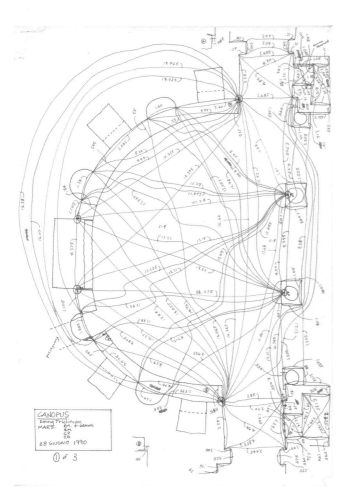

CANOPUS
Dining Triclinium
MARS: R.M. & DRAWN
B.M.
C.P.
Z.G.
28 GIUGNO 1990
① of 3

F

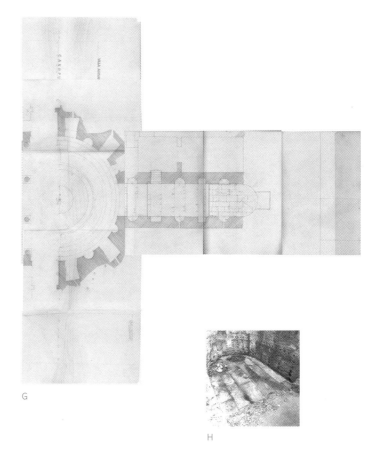

G

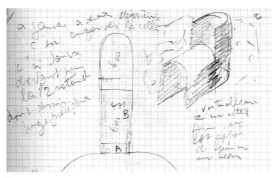

H

I

A

1   Anina Nosei operated an art gallery in the 1980s in SoHo and subsidized the early work of Jean-Michel Basquiat.

2   Paolo Igliori, at the time of our early use of Villa Lina, was married to the Italian painter Sandra Chia and could trace her family lineage to four "major" popes.

3   Villa Lina was established in the nineteenth century and is a large hazelnut farm. Paola once described a lunch at Villa Lina where her mother, a child at the time, helped serve tea to guests including Mussolini and Hitler.

4   When we began in earnest with our work in late June of 1986, our first day out at the Villa was immediately halted due to the lack of a *permesso,* which we subsequently obtained that summer and for future summers from the Superintendent's Office for Lazio in Rome.

5   In subsequent years our techniques improved vastly. In addition to changing from cloth tapes to 25-meter steel German tapes, wooden carpenter folding measuring sticks, bubble levels custom made at the Atelier, assorted plumb bobs, line levels, hand levels, planing one-meter and two-meter sticks, marking crayons, and brightly colored mason's lines all found their way into our two heavy tool kits. In the early 1990s we acquired electronic surveying equipment, on loan from Sokkia, and on one occasion a very early Garmin GPS (used to find true north—not easy). For photo documentation we utilized Hasselblads and fine-grain black-and-white film, as well as hand drawings linking each photograph to the position of the camera and direction of the photograph. In addition, we developed a careful system of keeping records based on the original measurement sheets for a project: A4 enlarged to A3 for corrections, daily logs, and the occasional color composite photograph.

6   Our measuring years ran from 1985 (first trials) through 1986 to 1995—ten summers of ten plus weeks with a team of fifteen mostly graduate students of architecture, and our invaluable collaborator George Newburn and assistants David Hecht, Tomaso Bradshaw, Kai Uwe-Bergman, Alexander Kitchin, and Eric Vogel.

7   Our days at the Villa were Mondays, Thursdays, and Saturdays. Before starting work, there were always the *cappucini* at Nilla's coffee bar adjacent to the Villa. Lunch was brought from Villa Lina in a red Coleman-like cooler. We always found near to our measuring places an appropriate place to eat. Surprisingly, these often turned out to be Triclinio (that is, dining structures) at the Villa! Two "famous" Coleman 10-liter water coolers were filled with ice and the best water in all of Lazio—water at the Villa from Aqua Marcia. Our days most often ended with a tour and close reading of part of the Villa, followed by endless Peronis and salted peanuts at Bar Belli, and then the fifty-minute drive back to cooler Ronciglione and Villa Lina.

8   This account is from a classical text written in the fourth century A.D. The first modern text mentioning and describing the Villa was written by Pope Pius II in 1461 as follows:
"About three miles from Tivoli the Emperor Hadrian built a magnificent Villa like a big town. Lofty vaults of great temples still stand and the half-ruined structures of halls and chambers are to be seen. There are also remains of peristyles and huge columned porticoes and swimming pools and baths, into which part of the Aniene was once turned to cool the summer heat. Time has marred everything. The walls once covered with embroidered tapestries and hangings threaded with gold are now clothed with ivy. Briars and brambles have sprung up where purle-robed tribunes sat and queens' chambers are the lairs of serpents. So fleeting are mortal things!"

9   Ligorio's text is the first extensive description of Villa Adriana, but his drawings, which many think were linked to this text, remain lost. The first plan of Villa Adriana is by the noted Baroque architect Francesco Contini (published in 1668 along with the first appearance of Ligorio's text). The next full documentation of the Villa is by Augustino Penna in his *Viaggio pittorico della Villa Adriana Roma* (1831–36).

10   One of the six sketchbooks Le Corbusier carried on his "Voyage to the Orient" contains thirty-seven pages of pencil sketches of the ruins of Villa Adriana, complete with captions and notes.

11   Since that time, there have been three major excavations at Villa Adriana. The first was at our dear Temple of Pluto, where we measured and dug within deep blackberry and other growth for three summers. The Soprintenza's office sponsored a clean sweep, including all marble bits, etc., that were subsequently used as fill under the new tourist parking lot at the base of the Villa. We completed our work here in 1997. The very major new excavation involves the area between the Vestibolo and the Pecile and west of the Small and Large Baths. This area was the dumping ground for earth during the Canopus excavation in the late 1950s, and when carefully excavated in the early 2000s this area revealed a fantastic temple and perhaps the burial ground of Hadrian's lover Antoninous. We have yet to measure this area, but it has been well documented by our friend the archaeologist Zaccaria Mari. The final area excavated lies at the eastern base of the Villa known by us as Count Centini. This area we measured during the Atelier years, mostly underground in muddy *criptoportici* (tunnels).

12   The Lolli and Bulgarini families own about half of Villa Adriana, and have for about five hundred years. Tiburtini Olive Oil has been imported into the U.S. since the early 2000s.

13   See William J. MacDonald and John A. Pinto, *Hadrian's Villa and Its Legacy* (New Haven, Conn.: Yale, 1997), and in particular chapters nine and twelve for the accounts of architects Ligorio, Contini, Piranesi, Le Corbusier, and Kahn, and the effect the Villa had directly on their work.

14   The "architectures of note" are clearly a moving target. Terragni's Casa del Fascio was resurrected by Peter Eisenman in the later part of the twentieth century.

A   Views of the "Eyeball Terrace" at Piazza d'Oro looking south, north, north, and northeast, showing "eyeball" reflecting pool and water trough feeding from the outer edge.

A

Caochangdi Village, Beijing, China, 2007–2008

MAR received an excited call from Drew Hammond in late November of 2002 stating that his friend Bernard Webb, living in Beijing, was hooked in with the leaders, and asking if we would be interested in heading an effort to introduce steel construction to China to build "endless" eighty-story buildings. We told Drew that three stories was our highest so far and suggested that contacting SOM would be more appropriate. Drew prevailed, and after meeting Bernard in Italy at the olive harvest, and after realizing we had Paola Igliori and Ronciglione in common, we found ourselves in Beijing in late February of 2003. After a one-and-half-year struggle, the steel introduction project evaporated. But on our first trip to Beijing, we visited the now famous 798 Arts District and became obsessed with the Bauhaus-engineered 1950s Factory 706. Two years later, we secured the lease for the 70,000-square-foot space, along with two partners: the research branch of the Ministry of Construction (CABR), and Liu Long Hua, chairman of Beijing Urban Construction Group (BUCG). The thought was to resurrect an idea first developed with architect Yung Ho Chang in 1993 for a kind of neutral ground space for American and Chinese schools of architecture. Something between a less elite Cranbrook and a public forum for architecture and design, in a country where architecture/construction was the number one business, emerged in the form of B. A. S. E. (Ji Di in Mandarin). The lease on the 706 space ended in February of 2006 after we had commitments from faculty and students from Michigan and Toronto who were arriving early May. Scrambling, we landed in Caochangdi Village, located adjacent to the 798 Arts District. Across the street from our friend artist/architect Ai Weiwei we rented the raw space of a bloated Quonset hut-like building, where we muddled through May and June, living and working at B. A. S. E. and becoming enamored with Caochangdi. In a conversation with Ai Weiwei, we remarked that we felt Caochangdi was a remarkable place, and he replied, "I never go there—I grew up in [an urban] village." Knowing Weiwei's history, we understood him to mean that Caochangdi was too much like the village he suffered through as a young boy during the Cultural Revolution. Last year, bumping into Ai Weiwei just before B. A. S. E. was again going to hold court, Weiwei proposed we collaborate on a "close read" of the remarkable space and place of Caochangdi.

Village in the City, Home to One in Every Ten Beijingers and Change

Caochangdi is one of more than three hundred urban villages, or "villages in the city" to more directly translate from Mandarin, in Beijing. These villages are the often illegal and ad hoc assemblages of structures that house an estimated 1.5 million people, or one in every ten Beijingers. Urban villages are common to all Chinese cities and bridge the gap between rural life and the mostly newly developed thriving cities. One of the beauties of the recent development of Caochangdi is that it has been spontaneous and illegal—a kind of people's architecture mixed with high art and architecture (e.g., Ai Weiwei and the art gallery culture), freed from the stifling constraints of large-scale developments guided by unyielding color-coded planning guidelines.

Caochangdi tells a specific story of itself and its four thousand to seven thousand residents, but it also has embedded within it the problems and possibilities of urbanism as they occur in this most unique and pivotal point in human history as increasing rural-urban migrations have produced, for the first time ever, a 50/50 split in urban and rural inhabitants. For us, watching Caochangdi over the course of the past two years has been like looking at a mad fast-motion video revealing not only the mechanisms of urban change as they are occurring in early twenty-first-century Asia, but also the human and spatial consequences of this change. In China, history is both deep and embedded while at the same time fleeting. It was difficult to find any historical accounts of the Village, but through the narration of the elected village leader, the history of Caochangdi began to unfold. It is a story of strange shifts that move with the tides of Beijing and of China.

Urban/Rural Conundrum

Situated in a pocket of land at the intersection of the 5th Ring Road and the Airport Expressway, Caochangdi is now in the midst of the encroaching city of Beijing. Located in the Chaoyang district—the largest revenue-producing district in all of China, accounting for 2½ percent of the entire GDP of the country—Caochangdi is minutes from the Central Business District and not far from the Olympic sites. And yet the economy and atmosphere of the Village itself operates more like a rural Chinese community than a community in a thriving global city. The only exception to this, and what produces a kind of strange urban conundrum and sets Caochangdi apart from the three hundred or so other urban villages in Beijing, is that since the beginning of the twenty-first century it has become a locus of art production and international art galleries mixed with the norm of the urban village.

Grassland and the Natural Village

Caochangdi translates into English as "grassland." The piece of land began as an unoccupied grazing land and was used by the Imperial Court as a hunting ground. There are still parts of the village, at the periphery, which are just vast empty fields. The first inhabitants were actually dead: once the site was determined to have excellent *feng shui*, the Imperial family began to use it as a grave site. They planted elaborate gardens that, if not wiped away during the Cultural Revolution, would have been a popular tourist site.

Two extended families, the Suns and the Zhangs, were responsible for building the Village. Caochangdi

Caochangdi Project Team: Darien Williams (project manager), John Beck, Sara Blumenstein, Jeannie Chung, Kevin Deng, Ellen Donnelly, Andrew Houlihan, Jesse Jackson, Wenyan Grace Ji, Harvey Krage, Sen Liu, Andrew Loh, Charlotte Nelms, Johnathan Puff, Song Chi, Robin Tregenza, Richard Tursky, Liam Woofer, Xu Yukun, Jason Song Jie Zhao.

FAKE Design Team: Andrew Lee, Nadine Stenke, Yuan Gao

A   Caochangdi Village. Aerial photograph taken prior to 2002 and before the construction of the 5th Ring Road and its interchange ramps with the Airport Expressway.

is known as a *zi ran cun,* or "natural village," which in Chinese refers to a settlement that naturally springs up in proximity to some opportunity in the environment to provide livelihood and sustenance. The Suns and the Zhangs serviced the tombs and the Imperial family members during their visits to the ancestors' graves.

People's Agricultural Commune Followed by the Deng Reforms and (Semi-) Privatization

During the Cultural Revolution, under Chairman Mao's orders, the imperial gardens were demolished and the Village became an agricultural People's Commune. The villagers' work went from manicuring imperial gardens to planting and harvesting crops cooperatively. At this time, as a part of the *Shang shan Xia xiang* campaign, when young people were sent "up to the mountains and down to the countryside," Caochangdi was considered far outside the city.

When Deng Xiaoping began to open the economy of China to the global market in 1978, some private companies moved into the Village and set up their head-quarters and factories in large compounds, or *da yuan.* Because of the need for more real estate to build these compounds, the farmlands diminished. The land, whether farm land or private compounds, was not privatized but remained under the control of the government, i.e., the People's Republic of China. This produced a kind of space under the influence of a hybrid experiment in conditions that are part capitalist, part communist, and part socialist. If we jump ahead in time, we will see that these large sheds and compounds are now being transformed into galleries and studios for the operation of the new entrepreneurial contemporary art scene that has emerged in recent years, sparked by the famous 798 complex.

Illegal Urbanism/Interior Real Estate

All of my buildings in the Village are illegal.
—Ai Weiwei on the projects by FAKE in Caochangdi Village.

The farmland still remaining after the large compounds were built was subleased to immigrants to the city. Freed from farming by passing the work on to these recent rural-urban migrants, the farmers now had time on their hands and cash in their pockets. To enhance their entrepreneurship and landlordship, they also began to rent out parts of their own houses or built larger (illegal) multistoried buildings where their one-story houses once stood. This phenomenon of new self-built, illegal, multistoried structures began over the past two to three years. We have learned that the rising middle class of China has little means of investment aside from acquiring, enhancing, and profiting from "interior real estate" by becoming landlords. We use the term "interior real estate" to distinguish traditional Western forms of real estate that involve land ownership from the Chinese version where land is held by the government (with land leases possible for a maximum of seventy years) but architectural space can be owned, sold, traded, and leased.

Art Superposes to Produce a Simultaneity without the Collapse of Difference, and Martha Stewart Pays a Visit to the Village

Early in the twenty-first century, Ai Weiwei moved to Caochangdi and built a compound of illegal structures to serve as a house and studio. An influx of other artists and galleries has followed in the past three years. At this time, of the sixty-five registered companies in the Village, forty are cultural enterprises. Many of the galleries have been opened by Europeans. This action has brought with it the sleek Mercedeses and Audis, designer-clad art patrons, and exhibitions of stunning art that share space with the rough-and-tumble Village, producing a kind of simultaneity without a collapse of difference. *Condé Nast Traveler* reported in their January 2006 issue that "Beijing may be the capital of the world's most populous nation, but it is also an underground favorite and a must-stop for the young and the art-collecting. The latest entry in the city's burgeoning arts scene is… the Caochangdi area, a nexus of up-and-coming artists." Since 2006, these artists have more than succeeded in living up to the hype. Recently, Martha Stewart paid a visit to the Village specifically to check in on Weiwei and his cool and edgy lifestyle and environment.

Fake Fake

The culture of the copy is alive and well in Caochangdi Village. Weiwei's FAKE design studio, located across the street from our B. A. S. E. space, has designed and built many projects here. Noticing the success of the FAKE projects in attracting foreign artists and galleries, local small landowners began to imitate form, materials, and details of the FAKE designs. We have tracked the "fakery" literally day by day. Having noticed a wall of intricately laid brick in a "real" FAKE project, we soon after spotted the farmer builders undertaking an alteration to their building under construction by chipping out bricks already laid to cosmetically imitate the pattern that FAKE had designed as an integral woven pattern. These are now known in Caochangdi as the Fake FAKEs.

Socialist New Village

In an attempt to capitalize upon the "natural" growth of architecture and the arts in Caochangdi, the Chinese Communist Party has given the Village leaders the mandate to make art and cultural enterprises contribute 70 percent of the Village's economy by the year 2009. The eleventh Five Year Plan of the party has as one of its primary agendas the goal of fostering invention and creativity through the development of cultural and creative

A

A Caochangdi Village. Aerial photograph taken after the construction of the 5th Ring Road reveals that an interchange ramp to the Airport Expressway was omitted, thereby sparing most of the Village from demolition.
B Courtyard houses in Caochangdi designed by FAKE and Ai Weiwei.
C Across the street from the FAKE compound shown above is this "fake FAKE" produced by a local entrepeneur who, having seen the immediate economic

success of the "real" FAKE projects, lost no time in imitating the form, material, and style to produce real estate attractive to foreigners and artists.
D Context map showing the city of Beijing and the location of Caochangdi at the intersection of the 5th Ring Road, which delineates the extent of present day Beijing's urbanism, and the Airport Expressway.

B   C

D

A

B

C

D

122   Re-writing Caochangdi Urban Village

industries. The purpose of this is to nudge China out of its role as "widget maker" for the rest of the world.

Also as a part of this most recent Five Year Plan, President Hu Jintao has called for the national development of the Socialist New Countryside, and Caochangdi has been discussed as a model Socialist New Village. While anything is possible, it appears that the mostly illegal structures of the Village will not be slated for demolition. In fact, as a part of the initiative of building the Socialist New Countryside, many improvements were made during the summer of 2007. New gas lines and storm and sanitary sewers were installed, and new roads, parks, and landscaping were added.

Caochangdi A–Z and 1–331

The streets of Caochangdi are not named, and the Village is like an undifferentiated numerical field with addresses being simply a number between 1 and 331. This gives the streets an oddly illegitimate quality. The house and building numbers are assigned spatially, sometimes, but more often are applied temporally, that is, in order over time as a new address becomes necessary. This makes wayfinding for outsiders with any conventional map impossible.

In an effort to turn Caochangdi into a "real" place, the Village leaders, as a part of their mandate to build and promote the Socialist New Village, plan to legitimize and name the streets next year. Local officials are considering naming the streets after famous artists because of the Village's recent prominence as a thriving arts district. They are unsure if they should use the names of famous European artists, Chinese artists, or some combination of the two. But they do seem to have settled upon artists' names as the way to go.

An A–Z alphabetical catalog of the numbered buildings in Caochangdi reveals a wild mix of programs that makes it, at least for us, a fantastic place to be. Buildings from a dog meat restaurant to a Korean Christian church operating under the cover of an animation training school, from a blue-chip art gallery based in Lucerne and Beijing to a Belgian foundation for cancer diagnosis and therapy, from the house and studio of Ai Weiwei and FAKE Design to IOWA, a compound of Quonset huts transformed into an American-style suburban subdivision complete with miniature golf and a Mongolian corn-fed beef restaurant. A driving school, boasting simulated on and off ramps for drivers new to freeways, and a taxi drivers' hotel (with time shared on twelve-hour intervals) coexist with small shops and traditional residences.

Urban Afforestation and the Green Screen

Also as part of the Socialist New Village campaign, but more directly related to the Central Party mandate for urban "afforestation" (especially in light of the 2008 Olympics), between three and four billion trees have been planted in Beijing. We have watched this tree planting effort transform Beijing. Afforestation is the word that the official Chinese press has adopted to use when speaking of the movement to counteract the massive deforestation that began with Chairman Mao's agricultural campaigns and continuing today mostly due to the tremendous demand for wooden chopsticks in China (think 1.3 billion people times two chopsticks times three times a day). Deforestation has caused the Gobi Desert to advance toward the city at the rate of one kilometer per year, producing dunes as high as 30 meters and spring sandstorms that have become known throughout Asia and beyond as the dreaded "fifth season." In order to water the trees in this desert environment, a contemporary form of engineered rainmaking has been implemented—seventy rockets of silver iodide fired from retired military antiaircraft equipment produce two days of rain, providing a good dose of "top down" irrigation.

The Village has benefited from some of the urban afforestation in Beijing. A mapping of the green space shows that 90 percent of the new trees and landscaping occur at the periphery of the Village, and this reveals an agenda not geared toward providing villagers with parks or street greenery but, rather, with a kind of "green screen" that masks the Village's mixed bag of architecture from the Airport Expressway and the 5th Ring Road. These two arteries are, respectively, visitors' first entry into the city and the way to the Olympic venues from most of the five-star hotels, making the scenes and impressions taken through the taxi or limo window most critical to the "powers that be," with their strong desire to impress. In fact, what these powers do not fully grasp is that the Village, which has been touted as one of the world's coolest art hot spots, attracts tourists and visitors who gain a lasting experience unique among visitors to the city.

A   Li Songsong, *Mist,* oil on canvas.
B   Wood Reclamation.
C   Beijing has about 660,000 registered dogs, a figure that has been growing by nearly 10,000 per month according to the municipal public security bureau. The city introduced a "one family, one dog" policy last year and launched a nationwide campaign against unregistered dogs.

This Siberian husky is just one representative of Caochangdi's diverse canine population.
D   Foundation Preparation.
E   Caochangdi 40.

E

A

Buzz

As the official planning mandates continue to come down from the top, a continual buzz is in the air, with the people of Caochangdi laboring to build and rebuild their "natural village" and artists continuing to make and sell new work. The top-down projects plant green screens to hide the village from visitors on the Airport Expressway, install oversized roads that go from nowhere to nowhere, and build museums that sit like empty modern dinosaurs. At the same time, and even in spite of this, the former farmers turned entrepreneurs, artists, and gallery owners are building a vital and profitable urbanism in Caochangdi at an astounding rate. Our work in Caochangdi has been focused on our fascination with the physical, social, economic, and human contributions of this grassroots urbanism that is growing before our very eyes. We are in the midst of trying to catch it while we can.

For us, the lessons of the Village have been a powerful antidote to the more publicized versions of urbanism that we know from wearing our architect and planner hats, looking at magazines, and moving around "well-to-do" parts of the city. Caochangdi's ad hoc urbanism has an economy (and a resulting environmental soundness), a sense of humor, and a direct placement of energies toward things that will affect us and our daily city lives. Art curator Pi Li once said that private space did not exist in China until the late 1980s, when the government began to sell housing units to individual families. There is a phrase in Mandarin, *li wai bu fen*—it means a lack of a clear division or clarity about what is inside and what is outside. It can refer to your clothes being worn inside-out, to not knowing the difference between a friend or an enemy, or between home affairs and external affairs. Surrounded by an urbanism of "object buildings," to borrow a term from Yung Ho Chang, Caochangdi has produced a kind of *li wai bu fen* urbanism where even when we are outside, we can be inside the city and the city can be inside of us.

A   New Socialist Village Central Party Projects (see p. 102, A).
B   Liu Quan Xi , also known as Xiao Liu (Young Liu) or XL, is a builder who runs his own business with a staff of about thirty-five men. His work is mostly in the city of Beijing, which is where he and his workers live. He is from Lin Quan Village in Anhui Province, as are many of his men. He and his workers are what is called in China the Nong min gong or farmer workers. They are also sometimes called Bei piao (Beijing floaters). They are migrants to the city whose move from rural to urban areas was made at the same time that the world's

urban population reached 50 percent of the total global population.
    Chain migration refers to the mechanism by which rural residents from the same village make the move to a large urban area, usually in search of work and better opportunities, aided by previous immigrants from their village. Xiao Liu began a chain migration from his home village in Anhui Province. Most of his workers are from his village, and some are even family members. Xiao Liu has also been hiring workers from Hebei Province, provoking another chain migration to form.

B

Venturi Scott Brown at Home

Perspecta 41 interviewed Robert Venturi and Denise Scott Brown at their home in northwest Philadelphia. Forty years after *Learning from Las Vegas*, we spoke with them about the ways in which their work has redefined the relationship between architecture and travel. Venturi and Scott Brown's living room is a reflection of their own travels, personal and professional. They have surrounded themselves with thrift store ceramics, Lichtenstein and Warhol prints, a tribute to the titans of Mannerism and the Baroque, and, of course, lots of neon. The high, the low, the historic, the generic, and the everyday are given equal weight, a perfect illustration of the architects' Pop, and populist, sensibilities.

All images © Colin Montgomery

For an interview with Denise Scott Brown and Robert Venturi and photos from the VSBA archives, see pages 36–41.

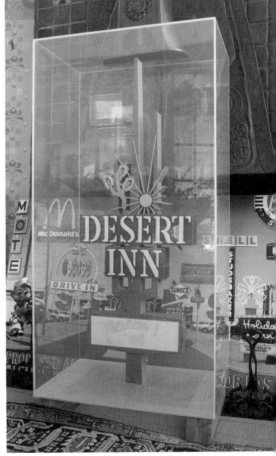

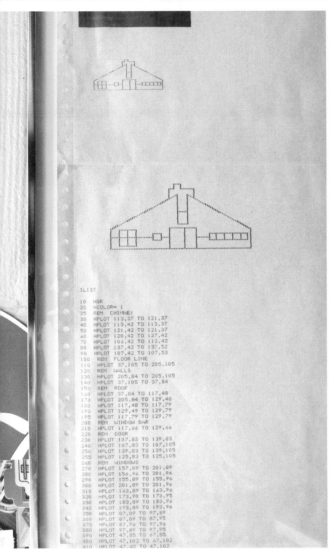

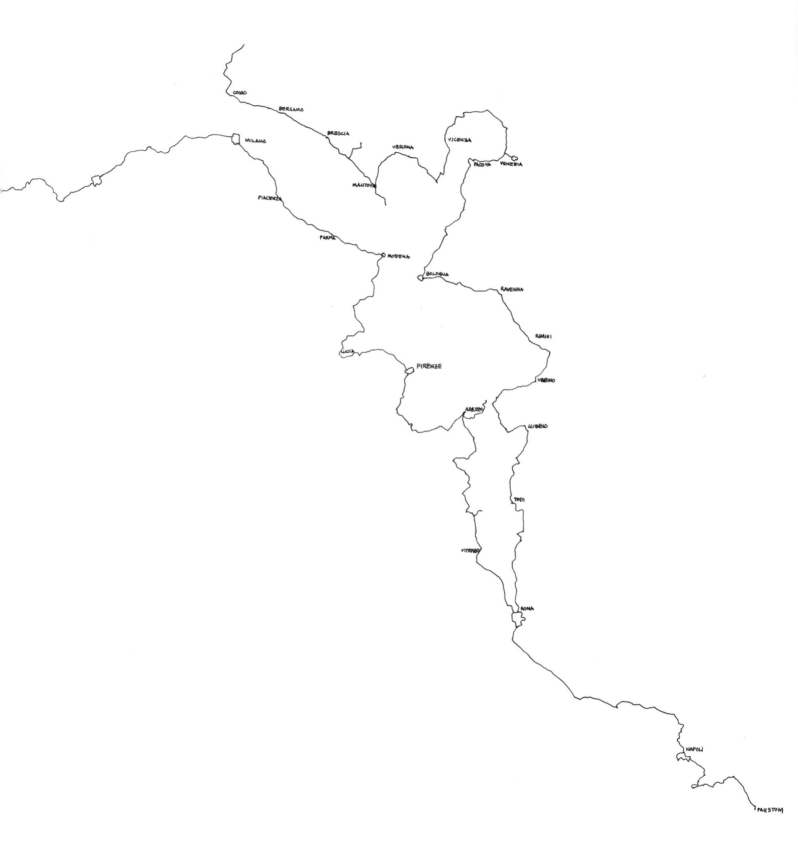

COMO
BERGAMO
BRESCIA
VICENZA
MILANO
VERONA
PADOVA
VENEZIA
MANTOVA
PIACENZA
PARMA
MODENA
BOLOGNA
RAVENNA
RIMINI
LUCCA
FIRENZE
UBBINO
AREZZO
GUBBIO
TODI
VITERBO
ROMA
NAPOLI
PAESTUM

INTERVIEW WITH PETER EISENMAN

THE LAST GRAND TOURIST: TRAVELS WITH COLIN ROWE

P41

PE

The idea of the grand tour in architecture is an English—if not a European—tradition, in which an older experienced traveler initiates a young person to the cultural splendors of southern Europe. In the mid-eighteenth century, Robert Adam established his architectural practice in London after traveling extensively in Italy with his tutors, and Goethe described his 1786–87 travels to Italy in his book *Italienische Reise,* published in 1816–17. While the Grand Tour has come to be seen as an essential part of an architect's education, my travels with Colin Rowe were part of an "accidental" education, but they had a profound impact on the manner in which I would subsequently practice.

In the spring and summer of 1959, I was working for The Architects' Collaborative in Cambridge, Massachusetts. At the time it seemed like heaven, working for Walter Gropius and living in Cambridge. This was supposedly the *summa* of an architect's life, but I soon realized that even Gropius and his associates had no real ideological or philosophic commitment to what I thought was architecture. TAC was so unsatisfying that I went to see a former employer, the architect Percival Goodman. Percy said, "Look Peter, why work your way up the ladder in an office to become a junior partner or maybe a partner? Why don't you come back to graduate school at Columbia?" At the time I was twenty-seven years old. I had been in the army for two years in Korea, I had done my three years of apprenticeship, and I was studying for my architectural license. Because I was in Boston, I applied to MIT as well as Columbia. I was accepted at both, but Goodman wanted me back at Columbia. He said, "You can graduate in one year rather than two." At the time, this was important to me.

But I need to go back to the fall of 1959, when Jim Stirling came to Yale for his first visit. Stirling came down to New York and I was introduced to him through my then roommates, John Fowler (who went on to work with Paul Rudolph) and Michael McKinnell. Jim said, "You know, you ought to go to England. That's where things are happening." New Brutalism was in vogue, and the Smithsons and Team 10 were generating a new energy in England. In the spring of 1960, I applied for a Kinney traveling fellowship, which was worth $7,500, which in today's dollars was a lot of money. At the same time I also applied for a Fulbright to France. I received both fellowships and decided to go to France. My brother was living in Paris at the time. I arrived on the *Flandre* in Le Havre and took the "boat train" to the Gare du Nord. When I asked a taxi driver, in French, to take me to Rue Git-Le-Coeur, where my brother was living, the driver turned to me and, in the most condescending tone possible, suggested that it would be better if I spoke English. At that moment, I realized that France was not for me. I spent a night with my brother, then turned around and accepted this other fellowship at Cambridge to be a research assistant. Unwittingly, of course, this decision would lead me to Colin Rowe.

I remember our first meetings. I would go to Colin's flat two or three times a week, and he would pull out books, Campbell's *Vitruvius Britannicus,* Letarouilly's *Edifices de Rome Moderne,* and other books with a series of fantastic plans from the Renaissance. I was taught how to read these plans and to see that specific plans showed certain ideas. I was taught how to understand the nuances of these plans, how they constituted the essence of what is architectural, of what has become the persistencies of architecture. We were not analyzing their function but rather the architectural relationships in these plans. This lay the groundwork for the trip. After several months, Colin suggested that I was the "noble savage" to his Robert Adam, and proposed that we travel in Europe for the summer.

Where did you go?

I was the one who researched the trip. As I was interested in De Stijl and the Bauhaus, we started off in Holland, against Colin's better judgment. We saw all of Rietveld, Van Tijen and Maaskant, Bijvoet and Duiker at a time when rarely anybody had gone to see this work. We saw the Van Nelle Factory, the Oud Siedlung, Bijvoet and Duiker's Zonnestraal Sanatorium, and of course the Schroeder House. It was then that I realized how much Colin did not like modern architecture.

After Holland, we went down the Rhine, stopping in Krefeld to see Mies's Lange and Ersters houses, which Colin had never seen. In Stuttgart, we saw the Weissenhofsiedlung. I did all the driving in my white Volkswagen Bug while Colin read incessantly to me. Twelve hours, night and day, we did nothing but look, and I would drive while he read, much of it useless trivia, like the shields of popes, the number of Piccolomini popes, etc. It was a total immersion experience. Next came Zurich, where Colin wanted to visit one of the old Texas Rangers, Bernhard Hoesli, who had worked with Le Corbusier and had taught at Texas with Rowe.

In Zurich, we had dinner with Hoesli and his wife. Hoesli had taken us around to see Le Corbusier's work in Zurich, and then showed us his own work in his office. Hoesli was a very bright person, but on this occasion, I became Colin's attack dog. Bernhard asked me, "Well, what do you think of my work?" We had seen that his work was a cross between Wright and Le Corbusier. I immediately said, "Bernhard"—and this is what endeared me to Colin—"Bernhard, I have never had a more exhilarating day. It was the most amazing experience looking at Le Corbusier with you. But I cannot understand how a person who knows so much about architecture can do such bad work." And there was silence. Boom…it was an amazing moment.

Leaving Zurich, we proceeded south through Switzerland to Como. Now we need to go back to Como because that is a major part of my story. Unlike Goethe, who reveled at the Lago di Garda, Colin said it was to be avoided at all costs, except for a brief stop in Sirmione at the foot of the lake, because it was now full of *Tedeschis* of a somewhat different ilk than Goethe. Mussolini had ruled from Salo, on Lago di Garda, in 1944–45, just north of Sirmione. Such was the kind of history that Colin would read as we traveled. I, this so-called noble savage who did not know anything, even though I had been reading *AD* during my year at Columbia and had learned about Brutalism, and even though I had been meeting regularly with Stirling, Smithson, Banham, and other members of the English scene in London, I was still a neophyte.

When Sandy Wilson had come back from Yale, he gave me, as a present for filling in for him, the *Encyclopédie de L'Architecture Nouvelle* by Alberto Sartoris. In that book I saw Giuseppe Terragni's work for the first time—his Casa del Fascio, the Asilo Infantile, and the Giuliani Frigerio apartment block. There was also Cesare Cattaneo's apartment block in Cernobbio just up the road from Como. This fired my imagination and my desire to see these buildings. Thus, when we arrived in Como, we immediately went to the square in front of Casa del Fascio, and, as Colin said, I had a revelation. After having seen De Stijl, Mies, Corbu, the Weissenhofsiedlung, all of these monuments of modern architecture, to see the Casa del Fascio in the flesh was amazing. I was blown away. After Como, we drove to Milano, where we saw the Terragni apartment buildings which nobody really knew at the time. They were only in the Sartoris book. We also saw Terragni's two houses in Seveso and Rebbio on the way.

My mania for collecting architectural magazines from 1918–39 began in Milano. Much of what was modern prewar architecture had been published in Giuseppe Pagano's magazine *Casabella*. This was the focus of my search in used bookstores. I would walk in and say, "Vecchie riviste di Casabella della prima della guerra?" I looked in every little bookstore from Milan to Naples and back to Torino. During that time we discovered many small antiquarian bookstores, some of which I can still visit to this day. But it was only on our last day in Italy that we hit the jackpot in the galleria in Torino, but that is another story.

After Milan, Colin programmed the rest of the trip with High Renaissance and Mannerist architecture and painting, but very little Baroque. I was not allowed to look at Borromini or Bernini. The work we had to see was the basis of the Cambridge course that Colin was giving, called "From Bramante to Vignola," that is, from 1520 to 1570 in northern Italy, both painting and architecture. Of course, this was all new material for me.

We went east to Bergamo to see the *citta alta* and the Scamozzi loggia on the way to the Veneto. We also detoured below the Milano-Venezia autostrada to Mantova, where we stayed for three days. We were now in the heart of Colin Rowe country. We saw Giulio Romano's Palazzo del Te, with the faux rustication and the giant frescoes bursting out of their panels. We spent an afternoon sipping San Pellegrino Aranciatas in front of Alberti's facade for San Andrea. We went to see the little-known church of San Benedetto Po, with its interior by Giulio Romano and its baptistery covered with his frescoes. Twenty years later, when I returned, there were no frescoes, only a restored "original" Romanesque baptistery. The work by Giulio Romano had fallen victim to the "restoration" impulse. Next came the Veneto and the Palladian villas. At that time none of the villas had been documented or catalogued, but Colin knew their locations from his previous visits. We would ask for directions in our primitive Italian and we found—and I still have the slides—ten or twelve Palladian villas that had been previously undocumented in any books at the time, certainly not in the old Baedeker and Michelin Guida Rossa guides that were our constant companions.

How were you documenting the buildings? Were you taking slides or drawing?

I was taking slides, but not drawing. Learning to see requires something other than slides or drawings. My most important lesson in architecture was the first time I saw a Palladian villa. I cannot remember which one, somewhere in the Veneto. It was hot, probably ninety-six or ninety-seven degrees, and humid, and Colin said, "Sit in front of that facade until you can tell me something that you can't see. In other words, I don't want to know about the rustication, I don't want to know about the proportion of the windows, I don't want to know about the ABA symmetries, or any of those things that Wittkower talks about. I want you to tell me something that is implied in the facade." I remember this moment as if it were yesterday. This is how Colin began to teach me to see as an architect. Anyone can look at window-to-wall relationships, but can anyone see edge stress, the fact that the Venetian windows are moved outboard from the center to create a blank space—a void between the windows—which acts as a negative energy? Such ideas are not found in any books. They are found in seeing architecture.

In this way I began to understand how to look at Palladio, at a portico in relationship to the main body of the building, at the flatness of the facade and its layering. Of course it was very different from looking at Giulio Romano's Palazzo del Te, which displayed different kinds of architectural tropes: a different flatness, a different layering, the implied peeling away of the stone, and the real stone making stone appear thin. We talked about frontality, rotation, and the difference between Greek and Roman space. All of these lessons I learned through looking at the subtleties of the Palladian villas. In Vicenza we saw the Palazzo Godi, which Scamozzi finished after Palladio's death. We saw how much drier Scamozzi was than Palladio. To be able to see dryness was as important as being able to taste dryness in a wine.

We then went to Venice. In retrospect, in Venice, interesting differences between Rowe and Tafuri became clear. Tafuri thought that Sansovino was important, while Rowe infinitely preferred Scamozzi. We saw two Palladian churches, San Giorgio and Redentore, and the layering and compression that occurred on the facades, their frontality. Now I was beginning to see things. And of course we were still doing twelve hours a day. I said, "Hey Colin, come on, let's go to the beach." But no, we could not go to the beach. For Colin, it had to be total immersion. This kind of mentoring would be absolutely impossible today.

We went into the Veneto, then down to Vicenza, to Verona to see Sanmicheli's city gates, to Padua to see the cathedral. This is where the story also gets interesting, as far as Colin is concerned. He said we could not go to Florence until we had seen Rome, because I needed to understand the influence of Rome on Florentine and Bolognese painting, what he would later call Mannerist painting. In other words, we had to see Raphael, Michelangelo, and Peruzzi before going to Florence. On the way to Rome, we went to Urbino to see the *cortile* of the Ducal Palace and the Piero della Francescas. The next stop was Arezzo, where we ate in the Buca di San Francesco, across from the Vasari Loggia. We went to Borgo San Sepolcro—another one of the things that only Colin would know—which is a little town near Arezzo, with a small church, not yet restored, with frescos done by Piero della Francesca. Many years later I went back and saw them when they were completely restored. But who had been to Borgo San Sepolcro? Colin was meticulous in knowing what to see and where to see it.

Down through Toscana we went. We made an important stop in Gubbio, which is a tough hill town lacking the saccharine qualities of Assisi and San Gimignano. From there we went to Todi, where I had my first *spaghetti carbonara* in a restaurant called Da Umbria, with a magnificent view of the valley. Of course, we made the obligatory stop at Sangallo's Santa Maria della Consolazione. From Todi we went to Perugia, Orvieto, and Viterbo, to the Villa Lante, to, finally, Rome, which was a literal feast for Colin. We saw the *Stanze di Raffaelo,* in which I began to understand the three periods of Raphael's paintings, and *The Fire in the Borgo* by Giulio Romano. I began to understand how this late period led to the painting of Parmigianino, Pontormo, and Bronzino. Painters were an integral part of understanding the architecture. Piero della Francesca was the first to bring a certain layered frontality of space that architects like Bramante pick up. Rome is a chapter by itself. Included in our tour was every Roman wall church of the sixteenth and seventeenth centuries, including Carlo Rainaldi's Santa Maria in Campitelli. It was in Rome that I got my first introduction to Luigi Moretti. We went to the Fencing Academy, which was in pristine condition, then to Casa Girasole and Casa Astrea. Colin had been impressed by Moretti's magazine, *Spazio.*

After a detour to Naples, we started north from Rome. I remember this was one of the highlights outside of Siena. By this time I was pretty beat, really exhausted, and particularly tired of being lectured, read to, and told what to do twelve hours of every day. We were driving along just outside of Siena when Colin said—and this was the way he would say things—"In 2 kilometers we're going to take the right bifurcation." A couple of minutes later he said, "Now remember, in 1 kilometer we're going to take the bifurcation to the right." And I began to steam. So when we reached the bifurcation, I went speeding by to the left. I had had it. It was done. And Colin said, "I said right." I said, "I heard you." He said, "I said right," again. I said, "I heard you." He said, "Stop the car." So I said OK. I stopped the car. And he got out, closed the door, and I continued on.

He walked back?

No, he hitchhiked to Siena, where we met up at the hotel, both having cooled off. After Siena we went to Florence, then Bologna. Bologna is memorable because we looked at Vignola's Loggia dei Banchi and at the Carraccis and Guido Reni in the Bologna Gallery. Then we went to Lucca to see the Pontormos. We looked at a lot of painting, but at the same time, I was trying to collect issues of *Casabella*. We arrived in Torino on our last day in Italy. I remember this distinctly. We went to a shop in the glass galleria in Torino, an old white-haired man with a fascist beard, split in the middle—clearly an old fascist—was sitting outside the bookstore. We asked him if he had any old *Casabella* magazines, and he replied that yes, he did. And I said, "Could we see them?" So he goes into the store and tells the assistant to go downstairs to the basement. And he said, "Look, I don't want to bring them all up, which ones specifically are you looking for?" And I said, "Why don't you just bring up some magazines from 1932?" So he brings up a complete year, in mint condition. So I asked if there were more,

and he said yes. So I said, "Why don't you bring them all up?" He brings up a hundred plus issues. It was amazing. I mean, a trove of mint-condition magazines from the 1930s. Now, I knew they were worth $10 apiece, that is, 6,000 lire. But if I bought a hundred magazines, that would be $1,000. I didn't have that much. I was making the equivalent of $2,000 a year, and with my fellowship for $7,500 we had bought a car, traveled, etc. We did not have much money at that point. So I asked what he wanted for them. He said, really quickly, 60 lire a piece. Not 600 but 60. I said, "Too much, I'll give you 20." We agreed on 20 lire a copy. He had never sold these magazines, nobody had ever asked for them. I could have bought the entire store, which had all of the Futurist and Fascist material one could ever want.

After Torino, we went back up through France, to Chambéry and Nancy—a city Colin loved. Then we went into Paris and looked at what he considered to be French neoclassical architecture by the architects Duc and Duban, people who are hardly known. We looked at Le Corbusier, of course. And I remember, also going to his office at 35, Rue de Sevres. We stood outside on the doorstep, and I looked at Colin and said, "What the hell am I gonna say to this guy?" He said, "Ring the doorbell, come on, come on." And I said, "No, no, no, I can't do that, I don't know what to do." So we turned around and walked away.

What happened when you returned to Cambridge?

Leslie Martin, asked me if I would stay on to teach a second year. At the time I did not want to be a teacher, I wanted to be an architect, so I asked if I could work as an architect. Martin suggested that since I already had my license, I would not want to work as a draftsman, and that it would be difficult to find any other architectural work. Then he said, "I will do something which is highly irregular. Why don't you do a Ph.D.? You can do it in two years instead of three and still teach first year." Being a teacher at Cambridge, one was supposed to be sitting at high table in college, but as a research student, one was supposed to be sitting with lesser mortals. Martin, with his political acumen, was able to work it out, suggesting I do a Ph.D. under his guidance.

I had never thought about getting a Ph.D., but I decided to do the thesis. This was perhaps another example of my accidental education. I also saw that there would be some problem for me in establishing my distance from Colin Rowe. Rowe's last year in Cambridge was from the fall of 1961 to the spring of 1962. During that time I decided to write about the formal basis of modern architecture as an analytic work on four distinct architects: Terragni, Le Corbusier, Aalto, and Wright, much to Rowe's chagrin. I finished my Ph.D. in 1963, the year after Colin left.

How did the trip with Rowe influence your work?

Without it, I would not be who I am today. There is no question that my education made it impossible for me to be what I would call an ordinary practicing architect. The two trips—Colin and I made a second tour in the summer of 1962—and the Ph.D. were all part of it. My idea of what it was to be a practicing architect changed completely. Even today, I am amazed that I have done major buildings.

Being mentored by one of the three great historians and critics of the latter part of the twentieth century—those being Banham, Rowe, and Tafuri—was the most intensive experience I had. The time I spent with Rowe was my education. In those two years, those two trips, I received an education that would be impossible to have in any other way. I both carried this education forward and needed to react against it.

Later, there were other mentors, Tafuri and Jacques Derrida. Percival Goodman had been my first mentor. I was open to being mentored, and the times were such that mentoring was possible. This would be impossible today. With Rowe I learned about much more than architecture, from the Carraccis and Guido Reni in the Bologna gallery to the Vignola loggia in Bologna.

This was the time that Rowe was writing about Le Corbusier's La Tourette. He took me to the Cistercian monastery Le Thoronet, which is the formal underpinning of La Tourette. How many students even know about this, much less have been there? All of this information was practically imprinted on my brain, because it was passed to me in a very passionate way. I truly was a "noble savage," like a sponge soaking up this material. The thought of having a Ph.D., the thought of teaching had never ever occurred to me. I also did not realize that it was going to put me off of the conventional route to becoming a practicing architect.

Why did you decide to leave England?

First of all, it was too claustrophobic, too homogeneous. I missed a certain sense of humor that was American. I also missed a certain capacity to be able to be "me." I could not live forever as an expatriate. Even though I could have stayed, I never would have practiced architecture in England. I knew I wanted someday to build buildings. That was very important. I could not become a historian like Colin.

Is this kind of learning still possible? Why don't you travel with your advanced studios, if you are trying to teach your students to see in the same way that Colin taught you? Or maybe you're not trying to do the same thing?

The first-year class that I teach at Yale is an attempt to teach students how to see architecture as architects. It is something that does not come naturally. Yale's Dean Robert Stern has said there is a disjunction between the first and third year in the studio. We needed to find a course that mediated between first year and third year. How does that knowledge move into the studio?

I am trying to set up a series of case studies to show how Rem Koolhaas moves from Palladio and Schinkel to Le Corbusier to Rem Koolhaas. I am trying to define the persistencies of architecture. What are those things that do not change, what things have changed, where are the fertile areas for change? How do you take the knowledge of Bramante and Palladio and use it in a studio with Zaha Hadid? How does Hadid do it? How does Frank Gehry do it? I want to show examples where masters have been able to take material from the discipline of architecture and manipulate it so that it becomes present. How do you produce work that does not rely on graphics or Photoshop or computers, work that relies on the capacity to integrate architectural knowledge into the present? In other words, what are the present situations? Venturi, Moneo, Koolhaas, Porphyrios, Krier, Graves, all these architects have had very good educations and have integrated that education into their practice, whether you agree or not with their current directions.

You said earlier that this kind of travel is no longer possible, that you cannot travel today the way that you traveled with Colin Rowe as your *"cicerone."* Is it not desirable, or is it simply not possible? And if it is not possible, why is that? What has changed?

The world was much smaller in those days, and slower. One knew everybody that there was to know. One does not know everybody in the world anymore. In those days you either went to college at Harvard, Yale, or Princeton, or you were out. When I applied to college, for example, I applied to Harvard and Cornell—that was it. I did not apply to six schools or eight schools. The world has become more varied and diffuse and the old days of what it was like at Yale are not same as what it is like today. Peter Eisenman, for one, does not have the time or money to take off and travel for two or three months. And I am married. You have to be an unmarried architectural critic who is willing to spend their time for nothing, *for nothing,* to do this. Nobody paid Colin to do it. We each paid our own way. Do I think that it is a way to learn? Absolutely. Do I think one should be paid to mentor? Absolutely. But I think the world has changed.

What is interesting is that I married my first wife that summer after Rowe left. We were on the road going from Florence to Arezzo, repeating, as our honeymoon, the trip that Rowe and I had taken. We drive off the main road to a little place, and there is a side road coming in from Cortona. We go by and I pull up in the parking lot of this restaurant where there are no other cars, and I look in the rear view mirror and there is a little green MG, which is what Rowe was driving, and I said to my wife, "Liz, you won't believe this but Colin Rowe has just pulled up behind us!" And it was true. Rowe was with Alvin Boyarsky, who was then the next in line to take this grand tour. The danger about mentoring is the risk that you never get out from under it.

Because the mentor is doctrinaire, or because it is an intellectual shadow?

Usually the mentor produces an intellectual shadow. Colin Rowe was never doctrinaire. He never insisted on anything but the way you learned. The way the trip was programmed was according to an attitude that Colin had about Mannerist painting and architecture and the way it related to modernism. I still see through Mannerist eyes. For example, when we were in Rome the first time, we saw no Borromini and no Bernini. Instead, we saw Carlo Rainaldi and Vignola. We went to Santa Maria in Campitelli, by Rainaldi. It was only a few years ago that I realized that Rudolf Wittkower, Rowe's mentor, had written a long article on the intersection of Palladio and Borromini with Rainaldi in 1935. Rainaldi had haunted me without my understanding until I read Wittkower's article, which Rowe never told me about.

If it had not been for Rowe, I would not be who I am today. But also, if I had not escaped from Rowe, I would not be who I am today.

It seems that architects today are traveling out of a professional rather than an intellectual interest. For example, many architects from our generation are building their careers in European offices. A stop in Rotterdam has become *de rigeur*. Do you think that travel has become more of a tool for professional advancement than intellectual development?

There is a reason for this kind of travel, and that is because people do not know how or what to see today. I know people who have spent a year in Rotterdam and have never gone to see the Zonnestraal, for example. They would not even know where the hell it is. They haven't gone to see Oud's houses in Scheveningen because for some reason that history has eluded them. Nobody has taught them about those things. In other words, nobody has analyzed Johnson's International Style show and asked "Where did he get these things? Where did he pick up these pieces? Johnson was so literate, he saw and knew everything. Just being around Philip, I learned a lot about the 1930s in Europe and his travels and why he made the choices he made for the 1932 show. Students today can go and work with Rem, Zaha, Herzog and de Meuron, but students are not curious as to how these architects put this information together.

Meaning the source material that supports the intellectual position of these architects?

How else does one become free of stylisms of convention, unless one has an education? To me education is the most important thing.

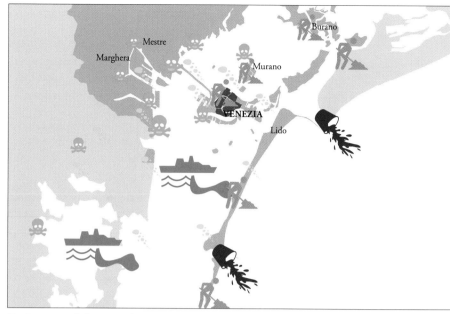

Environmental threats and interventions

Degradation from shipping
Pollution
MOSE Barrier
Erosion
Local Interventions
Flood Levels 100 cm
Flood levels 120 cm
Flood levels 140 cm
Comune di Venezia

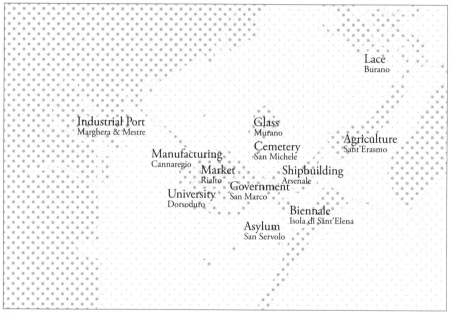

Lace
Burano

Industrial Port
Marghera & Mestre

Glass
Murano

Agriculture
Sant'Erasmo

Cemetery
San Michele

Manufacturing
Cannaregio

Market
Rialto

Shipbuilding
Arsenale

Government
San Marco

University
Dorsoduro

Biennale
Isola di Sant'Elena

Asylum
San Servolo

Venice programs

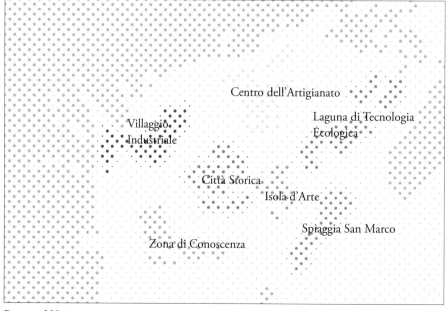

Centro dell'Artigianato

Laguna di Tecnologia
Ecologica

Villaggio
Industriale

Città Storica

Isola d'Arte

Spiaggia San Marco

Zona di Conoscenza

Proposed Venice

Learning from Venice

Jeffrey Inaba/C-Lab
C-Lab: Jeffrey Inaba, Benedict Clouette, Elizabeth
Knotts, Jesse Seegers, Kristina Blazevski

Cities that barely survive are as interesting as cities that thrive. The responses in Venice to simply survive are strategies of urbanization that are as useful to know as the ones that can be gained from rapidly developing cities. There is value in circling back to contemplate old cities struggling to stay alive, rather than only studying new, fast growing areas. It's a different way to appreciate cities than the predetermined learning-through-travel mode that might be best called the Rome syndrome. The 1968 Venturi Scott Brown/Yale trip to Las Vegas is the prototype of the "travel studio," and *Learning from Las Vegas* is the prototype of the "travel studio" publication. Both are as much about Rome as they are about Vegas. Venturi and Scott Brown's study references Rome to interpret Sin City, but more importantly it references the "learning experience" of the architect's journey to Rome—the excursion undertaken by generations seeking to cultivate a bona fide relation to The City. Rome is the architect's pilgrimage site to apprehend the sacred link between architecture and urbanity. It is the source guide and model city of architectural education, and the firsthand experience of walking its streets and encountering its buildings and public spaces is essential to the formation of the architect. Not only is Rome the city of eternal architectural lessons, but it is also the eternal travel experience that can be reenacted in any city, new or old, with the preordained outcome of discovering positive architectural traits through the observational filters of urban emergence, expansion, and excessive symbolism.[1] In this sense, the Rome of *Learning from Las Vegas* is the prototypical travel state of mind in which the architect unearths new patterns of urban growth and architectural innovation in any rapidly changing context, be it Las Vegas, Shenzhen, Dubai, or Mumbai.

The flip side of the Roman mode of experience is to learn from the urbanism of stasis. There are cities that by comparison have remained mostly the same, whose ambition is to preserve and endure—not to evolve and grow. Venice is a city that tries to maintain rather than change what is there. It plans for continual retreat instead of expansion and is defined by entropy not vitality. The pacing of urbanization is not dictated by the short-term demands of return-on-investment cycles, but by the long-term need to protect against slow but inevitable decay. Vegas was built in a day, whereas Venice has been successfully falling apart for centuries. Unlike other cities that try to conserve their architectural heritage and to reincarnate the urban center as a museum for tourism, Venice's precarious siting makes it more challenging to preserve and maintain a living past. The initial act of building the city in a lagoon to protect against military invasion from land has led to an unending battle with the sea and the technologies that respond to it. Silt accumulation, erosion, changes of sea water level, and tidal patterns continually jeopardize its existence. Technologies that have been applied over the centuries to respond to these forces have had to work antagonistically against nature. They tend to prevent natural systems from evolving in a sustainable way in order to keep alive a city founded on an unsustainable premise.

Preserving Venice requires balancing its supernatural ecology. It is supernatural in that both nature and technology have altered the lagoon system to the extent that their roles, effects, and reactions are indistinguishable from one another. As nature in and around Venice threatens the city, a technology is implemented to respond against it. This results in more complex mutations to the environment that in turn require the need for a more advanced responsive technology, all in order to preserve the experience of a seemingly unchanging urban mise-en-scène. While each engineering intervention in the lagoon seeks to uphold an imagined harmony with the sea, the attempts seem to inevitably produce a more hazardous and entropic situation, introducing further environmental threats instead of conserving Venice's urban and architectural integrity. For example, to reduce urban flooding, the inflow of water to the lagoon has been limited to such a degree that it has also reduced the outflow of water, consequently debilitating the ecosystem's ability to clean itself, which in turn has allowed for the growth of organisms that threaten the city's wood foundations. Now further technologies must be devised to counteract the lagoon's new organic profile without increasing the inflow of seawater. Stasis.

This supernatural dynamic works against both change and preservation. Venice simultaneously resists the inevitability of ecological flux and the technologies devised to conserve its history. Corrective actions that successfully reduce harmful environmental forces but also alter the integrity of the historical image of the city are themselves at risk of peril. Schemes that preserve the functions of the city face compromise if they endanger the city's patina of decay. There is self-assurance that when things get close to the point of irreversible implosion a new fix will help perpetuate the city's unique condition of ecological instability and timeless appearance. At the same time, the constant cautionary refrain that Venice is exposed to forces that may lead to its extinction increases its value as an urban artifact. The longer its collapse is deferred, the more appreciated its tenuous existence. It may not sink tomorrow, but the notion that soon it may is the source of its appeal.

As part of a self-initiated plan to help preserve Venice, we propose to apply the Venetian method back onto the city, inducing menacing forces in order to expose it to peril and thus prolong its existence and value. By gradually yielding to the encroachment of the sea, we envision a partially flooded Venice resulting in the dissolution of the urban figure-ground. New islands of consolidated program will form flotsam of a historic ruinous fabric that will increase the city's desirability and initiate actions to preserve it, setting in motion further catastrophes in need of preservation.

---

1 See Rem Koolhaas, Robert Somol, and Jeffrey Inaba, eds., *R O/S, Roman Operating System*, unpublished manuscript, 2000, Loeb Library Special Collections, Harvard University.

For an illustration of the proposed application of the Venetian method, see pages 142–143.

1   By concentrating Venice's historical sites into a single island, **Città Storica** consolidates risk and value.

2   **Isola d'Arte** groups Venice's major collections and exhibition spaces, including the Accademia Museum, François Pinault's Palazzo Grassi, the Peggy Guggenheim Collection, and the Biennale di Venezia.

3   **Laguna di Tecnologia Ecologica** is a 'supernaturally' regulated site for agriculture and aquaculture in lagoon ecologies. The Laguna employs environmental infrastructure, such as the MOSE project, to model various conditions through selective flooding.

4   With many of the industrial plants of Marghera and Mestre too outmoded to be upgraded for future uses, **Villaggio Industriale** presents an opportunity for new facilities to be constructed in the lagoon, affording better access to shipping routes for their products.

5 **Centro dell'Artigianato** is a destination for high-quality handmade goods, including Murano glass and Burano lace, two of Venice's historical artisan industries.

6 **Zona di Conoscenza** brings together Venice's research and educational institutions, such as the Università Ca' Foscari, Fondazione Querini Stampalia, and the Biblioteca Nazionale Marciana.

7 **Spiaggia San Marco** is the resort district, combining the Lido's famous hotels, entertainment events like Carnevale, and innovations drawn from simulated Venices, such as the Venetian Hotel in Las Vegas.

READING THE GENERIC CITY

RETROACTIVE MANIFESTOS FOR GLOBAL CITIES OF THE TWENTY-FIRST CENTURY

Esra Akcan

I.

In 1993, Rem Koolhaas traveled 360,000 kilometers, spent 305 nights in a hotel, and made the information public to call attention to the rising impact of traveling on the architectural profession in the age of globalization.[1] Ever since, he has published copious books, essays, and exhibition pamphlets that have gone well beyond travel diaries and have come to illustrate a new type of *research* on the city. This research is collected in publications that are no longer written by an author but by a big team, AMO, which defines itself as a research and design studio that applies architectural thinking to disciplines beyond the borders of architecture and urbanism.[2]

Why do architects travel and record what they see? Three impulses suggest themselves: The first is the impulse of the Grand Tour. Architects travel to study the masterpieces of Architecture, to learn from the great minds of the past. They record what they see in order to remember the buildings that have somehow proved their worthwhile existence. Such travel notes will provide the confidence that any architect needs in moments of weakness, ensuring them that it has once been possible to build artifacts with an aura, and it should thus be possible again. The second is the impulse of the meticulous and persistent diary keeper. Everything is worth recording in this case. Small vernacular buildings, buildings with no name, randomly created irregular streets are no less collectible than monuments with an aura. Unlike the permanent residents of the town who go ahead with their usual lives without paying attention to the mundane details, the traveler-architects with this sensibility record everything they see. They collect unconditionally, regardless of privilege. Everything is equally important, perhaps too important, by virtue of the fact that they

are there. There is nevertheless a third type: travelers that have an uneasy dissatisfaction with their own world, whose reflections or alternatives they seek in the travel destination.

These impulses map concurrently with Friedrich Nietzsche's theories of writing about the past. In his book *On the Advantage and Disadvantage of History for Life,* the philosopher specified three genres of history that would be applied by three types of individuals with different sensibilities.[3] Those who want to be powerful lean toward monumental history and consider only the major accomplishments and heroes of the past worthy of study. The errors of great heroes are excused in monumental history for the sake of maintaining their mythic status. Here "the past must be described as something worthy of imitation, something that can be imitated for the second time, so long, at least, is the past in danger of being somewhat distorted, of being reinterpreted according to aesthetic criteria and so brought closer to fiction."[4] The second type of history is favored by individuals with antiquarian sensibilities. This type of historians are patiently archivist; they collect all possible documents without official selection criteria, not realizing that it is impossible to run away from making choices.[5] The utopia of the antiquarian is to reconstruct the past without value judgment, even if it is categorically impossible to relive each and every second of life for the second time. In addition to monumental and antiquarian attitudes toward the past, there is also a legitimate need for a third kind of history, the critical history, written by those who feel the need to condemn the past. "[O]nly he who is oppressed by some present misery and wants to throw off the burden at all cost has a need for critical, that is judging and condemning history."[6] These are the creatively destructive or destructively creative historians who want change.

These three kinds of Nietzschean history mapped onto the three impulses of the traveler-architect can be summarized as follows: the impulse to record only the most important buildings, to record everything, and to record in order to change. A specific mixture of all three impulses can of course exist in the same traveler.

In his research on world cities, Rem Koolhaas is consistently attracted to "virtually unknown" architects rather than ones with an *aura,* he records buildings conceived and constructed by a mass of builders rather than stars, by producers rather than authors. His thick books with countless snapshots seem to have an antiquarian obsession with the ordinary bits and pieces of the city, rather than its most memorable monuments. How can one explain, then, Rem Koolhaas's own comfort in stardom, and his own desire to design buildings that always stand out in the crowd? Koolhaas seems to have antiquarian sensibilities as a researcher and monumental ones as an architect. Is he a monumental researcher staging as an antiquarian, or an antiquarian architect staging as a monumental? Or, may we say that the confrontational sensibilities in his writing and public persona best explain the work as a whole as some sort of criticism? Many of Koolhaas's texts, including the ones resulting from research travels, read like manifestos, throwing harsh assaults at the established values of the profession and, at times, at the choices of the majority.

Using the word "critical" today (in an age considered "postcritical" or "projective," but *only* based on two specific definitions of criticality), especially in relation to Koolhaas (the architect who is usually the first to be singled out by the advocates of postcriticality),[7] brings with it baggage, and that is exactly why I would like to insist on using it, albeit cautiously. As Nietzsche also warned in the same book, "much harm is caused by… the critic without need."[8] What is the "need" in Koolhaas's confrontational style? Is there a consistent position, a project for change that comes out of his *oeuvre?* Is Koolhaas's apparent confrontational style a veil to mask the end of the possibility of criticism in the "post-critical" age and turn this new condition into an opportunity for functioning as an architect in the market (a possible explanation of course, but one that will not be entertained in this article), or can we still define critical perspectives (by looking at Koolhaas or not) as long as we do not narrow down the meaning of criticality into a specific Western discourse? Let me take a detour by reading Koolhaas's article The Generic City in relation to his work on the generic cities of New York, Singapore, Lagos, the Pearl River Delta, and the Persian Gulf in order to answer this question. Even though Koolhaas openly declared inconsistency as a liberating impulse for the intellectual,[9] and at times retreated into ambivalence himself, it is nevertheless possible to observe repeating patterns in his publications on the city that lead to a consistent explanation.

II.

Rem Koolhaas's earliest manifesto on globalization (1993) was set next to a photograph of a very decipherable "anthropological" image, portraying a semidressed man and woman of color in a jungle standing in front of their basic shelter with primal tools in hand.[10] These formulaic signs of "primitive culture" must have meant to imply the coming of a new age when architects would be working with "other cultures," just like old-school anthropologists. And surely after a few pages, Koolhaas wrote: Sometime in 1987, in our office, international projects and collaborators began to form a majority. Suddenly OMA was global, not in the form of multiple offices turning out a single 'product' but of one involved more and more deeply in other cultures. We became experts in difference.[11] In one of the earliest accounts on the impact of globalization on architecture, Koolhaas thus spoke about globalization's professional possibilities that enabled architects to find a market of commissions in any part of the world on the one hand, and, on the other hand, the emerging necessity to understand the new contexts in which they would have to operate. In the next decade, Koolhaas's ideas on globalization gradually moved away from a fascination with professional opportunities toward an emphasis on learning "non-Western" cities.[12] In explaining his pedagogic activities at Harvard, Koolhaas stated that it would be probably much better to suspend design education for ten years, and to introduce ten years of solid research.[13] His book *Mutations* was not about design, he declared, in which the architect is asked to intervene in, but never to appreciate or understand a given situation; on the contrary, it was about pure research on the urban conditions of world cities.[14] This period of pure research soon came to a close when OMA secured major commissions in the places of research, such as CCTV in Beijing and eleven ongoing projects in the Middle East. Nevertheless, Koolhaas and AMO's activity to understand world cities is continuing. The books that come out of this exploration aim to overthrow the received values of the city and replace them with a new set of hitherto unusual ones.

However, "learning other cultures" is a fragile anthropological territory. Being interested in the "non-West" is not a value in itself, unless one can differ from the ages-old accounts of Orientalist writers and travelers who constructed the Western stereotypes about "exotic" lands, on the one hand, and unless one is genuinely committed to avoiding any cultural imperialist implication, on the other hand.

Koolhaas had already started research on cities in *Delirious New York* (1978), where he developed an argument that was never abandoned, and which therefore has to be treated as the foundational book of his theory on the global city.[15] Choosing Manhattan as the archetype of the Metropolitan Condition[16]—one that needed a different theoretization than the turn-of-the-century metropolis—Koolhaas observed high density and the resulting culture of congestion as the major metropolitan charm at the end of the twentieth century. In Manhattan, both the nameless yet experimental vacationing structures in Coney Island and the ideas of the skyscraper theorists, who stacked multiple realities and simultaneous private experiences on top of each other, created a culture of congestion that exploited density to inspire and support particular forms of social intercourse.[17] These unordinary, eccentric, and stimulating social intercourses were indeed illustrated with numerous examples in *Delirious New York:* Koolhaas demonstrated to us the charm of eating oysters with boxing gloves, naked, on the 9th floor of the Downtown

Athletic club; fighting the loneliness and alienation of the metropolis with the accidental partner with whom you have fallen into the same rotating horizontal cylinders of the Barrels of Love; coming to terms with the unnaturalness of the urban condition by sunbathing on the artificially lit beach of the electrifying Coney Island. *Delirious New York* was a historical research, albeit an unconventional one that was equally enthusiastic about obscure unbuilt projects in the depths of archives and architects' costume balls where they dressed up as skyscrapers. Koolhaas's usual confrontational style against the values of the architectural profession had transformed into a deep affection here for the informal products and practices of Manhattan, which received less disciplinary attention. Just as the avant-gardes of the early metropolitan condition, Koolhaas challenged the conventional view that undervalued the metropolis with a sense of anguish and dissent, instead suggesting that the unique metropolitan architecture would come out of this culture of congestion.

In New York, Koolhaas discovered two unconventional conditions that had transformed the way buildings were produced and consumed, and for which, I shall argue, he looked again and again in the "non-Western" global cities. The first was the decreasing role of the professional architects in shaping the interior performance of their buildings due to the high urban density that compressed multiple worlds and incommensurable individual lives in one skyscraper:

> Through the medium of the Skyscraper, each site in the Metropolis accommodates—in theory at least—an unstable and unforeseeable combination of superimposed and simultaneous activities whose configuration is fundamentally beyond the control of architect or planner.[18]

Architecture's conventional tools that aspired to shape the future and regulate lives by determining a stable physical order were now falling way short in living up to the instability of the metropolis. Later in *S,M,L,XL,* Koolhaas would summarize his argument for New York as follows: The permanence of even the most frivolous item of architecture and the instability of the metropolis are incompatible. In this conflict the metropolis is, by definition, the victor.[19] Architects were losing control and authorship. The resulting environment was much more charming.

The second related condition was the impossibility of imposing a prescriptive order on New York, which ended up being its asset rather than liability:

> …the authors of the Regional Plan know instinctively that it would be suicide to solve Manhattan's problems, that they exist by the grace of these problems, that it is their duty to make its problems, if anything, forever insurmountable, that the only solution for Manhattan is the extrapolation of its freakish history, that Manhattan is the city of the perpetual *flight forward*.[20]

For Koolhaas, New York in its heyday (i.e., not after the reactions to September 11)[21] was an archetype of the new city because it escaped human prediction, bureaucratic tidiness, and conventional organization logic, yet its residents always came up with a practical ad hoc solution. The strength of the metropolitan architects would be their ability to confront this disorder and messy conditions with no sense of determinist intervention, and to treat chaos as an opportunity for a new architecture that would embrace the instable and dynamic urban experience.

III.

Let me now suggest, with the unavoidable harshness of any containment act, that in his future work, Rem Koolhaas reworked these two related conditions, and theorized the first as junk and the second as mutant space, which together characterize the generic city. What unites Koolhaas's depiction of these cities is the fact that inhabitants in all of them have come up with creative ways of living in cultures of congestion and, especially, with forms of unspecific and unstable buildings.

The Generic City (1994), published in *S,M,L,XL,* was a depiction of the city that comes out of the global capital. Due to the impact of the economic transformations brought by globalization, some cities are expanding, others are shrinking. The Generic City seems to be a theory about the first category, and so are the exemplary cities Koolhaas picked to illustrate his theory that confirmed or adjusted his observations. The abstract account on the generic city was thus filled in with Koolhaas's "retroactive manifestos" on different world cities.

The Generic City was a testimony to the contemporary loss of identity as long as identity is created by the past. But the fact that human growth is exponential implies that the past will at some point become too 'small' to be inhabited and shared by those alive.[22] Koolhaas theorized the contemporary city, the one created by us in the present moment, as the city which is emancipated from an identity that imprisons…resists expansion, interpretation, renewal, contradiction, an identity that centralizes [and] insists on an essence.[23] The generic city is the city without history. It is big enough for everybody. It is easy. It does not need maintenance. If it gets too small it just expands. If it gets old it just self-destructs and renews. It is equally exciting—or unexciting—everywhere.[24]

The generic city, set against the artificially preserved traditional European city, such as Paris and Zurich—the two examples Koolhaas cited in the article—signaled the coming of a new age generating from America and Asia. Did the Generic City start in America? Is it so profoundly unoriginal that it can only be imported? In any case…a large proportion of Generic cities is Asian.[25]

Singapore was exemplified in *S,M,L,XL* as a generic city (the text was written in 1995, only a year after The Generic City), a city less than thirty years old, uncontaminated by contextual remnants,[26] a city without qualities,[27] a completely fabricated island that developed fast over a tabula rasa with unforeseen opportunities to build new vertical housing, mixed-use skyscrapers, tower car-parks, connected atriums with creative forms of urban linkages. Like the generic city, when Singapore got too small, it just expanded with the major landfills that significantly changed its natural geography. Koolhaas chose to bring to the fore SPUR (Singapore Planning and Urban Research Group, formed by William Lim and

Tay Kheng Soon) because the "Asian" as a sign of local identity was nothing but a "sentimental diversion" for them (in those days), while congestion and density were the true signifiers of their city. In Koolhaas's words, It is exactly this "new" density—the high-rise explosion of which the HBD housing blocks were only the beginning—that will be the sign of the Asian.[28] Koolhaas intuited the hints of Manhattan's early urban delirium in Singapore. In its heyday, Singapore was the first city where one could discover a new Asian self-awareness and confidence…they are containers of urban multiplicity, heroic captures and intensifications of urban life in architecture.[29]

Additionally, Koolhaas predicted Singapore as the Hermes of the next China, and by extension, as the model generic city where the majority of the world population would soon reside:

> In numerous architectural offices in Singapore, whose names few of us have ever heard, China's future is being prepared. In these countless new cities the skyscraper is the only surviving typology…Projecting outward from Singapore, an asymmetrical epicenter, there will be new Singapores across the entire mainland. Its model will be the stamp of China's modernization.
>
> Two billion people can't be wrong.[30]

The Generic City was more than its author's travel notes exploring reality, but rather a manifesto for the future coming out of the experience of traveling. Despite the lack of open reference, Aldo Rossi was the father figure that Koolhaas constantly rebelled against: the memory of the traditional European city was not at all worth preserving, and contemporary architects needed to be emancipated from the task of establishing continuity with the conventional urban environment. Rather than maintaining the unity, harmony, memory, or identity of historical cities, Koolhaas called for the metropolis of ultimate excitement, creative forgetting, disconnection from history, and unpredictability.

Nevertheless, the generic city in Koolhaas's observations was neither without new identities nor a homogenous whole. It was multiracial and multicultural.[31] Architectural reflections of different identities could thus be observed side by side in the most unexpected and unpredictable ways. The Generic City is the apotheosis of the multiple-choice concept: all boxes crossed, an anthology of all the options.[32] The category of difference needs some clarification in Koolhaas's various pieces. In his earlier accounts Koolhaas defined the generic city as the general city, the city without qualities, the city without identity,[33] but this was not meant as a call against difference. On the contrary, in his work on Lagos and the cities of Pearl River Delta and the Persian Gulf, Koolhaas differentiated the traditional city from the generic city in terms of the former's homogeneity as opposed to the latter's hybridity. Koolhaas identified the five Chinese cities of the Pearl River Delta as the City of Exacerbated Difference (COED), namely a new urban coexistence where every city defines itself in terms of difference from the other cities and always renews its differences in order to survive:[34]

> The traditional city strives for a condition of balance, harmony and a degree of homogeneity. The City of Exacerbated Difference, on the contrary, is based on the greatest possible difference between its parts—complementary or competitive.[35]

A few years later, Koolhaas made the same observation for Lagos: Lagos is perhaps very similar to the City of Exacerbated Difference (COED) that I identified in the Pearl River Delta in China. It is perhaps the only sustainable model of the city—a city that consists of radically different parts that define themselves in relation to all the others, and that coexist through the interactions between all components.[36]

The Generic City is thus not necessarily a familiar declaration on the homogenization of the world, but rather an abstraction—a theoretical statement—on the transformation of the concept of a city as a result of globalization's complex forces, both homogenizing and differentiating, as well as a statement on the differences between the global city and the conventional Eurocentric definition of "the city." What best defines the generic is not therefore the loss of difference and identity, but the elimination of identity defined by the past, and more significantly the loss of control that used to be attained with conventional architectural and urban planning tools. The generic city is unpredictable, it abandons what doesn't work,[37] its multiple centers can move anywhere, it can expand or shrink in any direction, it signals the death of city planning as we used to know it. Not because it is not planned…But its most dangerous and most exhilarating discovery is that planning makes no difference whatsoever.[38] In that sense, the generic city resembles the skyscraper, as Koolhaas once saw it. Architects and planners are now losing control and authorship in shaping not only the interior performance of their buildings, as they did in Manhattan, but also the overall environment.

In his essay What Ever Happened to Urbanism?—written in the same year as The Generic City, in 1994—Koolhaas pointed out the paradox that urban planning as a profession was becoming inadequate exactly at the moment when the population of world cities were tripling.[39] This was all the more reason to understand how these existing world cities worked and, through their appreciation, to offer alternative ways of approaching the city other than the modernist norms of city planning. What if we simply declare that there is no crisis—redefine our relationship with the city not as its makers but as its mere subjects, as its supporters?[40]

Junkspace was another Koolhaasian term that depicted the proliferation of anonymous and nameless buildings, as well as the decreasing control of the designer-architect. As part of his research on shopping, Koolhaas used it to come to terms with the abundance of shopping malls, airports, multistory car parks, and theme parks, about which he remained conflicted and ironic, half fascinated, half traumatized.[41] Junkspace is nothing mysterious; it is what we see when we look out of the window of any building in a modern city. The built product of modernization is not modern architecture, but Junkspace. The form of Koolhaas's text mimics its content: it is claustrophobic. Junkspace is composed of one single paragraph; page after page, sentence after sentence, one continuously reads about the repetitive cycles of endless, anonymous, unspecific junkspaces.

The text weighs on the reader like a David Lynch movie, where one feels trapped in a space with many exists but no exterior. Every time you burst out of a building (i.e., a junkspace), you find yourself in another one. Junkspace is everywhere. Yet, like all good fiction writers, Koolhaas is able to compose the most interesting story out of our least attractive real world and dull lives. Where you see a big flat building with no windows, or countless concrete apartment slabs with no differentiation, Rem sees a perpetual Jacuzzi with millions of your best friends.[42] And like all fiction novels or travel diaries that inherit their writer's imaginative twist, the readers should enjoy the text, get inspired if they wish, but be cautious of believing it.

The anonymity of junkspace does not mean it manifests itself as the same environment in every city. For instance, in their latest book *Al Manakh,* AMO members continued to identify the anonymous architecture of the Persian Gulf states, including Kuwait, Bahrain, Qatar, Abu Dhabi, Dubai, Sharjah, and Ras al-Khaimah, as the nameless but spectacular buildings conceived as a result of the collaboration between "virtually unknown" architects, engineers, and developers:

> Other architects are responsible for their own foundering in irrelevance. While Western architecture has focused on convincing itself on its singularity and pursuing the next strange form, a more intelligent system has perfected its so-called art into an algorithm. The building industry—where engineer, architect and even developer are once again united in one entity—has caught up to neutralize the difference between the brand name and a more efficient, generic alternative… In a time frame of three weeks, a Virtually Unknown can generate the thrill that the brand-name architect couldn't even do in twelve months…this is architecture's redefinition, whether it is welcome or not.[43]

The anonymous, neutral, and familiar space of Dubai is slick and sophisticated, while that of Lagos is chaotic and dynamic. In either case, however, the "junkspace" is created beyond the designer's control out of the complex global forces acting on that particular city. In summary, anonymous buildings, designed by virtually unknown professionals, are taking over the generic city regardless of their prescriptive urban plans. The death of the author has never been so evident.

If the elimination of a fixed, single, and past identity previously sought by using conventional tools is the first major attribute of the generic city, the capability to mutate and adapt to the fast and perpetually changing conditions is the second. In Manhattan, the impact of the unstable metropolis influenced only the interior performance of the skyscrapers, while the envelope remained fixed. Skyscrapers combined the aura of monumentality with the performance of instability because their interiors accommodate[d] compositions of program and activity that change constantly and independently of each other without affecting what is called, with accidental profundity, the envelope.[44] Manhattan thus kept the illusion of architecture intact,[45] whereas the Asian and African global cities make the disillusionment complete. In *Delirious New York,* Koolhaas illustrated examples of the ever-changing interior organizations that constantly adapted and re-adapted to the

instability of the metropolis. In *Mutations,* he came to terms with the practical ad hoc solutions of a city that escapes bureaucratic order. Cities of Pearl River Delta and Lagos—exemplary cities from Asia and Africa—are in constant mutation, and they rely on mutation as a new organizational skill, rather than a prescribed conventional order:

> The fundamental conundrum of Lagos, considered as both paradigm and pathological extreme of the West African city, is its continued existence and productivity in spite of a near-complete absence of those infrastructures, systems, organizations, and amenities that define the word "city" in terms of Western planning methodology. Lagos, as an icon of West African urbanity, inverts every essential characteristic of the so-called modern city. Yet, it is still—for the lack of a better word—a city that works.[46]

So, how does Lagos work, despite the apparent malfunctioning of the conventional infrastructures and urban organizations that make up a "city"? It works through mutating operations and adopting agents that would be considered "marginal, liminal, informal or illegal" according to Eurocentric definitions, but that together construct a totally exciting organizational system. Property lines constantly change in Lagos, so do the building typologies; crime prevention techniques have sparked new industries; the walls built as security gates host casual trades; informal public and commercial spaces never remain static; the garbage of the city is totally disassembled through semi-official businesses and reused in the Nigerian economy; the most crucial industries, storage and parking functions, take place by temporarily occupying the land underneath the highways or undersides of overpasses and by adhering to the highway columns as space regulators; major trade in the city happens during the manipulated traffic jams[47]: Jamspace, the totally negotiable, usually illegal and hugely productive space of the traffic jam, is not something to fix, solve or even rationalize.[48]

Koolhaas made similar observations for the Persian Gulf cities in *Al Manakh.* The Gulf city is no longer generated by a plan; it has become a patchwork of developers' increments…Infrastructure is no longer conceptual anticipation, but pragmatic afterthought.[49] Like major Chinese metropolises, the most determining actuality of the Persian Gulf's building practice is its overwhelming speed. In a series of interviews Koolhaas and AMO's Todd Reisz conducted with past and current planners of the Gulf cities, it is revealed that master plans get prepared on the basis of construction that had already started; coincidental anecdotes shape the future much more than plans.

The uniqueness of Koolhaas's travel and research accounts on Lagos and Dubai was not only his perceptive observations of these cities, but also his prediction that all cities, European cities included, would sooner or later adopt these mutant urban organization strategies. The Gulf is the current frontline of rampant modernization…If you want to be apocalyptic, you could construe Dubai as evidence of the end-of-architecture-and-the-city-as-we-know-them; more optimistically you could detect in the emerging substance of The Gulf—constructed and proposed—the beginnings of a new architecture and a new city.[50] Or should I have said that Koolhaas's desire to inflict a *change* so that the static and slow European cities also mutate into the dynamic and speedy Lagos and Dubai determined his descriptions? In Koolhaas's eyes, Lagos and the Persian Gulf are not the developing African and Middle Eastern cities on their way to Westernization. On the contrary,

> Lagos is not catching up with us. Rather we may be catching up with Lagos.[51]
>
> The Gulf is not just reconfiguring itself; it is reconfiguring the world.[52]

IV.

In the face of these copious, abundant, and accumulative data on world cities, the question remains: Despite their differences, why do generic cities saturate our planet at this particular moment in world history? Is this the natural result of our global age, of our technology, or of our political convictions? Namely, is this the unavoidable architecture of not only democracy and multinational capitalism, but also (ex-)socialism as well as monarchy? Is this the architecture of majority or of surplus value created by deviation from fair exchange now exerted at a global level? Even though Koolhaas continuously consoles himself that he is receptive to reality and turns it into an opportunity for his architectural practice, just as he did after his book *Delirious New York,* he is also aware of the claustrophobic oppression of junkspace. If we start seeing the generic city as a potentially oppressive force (whether Koolhaas agrees or not), would this make it a "tyranny of majority" or a tyranny of G8? In either case, this would mean that the built environment lacks some of the mediums that are analogous to the political spaces devised to contest these hegemonies, such as minority spaces, free speech, and the public sphere. If so, wouldn't this mean that architecture as a profession and discipline needs new mediums similar to the social institutions that create hope for a more functioning democracy, a less oppressive market, and global equality? Are we really over criticism?

Any research on globalization and global cities around the whole world can hardly escape geopolitical questions. The political implications of Koolhaas's work can best be discussed by tracing his statements chronologically, because it is possible to intuit a shift in his answers. While his descriptions of the cities remained more or less constant in relation to the two themes outlined above, his recent accounts began adopting a more explicitly stated political perspective.

The Generic City, written in 1994, asserted to be a neutral description of sheer facts, but it was written from the perspective of the global elite. The global elite travel for work from one generic city to another, which are all internationally connected with familiar airports. The global elite spend their nights at glamorous hotels—the quintessential places of domestic irresponsibility where customers do not have to make the bed, clean up, or hang the towel. And the global elite shop, not simply as a form of necessary exchange, which is painful if you have limited means, but as a form of leisure. These three programs that Koolhaas listed as the basic architectural types of the generic city—the airport, the hotel, and the shopping mall—are the most controlled and surveilled spaces of our times and are therefore unlikely to host a public sphere (i.e., a sphere for free speech).

In The Generic City, Koolhaas was evasive and ambivalent, refusing to take sides about the recent developments of globalization. The article can be read both as a satire and a celebration. Koolhaas's affection as a global *flâneur* for the generic city was sort of a Baudelairian "love at last sight," both outside and inside, both suspicious and fascinated, both resistant and welcoming, both reserved and seduced, both critical and antiquarian. However, unlike Benjamin's characterizations of Baudelaire's reception of mass culture in the metropolis, Koolhaas's ambivalence served to depoliticize the discourse at this stage. Koolhaas did not take sides; he could (and still can) work in any ideological context, with leaders from any mainstream or extreme political conviction; he could survive in any governmental structure.

Even though AMO's thick books record infinite data of the real, Koolhaas, like all committed avant-gardes perhaps, is persistently drawn to the concept of tabula rasa on which new identities can be inscribed.[53] All Generic Cities issue from the tabula rasa; if there was nothing, now they are there; if there was something, they have replaced it.[54] Koolhaas is most curious about cities at their moment of booming from a tabula rasa: New York in the 1920s and 1930s, Singapore in the 1960s, Lagos in the 1970s, the Pearl River Delta in the 1990s, Dubai in the 2000s. He dumps them once dynamism dies: New York after the World Trade Center architectural competition, Singapore after its Promethean hangover. When there is a chance to start over, Koolhaas is there.

However, many crucial issues get sidetracked during this fascination with cities that emerge or change suddenly. Anthony Vidler had already pointed out the facetious but ignorant tone in *Delirious New York:* "For how should we laugh, for example, at the spectacle of positive projects like that of the 'Fighting the Flames' event on Coney Island juxtaposed to the actual fire that destroyed the fairground in 1911, a fair created for pleasure at the expense of the masses and contrasting with their degradation?"[55] Many more examples can be listed: The ecological problems to be caused by Dubai's landfills were not even mentioned in *Al Manakh* during the applause for the mega projects "The World" and "The Palm," even though the data by AMO itself in the same book proves the alarming ecological footprint of the region.[56] To give another example, Koolhaas was bound to disregard any design potential in, for example, Singapore's tropical architecture as a result of his inflexible rejection of local identity.[57]

Koolhaas is usually reluctant to confront the serious problems of these generic cities, which in turn exoticizes them as the alternative to the conventional European city that he is so eager to contest. The biggest risk of such travelers' accounts is their exoticism. In looking for an alternative to their own world, they can so easily fall into the condescending exoticism of the Orientalist traveler.[58] For example, *S,M,L,XL* was embarrassingly filled with the cliché Orientalist stereotypes: If it [Generic City] is Asian, then 'delicate' (sensual, inscrutable) women appear in elastic poses, suggesting (religious, sexual) submission everywhere.[59] To give another example, Koolhaas whined over the fact that there were no sensual, demure, provocatively innocent pre-geishas any more.[60]

Residues of this exoticism remained in the future work. While this will likely be avoided in the forthcoming book on Lagos, in his earlier accounts Koolhaas aestheticized the city's slums as heavens of self-organization creatively mutating to cope with the extreme complexities of global conditions. However, other accounts tell a different story: "As a picture of the urban future, Lagos is fascinating only if you are able to leave it. After just a few days in the city's slums, it is hard to maintain Koolhaas's intellectual excitement. What he calls 'self-organization' is simply collective adaption to extreme hardship."[61] Or in Okwui Enwezor's words, "there is a sense that the attentiveness to these conditions in Lagos tends to focus less on a principle of empathy and more on the erotics of chaos and gigantic flux."[62] While the reader searches desperately in Koolhaas's early work for the voice of Lagos's inhabitants, their dilemmas, and economical, psychological, and health problems, complicated responses to the histories of colonization, and complex relations with the current world powers, Koolhaas loves Lagos because it is resilient, material-intensive, decentralized and congested, and because it does away with the inherited notion of 'city' once and for all.[63] Aren't these the very attributes he was promoting long before he went to Lagos? Lagos seems to justify and prove the necessity for the "new city" Koolhaas had been projecting for years.[64]

Similarly, AMO celebrates Dubai as the world's most intricate and simultaneously flat-footed system of cross-cultural coexistence.[65] However, this elite multinational population is maintained at the expanse of millions of guest workers whose immigration status and working and living conditions in this tax-free land do not match current standards for international workers' rights (even if, we are told, there is improvement in this area). While Koolhaas admits cosmopolitanism as the biggest asset of world cities, he is reluctant to expose the tensions in Dubai that prevent a true cosmopolitan coexistence, such as the continuing hierarchies of an ethnic caste that puts the South Asian groups (the majority in the overall population) at a disadvantage.

If, in fact, Koolhaas is seeking confirmation for his preceding ideas during his travels, he would be less a migrant traveler who learns and changes in relation to the place of arrival and more a nomad traveler who carries and brings his place of departure (i.e., his project) to the place of arrival.[66] This is the basic symptom of all imperial impulses when it is directed toward hitherto disenfranchised geographies, however hidden or involuntary it may be, and however sincerely committed Koolhaas may be to the production of a non-Eurocentric architecture culture.

P.S. Alternative Ending

It is only in some of his recent publications that Koolhaas, together with key figures in AMO, openly confronted the drawbacks of exoticism and a hidden epistemic hegemony. Signs of change radiated from Koolhaas after September 11 as well, when his political choices became a bit sharper. It is still unclear to me whether this shift was intentionally committed to a political and ethical responsibility or whether it was a natural result of Koolhaas's reactionary attitude to the authority figures of culture. In any event, after September 11, we found Koolhaas making more and more comments with a critical sensibility against North American cultural hegemony. Due to his work with the European Union, Koolhaas increasingly commented on Europe, but now with a decreased sense of appreciation for Western hegemony. The Europe of the EU would not be the Europe that Koolhaas openly found so boring in his early career. It would be a new Europe in the making; and meanwhile not only the American but also the "non-Western" cities would offer new possibilities for imagining the future of global cities. Koolhaas was exceptionally progressive (and deliberately fictional) in opening the borders of EU to practically any country who wants to be part of it: If I were the foreign minister of EU, I would ignore Europe. I would simply assume that, for my domain, bigger is better…I would work with the Chinese to construct a Eurasian arc, which would be a new inclusive framework that could eventually accommodate every nation belonging to this landmass into a Judeo-Christian-Islamic-Hindu-Confucian belt of compatibility.[67]

The forthcoming book on Lagos, prepared by Talia Dorsey from AMO, not only observes the current self-organizing systems, but also examines the city's large development projects in the 1970s, just a decade after it gained independence, as forms of a "higher intelligence." The two "blueprints" of the city, the one created in the 1970s by the urban planners, and the other one added in time by the residents, together create new forms of self-organization. AMO will argue that Lagos can function despite all odds thanks to the combined intelligence of the urban planners and the additions made afterward by the inhabitants.[68] The fact that a preemptive higher intelligence could be inscribed in the master plans, which later enabled the city to adjust to the demands of its own dynamism, may actually restore Koolhaas's disenchantment with urban planning, and may in turn change the tone about the perceived impossibility of the architect's critical participation.

To give another example, in an admirable essay, Koolhaas and Reinier de Graaf from AMO discuss the education policy in the Persian Gulf (as well as the dangers of the U. S.'s exclusionary practices in this field after September 11) and reach a point where they admit the necessity to question the Western narrowness of some of the very frameworks of knowledge:

Human rights, corruption, freedom of speech, free trade, nuclear arms proliferation, and copyright. Undoubtedly many of these values and concepts currently considered to be universal will, in the long run, turn out to have been too narrowly defined—i.e., only from a Western perspective. In order to acquire true universal status, they will have to be renegotiated and become subject of a global debate...Maybe the real Enlightenment is still ahead of us.[69]

If I am in fact correct that Koolhaas is envisioning a transformed world where ages-old cultural hegemonies and hierarchies are transformed, he would be doing far more than recording reality but engaging in a practice that is willing to try making a true change, i.e., critical practice *par excellence:*

Is it possible to view the Gulf's ongoing transformation in its own terms?

As an extraordinary attempt to change the fate of an entire region?

Is it possible to present a constructive criticism to these phenomena?

Is there something like a critical participation?[70]

A traveler who lands in "non-Western" countries today is faced with the double challenge of avoiding both exoticism and being judgmental based on Eurocentric values. In a world where societies are getting more and more immune to the wars that justify themselves with numerous stereotypes of the "clash of civilizations" ideology, this double challenge is tripled with a responsibility for criticism. While discussing forms of postcriticality and their limitations, Roemer van Toorn writes: "Instead of chasing after elusive ideals, we prefer to surf the turbulent waves of free-market global capitalism...Thus many reflective architects believe that it no longer makes any sense to spend time constructing new ideologies or criticizing the 'system'...[D]reaming is no longer necessary since even our wildest dreams are incapable of predicting how inspiring, chaotic, liberating and dynamic reality can be."[71] For a world citizen who is outside the global architectural elite, such as one living in the slums of Lagos partly because architecture/city culture stopped investing in alternatives, or another one who is under the continuous threat of being bombed in the name of "freedom" in Baghdad, Beirut, or another Middle Eastern city, or one who lived through the deadly earthquake in Istanbul in spite of the ignorance and corruption in building industry, or one who endured a similar negligence in New Orleans, the reality is obviously not as "inspiring and liberating." Nietzsche's critical historian does not take the world at face value, because the world is "oppressed by some present misery." Fighting against the "system" of capitalism or staying in the "autonomous" sphere of architecture are obviously not the only forms of criticality. Suggesting that "architects gave up the critical project because it proved to be too unrealistic and, besides, reality is gorgeous" may sound like a mean joke to those who are inside the oppressive reality or those who empathize. Observing and recording the reality of world cities today unavoidably calls for new forms of criticism.

1 Rem Koolhaas, *S,M,L,XL* (New York: Monacelli Press, 1998), xiii.
2 Ole Bouman, Mitra Khoubrou, and Rem Koolhaas, eds., *Al Manakh* (Amsterdam: Archis Foundation, 2007).
3 Friedrich Nietzsche, *On the Advantage and Disadvantage of History for Life,* trans. Peter Preuss (1874; reprint, Indianapolis and Cambridge, Mass.: Hackett Publishing, 1980).

4 As Nietzsche put it, in this case "there are no differences in value and no proportions for the things of the past which would truly do justice to those things in relation to each other; but only measures and proportions of those things in relation to the antiquarian individual or people looking back at them." Nietzsche, 17.
5 Nietzsche, 20.
6 Nietzsche, 19.

7 See essays in William Saunders, ed., *The New Architectural Pragmatism* (Minneapolis: University of Minnesota Press, 2007). This essay does not prioritize participating in the critical vs. projective debate, other than pointing out that this opposition does not have an explanatory power for Koolhaas, who has been perceived as the champion of the projective generation. I hope it will be clear at the end of the paper that, if I am

correct about what I sense as the new direction of Koolhaas's work, this would be a shift to a critical position after a decade of more conservative geopolitics. This is not necessarily a critical practice that resists or subverts capitalist production, but an equally important criticism nevertheless. In the aim to reduce the confusion that is continuing to burden the debate by conflating political (Tafuri) and aesthetic (Eisenman) criticality, as Reinhold Martin warned in his essay in the same volume, let me make clear that I am talking about a social, political criticality, not the criticality of "autonomous architecture."

8 Nietzsche, 19.

9 Rem Koolhaas, online interview by Tom Fecht, for Hybrid Workspace (http://www.medialounge.net/lounge/workspace/main/general.html), June 26, 1997. Scholars also often criticize Koolhaas for being inconsistent and evasive. See George Baird, "An Open Letter to Rem Koolhaas," Harvard Design Magazine 27 (2007): 30–33.

10 Koolhaas, "Globalization," in S,M,L,XL, 362–69. See photograph, 362.

11 Ibid., 369.

12 Rem Koolhaas, "On the Harvard Design School Project on the City," Harvard Design Magazine 17 (Fall 2002–Winter 2003): 91–92.

13 Rem Koolhaas, online interview by Tom Fecht, for Hybrid Workspace (http://www.medialounge.net/lounge/workspace/main/general.html), June 26, 1997.

14 Rem Koolhaas, "Harvard Project on the City," Mutations (Barcelona: Actar, 2001): 116–17.

15 Aaron Betsky also commented that Koolhaas's theory on the city was original because he "extracted an essence of metropolitanism that is portable and packagable." Koolhaas defined a city that can "be built anywhere in the world." Aaron Betsky, "Rem Koolhaas: The Fire of Manhattanism Inside the Iceberg of Modernism," in What is OMA?, ed. Véronique Patteeuw (Rotterdam: NAi Publishers, 2003): 25–39. See quotation, 30.

16 Rem Koolhaas, "Life in the Metropolis or The Culture of Congestion" in Architecture Theory since 1968, ed. Michael Hays (Cambridge, Mass.: MIT Press, 1998): 320–31. See quotation, 322.

17 Ibid., 322.

18 Ibid., 328.

19 Koolhaas, S,M,L,XL, 23–26.

20 Rem Koolhaas, Delirious New York (1978; reprint, New York: Monacelli Press, 1994), 123.

21 Rem Koolhaas, "Delirious No More," Wired (June 2003): 166–68. Interview by Charlie Rose, Charlie Rose, Public Broadcasting System.

22 Koolhaas, "The Generic City," in S,M,L,XL, 1248.

23 Ibid., 1248.

24 Ibid., 1250.

25 Ibid., 1250.

26 Koolhaas, "Singapore: Portrait of a Potemkin Metropolis," in S,M,L,XL, 1008–89. See quotation, 1011.

27 Ibid.,1077.

28 Ibid.,1057.

29 Ibid.,1073.

30 Ibid.,1087.

31 Koolhaas, "The Generic City," 1252.

32 Ibid.,1253.

33 Rem Koolhaas, online interview by Tom Fecht, for Hybrid Workspace (http://www.medialounge.net/lounge/workspace/main/general.html), June 26, 1997.

34 Koolhaas, "Pearl River Delta," in Mutations, 334.

35 Rem Koolhaas, "Introduction: City of Exacerbated Difference," in Great Leap Forward: Harvard Project on the City (Cologne: Taschen, 2001).

36 Rem Koolhaas, "Rem Koolhaas," in Anymore, ed. Cynthia Davidson (Cambridge, Mass., and London: MIT Press, 2000).

37 Koolhaas, "The Generic City," 1252.

38 Ibid., 1255.

39 Koolhaas, "What Ever Happened to Urbanism?," in S,M,L,XL, 961–71.

40 Ibid., 971.

41 Rem Koolhaas, "Junkspace," in Chuihua Judy Chung, Jeffrey Inaba, Rem Koolhaas, and Sze Tsung Leong, Harvard Design School Guide to Shopping (Cologne: Taschen, 2002), 408–21. Also published in Content (Cologne: Taschen, 2004), 162–71.

42 Koolhaas, "Junkspace," 409.

43 AMO, "Argument: Introducing...," in Al Manakh, 198.

44 Koolhaas, S,M,L,XL, 31–37.

45 Ibid., 39–40.

46 Koolhaas, "Lagos," in Mutations, 652.

47 Koolhaas, "Lagos," 651–700; "Rem Koolhaas," in Anymore.

48 Koolhaas, "Lagos," 685.

49 Koolhaas, "Frontline," in Al Manakh, 194.

50 Ibid., 194.

51 Koolhaas, "Lagos," 653.

52 Koolhaas, "Last Chance?", in Al Manakh, 7.

53 Rem Koolhaas/AMO, The Gulf (Stuttgart: Lars Müller Publishers, 2007). Quotation from back cover.

54 Koolhaas, "The Generic City," 1253.

55 Anthony Vidler, "Psychometropolis," in Architectural Uncanny: Essays in the Modern Unhomely (Cambridge, Mass.: MIT Press, 1992), 192.

56 "Ecological Footprint per Capita" (map produced by AMO), in Al Manakh, 71. Estimates for the size of these landfill projects are alarming: 1.1 billion cubic meters of sand and stone are to be filled in water, 520 kilometers of beaches are to be constructed for The Palm; 232 kilometers of shoreline will be created for The World islands. As promoters of the project proudly state, the whole city of Venice fits into just a quarter of The World (Al Manakh, 275). The damaging effects of these megascale artificial islands on the microclimate of the oasis or the ecology of the Gulf water are yet to be analyzed.

57 Koolhaas, "Singapore," 1082–83.

58 The research on Orientalism in literature and visual arts is quite comprehensive. The foundational book that shifted the paradigm and rose a critical consciousness against the separatist, exoticizing, and ultimately imperialist impacts of Orientalist studies was Edward Said's book Orientalism. Edward Said, Orientalism (New York: Vintage Books, 1978).

59 Koolhaas, "The Generic City," 1263.

60 Koolhaas, "Learning Japanese," in S,M,L,XL, 106.

61 George Packer, "The Megacity: Decoding the Chaos of Lagos," New Yorker (November 3, 2006): 62–75. See quotation: 66, 75.

62 Okwui Enwezor, "Terminal Modernity: Rem Koolhaas's Discourse on Entropy," in What is OMA?, ed. Véronique Patteeuw (Rotterdam: NAi Publishers, 2003): 103–19. See quotation, 113, 116.

63 Koolhaas, Mutations, 718, 653.

64 AMO's book Lagos: How it Works was not published, and the manuscript was not ready for review during the writing of this essay. These ideas are thus based on Koolhaas's and AMO's earlier articles and lectures on Lagos.

65 Koolhaas, "Gulf Survey," in Al Manakh, 138.

66 For more about the differentiation between a migrant and a nomad traveler, see: Esra Akcan, "Nomads and Migrants: A Comparative Reading of Sedad Eldem's and Le Corbusier's Travel Diaries," in Travel Space and Architecture, eds. Jilly Traganou, Miodrag Mitrasinovic, and Samer Akkach (Aldershot, U.K.: Ashgate, forthcoming).

67 Rem Koolhaas, ". . . If," in Content (Cologne: Taschen, 2004). Originally written in May 2003.

68 Talia Dorsey, interview by author, April 16, 2008.

69 Koolhaas and Reiner de Graaf, "The Future of Knowledge," in Al Manakh, 329.

70 Koolhaas, "Last Chance?", 7.

71 Roemer van Toorn, "No More Dreams? The Passion for Reality in Recent Dutch Architecture and Its Limitations," in The New Architectural Pragmatism, ed. William Saunders (Minneapolis: University of Minnesota Press, 2007), 54–74. See quote, 54, 55, 60.

154 Interview with Edward Burtynsky

INTERVIEW WITH EDWARD BURTYNSKY

P41

Your work has been about charting human interaction with nature. In your early work we've noticed a ratio of about ten parts nature to one part man. This is certainly the case in the *Railcuts* series, where it is not clear where nature stops and man's intervention begins. Your *Oil Fields* series makes the distinction more apparent, but the images are still fundamentally set in nature. Your latest photographs are almost completely interior, entirely about architecture and the man-made world. How has the evolution of your photographic project shaped your travel itinerary? What drives your selection of sites?

What was it that brought your work inside, out of nature and into man made spaces?

You mention that you are more interested in factories in non-Western settings. What makes a Chinese appliance factory more compelling to you than a Canadian Toyota factory? Is it the extreme scale of the former, or is there something else at work?

Your photographs of China can be seen as a visualization of a news story that we are all following, about manufacturing moving overseas. On the other hand, your pictures of the shipbreaking and rebar industries in Bangladesh document a more unfamiliar story. Are you interested in giving images to stories that are even less visible, like the infrastructure of telecommunications or the service industry? How do you visualize these less tangible stories?

Why has it been difficult?

EB

What I did before the *Railcuts* series was pure landscape. This is work from twenty-five years ago, and it was more like painting, like abstract expressionism. It was about raw wilderness, the complexity of it, and finding a language in that complexity. The United States and Canada are blessed with large tracts of wilderness and this was a reference point for what the world looked like before we put our imprint on it. I think that understanding that reference point and appreciating it for what it was, and what it is, was a necessary prologue to looking at how we mark that place and shape it to our own purposes. My work is a progression from an appreciation of landscape to an appreciation of how we shape that landscape to meet our needs.

I used to work in factories. I tried to photograph factories in the United States and Canada, but finding a compelling reason for doing it always eluded me. When I started doing work on the Three Gorges Dam, I saw China becoming the manufacturer to the world. Suddenly I realized that the interior landscape of machinery and production had been transposed from North American and Western societies, and remade larger than life in China. This realization loaded that space with the tension that I felt it needed for me to do an in-depth exploration.

I think there's something else about it. These Chinese factories have a direct impact on places like Toronto and Montreal and a province like Ontario. There's a direct relationship between what's happening in China and what's happening in Ontario in the manufacturing sector that has reshaped the kinds of economies we have in Canada. Now we're far more engaged in the service industry, the financial industry, software, design, and creative cultures. All the manufacturing is happening in China. So the whole world order has been rejigged if you come from a manufacturing economy, which Ontario was. To me, these places are charged. I'm taking pictures of something we used to do here and now they do over there.

I have tried to find images in the telecommunications industry, albeit without great success.

It was hard to find ways to bring form to that kind of idea. The service industry is very hard to capture with a camera. One exception is Robert Polidori's latest work. He's photographing trading floors in stock exchanges around the world: Chicago, Kuwait, São Paolo, Hong Kong. These spaces are a dying breed. They are disappearing as we become more electronic. Chicago gave up its trading floor eight years ago. He's documenting the remains of a particular activity. That's one way of visualizing a service sector.

My current approach has been to see the last century as having been brought to us by the good graces of oil, which also brought with it a slew of problems, climate change being one of the most frightening of these problems. At the same time we can't deny that oil has brought about what I would consider the main ingredient for creating a middle class and the largest contributor to global expansion and the population explosion: a cheap

p. 153   Edward Burtynsky, *C. N. Track No. 4*, Thompson River, British Columbia 1985;   p. 154   Edward Burtynsky, *Manufacturing #10A* (detail), Cankun Factory, Xiamen City, 2005.

For an additional photo by Edward Burtynsky, see pages 72–73.

source of energy. Today less than 2 percent of Americans are involved in making the food supply to feed the whole country, as opposed to when people were in the fields with horses and it took two people to feed every one person. I've been photographing not only the sources of oil, the oil fields, but also the oil refineries, the transportation industry, and the way transportation has shaped our cities. Again, I'm trying to understand our cities as a product of oil. I'm moving through a visual diary or catalogue of things that are directly attributable to oil.

To follow these stories you need access to many sensitive sites. We're curious about the relationships you have with the corporations and governments whose property you are photographing. In the film *Manufactured Landscapes* there is a scene in which you're trying to get access to a large Chinese coal concern, but the management is worried about how they will be portrayed in your photographs. Were they right to be worried? You clearly do not have a confrontational style.

My work has a conscious ambiguity to it. It can be read in many different ways. A still image has the capacity to be understood by different people differently, and differently by the same person. One day you might appreciate it for the content, and another day for the form or the color. To me it makes sense to keep the work in a state of open narrative. Ultimately that doesn't define it as a direct indictment of an activity. I personally think that using the work as a direct indictment wouldn't be correct. First of all, it wouldn't be correct in terms of the relationships I have established with the places I've photographed. Secondly, these corporations are still an extension of the human experience. They are providing what they feel are necessary ingredients for urban existence and for our population. It's too simplistic to say, "This is bad, cease and desist." By saying that, you're basically saying we're going to turn ourselves back—back to where? How do we reverse out of this situation? I think its far more interesting to engage with themes of sustainability. How do we continue to live productive and healthy lives and not destroy the planet in the process?

Environmentalism has often taken the "cease and desist" position, and corporations say, "Well, that's not going to happen," and the two just ignore each other. That's been the situation for the past twenty-five years. We've known that these environmental problems exist, but no one has taken environmentalism seriously. It's a situation where perfection has been the enemy of the good. The problem won't be solved without the corporations. You don't want a world where everything comes to a halt—that's called rocks going through plate glass.

As architects, we are sympathetic to the idea that you have to work with people to get things done. But where do you draw the line? Would you sell one of your images to a corporation for the cover of an annual report?

Corporations have bought my work and put it up in board rooms. There is an interesting irony to that. If you look at the whole range of my work, it takes a sobering look at the scale at which we are affecting the natural world. I see these images not as an indictment, but as a lament for a loss of nature. We are supplanting the natural world for our man-made world at a great cost. We are polluting the water, we are clear-cutting forests, we are changing complete environments and damaging entire ecosystems. If someone looked at the arc of my work and didn't get that, they would be missing the fact that it takes a sobering look at the human experience.

Can we compare your work to the imagery of some of the early naturalists who also had political motivations? We're thinking of Thomas Moran and Ansel Adams, whose work helped create America's national parks. Do you see your work as a continuation of that kind of activist imagery?

You can look at Ansel Adams in Yosemite or you can go to the early Watkins and O'Sullivan. The massive plate work of Carleton Watkins and Timothy O'Sullivan was used in the U. S. Senate to help establish the National Park Service. The work of Lewis Hine was used to pass laws banning child labor in America. This type of work is interventionist, in other words, it intervened within the social order and was used as leverage to show people what was happening or what needed to be preserved. It convinced people by showing photographs of child labor and asking, "Is this the right thing to be doing with our children?" Or showing wilderness that should be preserved, and winning the case for nature.

Recently I was at a conference where we discussed whether photography today can have an interventionist effect. Can our work, in a world of media saturation, be meaningful? There are a couple of examples, but they are not created by professionals. The images of Abu Ghraib are definitely interventionist. The raw footage of the Rodney King beating literally shocked the world. These types of images bring attention to issues and create great problems for those in power. But it is interesting that it is not work coming from professional photographers.

One great success of your images is that they do intellectual work. We've spent this entire conversation talking about the ideas they raise and the conversations they start. But it has to be said that your photographs are also overwhelmingly beautiful, and you obviously have an eye for their aesthetic impact. You have called the beauty of images a "forbidden pleasure." Can you talk about the craft of making these images?

As an image maker I have always believed that one of the core capacities of the medium of photography is, in a fraction of a second, to render our world in exquisite detail. A print is a way to experience that world in a stillness that we don't ordinarily see. Our peripheral vision and the way we interpret space works in a completely different way than a photograph. In a still image, we can look at the world, think about it and analyze it, break it apart and understand it. You can find details in images that you would never understand if you were watching them on film, because when you see in three dimensions you pan. We don't analyze a film frame by frame; we analyze the narrative, the characters. Still images hold our world still long enough to be able to think about it. They lodge themselves in our memory in a different way.

I look for subjects that operate on the scale where those details are critical. I look for Lilliputian worlds in which we are dwarfs in our own creation. For instance, the figures in a mine landscape are small, they're only a quarter of an inch high in a fifty-inch print. That's a significant detail, and that detail only comes from looking at the print. You begin to understand the landscape through that detail.

The sublime used to be man dwarfed by nature, whether it's Turner's ship being tossed by the sea or Ahab taken down by the whale in *Moby Dick*. Nature is the omnipresent force, and man is dwarfed by that force, and often loses to that force. But in this image the figure is dwarfed by a man-made landscape. I think that what I am introducing through my work is a new notion of the sublime, the inversion of the sublime, where humans have become the omnipresent force, and we are dwarfed within our own creation. We have created architecture, cars, and jets that protect and isolate us from the forces of nature. But in the process, we've created a force that is now an element, like wind or fire. We can change the world, we can change the atmosphere, we can change the water. We are now a force in nature.

I'm trying to create prints where you first get taken in by the whole image and the largeness of the place that's being described, and then you reread the image and pick apart the small details that tell the story. There's a second narrative within the piece that you can use to understand the scale of a place. But the first impression of the image that makes you come to it, and makes you want to look at it, is a fundamental thing that I always try to do with my work. Because if somebody doesn't stop to look, they miss the whole point.

p. 158 Edward Burtynsky, *Manufacturing #10A*, Cankun Factory, Xiamen City, 2005; p. 159 Edward Burtynsky, *Manufacturing #10B*, Cankun Factory, Xiamen City, 2005; p. 160–161 Edward Burtynsky, *Shipbreaking No. 13*, Chittagong, Bangladesh 2000.

Commentary on *Travel*
Yuichi Yokoyama
Translated by Taro Nettleton

46   A mass of rocks is visible on the mountaintop. The landscape seems to symbolize something. A new house can be seen at the foot of the mountain.

48   This strange landscape, dotted with low conifers, residential structures, and boulders, is neither Oriental nor Occidental. It belongs to no continent. It is an unknown land. Originally, the current work ended with this scene. Therefore, one may consider what comes prior to this page as Part One, and what follows it as Part Two.

49   Buildings with large, heavy-looking roofs and built-for-sale homes are visible.

51   The house in the first panel is covered by vegetation. Its foundation is built lower than the ground, leaving only the roof visible. The house in the second panel has a ramp running from the entrance up to the second floor. Although one tends to see structures like this in areas of heavy snow, it is unclear whether this is such an area. The house in the third panel is an actual house in Sayama, Saitama prefecture, where the author's office is located.

52   This is a very narrow house. The rooms are presumably narrow as well. All the houses seem to be new and vacant.

53   These covered buildings may be abandoned. There is grass growing over even the electrical wires hanging above the ground.

60   If this is indeed a flower field, one would be remiss to not note that the flowers grow too close to the train tracks.

61   The train, kicking up ballasts as it runs, crosses the lake.

63   All of the passengers in the passing train are looking this way. Whether the naked eye would actually instantaneously register these individuals' faces is questionable, but this scene may not represent a human perspective at all.

66   Riding on the train for a long time, one can travel enough distance to enter a new weather map.

For the an excerpt from the book *Travel* by Yuichi Yokoyama, see pages 1–6.

An
American
Pastoral

AUDC
Robert
Sumrell
and
Kazys
Varnelis

What is the point of constructing a Grand Tour today? What are the monuments for an era immune to solidity and absent of lasting meaning, when any sense of place is evacuated by the logic of the virtual, in which architecture itself has become immaterial by being thoroughly leveraged in a delirious calculus of speculation?

The first Grand Tour was an antidote to the excesses of capital. Providing a first-hand demonstration of enduring values, the Grand Tour was originally not a finishing school for architects but rather a rite of passage for the British aristocracy and rising mercantile classes. The Grand Tour offered its participants an anthropological diagram of an earlier Empire that demonstrated not only economic and military but also cultural success. In contrast to the rough, provincial culture of a rapidly industrializing island nation on the outskirts of Europe, the ruins of Rome underscored the importance of the pursuit of virtue while emphasizing the fatal dangers of decadence and overindulgence.

But where to go now? Today, the global economic order of Empire embraces everything, leaving no exterior. Diffuse, global, uncontainable, Empire operates on the illusion that the economy is divesting from the physical and that the world is dominated by the virtual. Thus, a defining feature of Empire is that it is placeless. There is no one Rome anymore: no capital for Empire and no one place to see the ruins of the previous order.[1] Of course there are obvious choices like Detroit, but these are the ruins of the earlier era of Fordism, obsolete except for a nostalgic interest. Today Rome is both nowhere and everywhere. Like Piranesi's Romans, we live within the ruins of the world, undone for momentary profit, the best materials carted away by barbarians. Wherever we find Empire's most advanced form, whatever its diverse manifestation—the European Union, China, Japan, the United States, the former Soviet Union—we also uncover its ruins. Like Robert Smithson's Passaic, the superpowers of our day rise up into ruin, their currency eviscerated, economies emptied out by overinvestment. Forty years later, Passaic is everywhere.

The following tour is generic, uncovering everyday locations that describe the evacuation of values under Empire. Each of the stops isolates a place in transition, a node where the physical form of Empire's evacuated body lies in decay, disguise, or neglect. Each of these stops is crucial in a survey of contemporary urban life, but each can be found virtually anywhere.

1   Michael Hardt and Antonio Negri,
Empire (Cambridge, Mass.: Harvard University Press, 2000).

All images © AUDC/Kazys Varnelis

Airports

Our contemporary Grand Tour must begin at the airport.

During the process of modernization, airports were glamorous harbingers of modernity designed by cutting-edge architects. Eero Saarinen built the main terminal at Dulles and the TWA terminal at JFK; Charles Luckman and William Pereira built the UFO-shaped "Theme Building" as the centerpiece of LAX (Pereira's brother Hal, a Hollywood art director, provided inspiration with the flying saucer he designed for the film *The War of the Worlds*); and Paul Andreu (a student of Gilles Deleuze) built Terminal 1 at Charles de Gaulle, embodying the philosopher's hopes for a more fluid order in an arrival and departure machine. Built to operate as special zones within the city, such structures were the last modernist utopias, freed of the need to cater to place or history.

But with the introduction of wide-body planes and the deregulation of passenger airlines, flying became as banal as riding the bus. It wasn't until the mid-1990s that the promise of globalizing modernity was nostalgically recaptured by *Wallpaper* magazine and its heady advocacy of a slick, jet-setting consumer avant-garde. Corresponding to this was the fleeting architectural fancy for Supermodernism and the belief that the virtuoso architecture of the airport could extend into cultural attractions in city centers to magically bring tourists into decayed urban milieus.

After 9/11, even this temporary suspension of disbelief turned hollow. As the global elite turned to private jets boarded at smaller, more discreet airports, the rest of us find Supermodernism at a dead end. To perpetuate a state of terror and to remind travelers of their humbled position in the world, security regulations now demand that elegant leather Dopp kits be replaced by primitive Ziploc bags. The passage to modernity is now done barefoot, with your pants hanging off your ass. Here, the excitement of travel finally runs aground. If there is any comfort, it is that the security teams exude ineffectiveness, suggesting that there will likely be more excitement in the future.

In contrast to the degraded airlines, overnight couriers such as FedEx are more efficient and reliable for sending important information and expensive goods. However, even with the more flexible use of larger planes on additional routes, the majority of cheap imports still flood the developed world through a massive and ever-growing system of ports. Packed in universally sized shipping containers stacked up to 15,000 to a ship, goods move overseas at a leisurely pace only to be rapidly unloaded and hustled across the country by trucks and train lines to distribution centers from which they often are sent directly to the home, leaving the marketplace and agora as distant memories. With the United States having few marketable exports, the same ships return empty, their decks frequently bare even of shipping containers. Electronic funds transfers flow outward, from West to East, but with currency now a matter of euphoric speculation, and global trade based on a vast pyramid scheme, no one can question the madness.

Scores of containers build up in massive graveyards, reflecting the imbalance of trade. For many architects, this is a new source of dreams. As inspirational today as Henry Ford's Model T was for the modernists, the shipping container plays to our fantasies of responsible reuse while appealing to our childhood dreams of playing with building blocks.

Nevertheless, the productive culture of modernization is long gone. A house built of shipping containers is nothing but a device for storage, a place to put the interchangeable junk that the container brought in the first place. But we hardly need to build houses out of shipping containers in order to understand this. Our dwellings are already little more than that, containers devoid of any romance, empty vessels waiting for us to fill them until one day we take our junk elsewhere and leave them behind, valueless, discarded shells.

Highways

Containers and the goods they hold generally reach their final destinations via the interstate highway system. Built for high-speed travel, the highways were places in which a postwar generation tasted unfettered freedom. Driving on the unfinished New Jersey Turnpike, Tony Smith was awed by an experience so large that it couldn't be framed. Art, he concluded, could no longer compete with a culture that could produce such intense experiences.[2] In *The White Album,* Joan Didion described driving as "a total surrender, a concentration so intense as to seem a kind of narcosis, a rapture-of-the-freeway. The mind goes clean. The rhythm takes over."[3] Songs like Steppenwolf's "Born to Be Wild," Rush's "Red Barchetta," and Judas Priest's "Heading Out to the Highway" were recorded in order to be played loudly on the road, romanticizing the solitary freedom of the road, much as films like *Smokey and the Bandi*t and television shows like *B. J. and the Bear* did.

Today, with roads perpetually jammed by numbers they were never intended to carry, surfing the freeway is gone. Instead of communion with the flow there is only stasis amidst the fumes of the highway. Instead of solitude, only frustration expressed into the cell phone.

Nor is there any hope for a smoother-flowing future. To the contrary, traffic engineers now recognize jams as part of the solution, encouraging drivers to take shorter trips by frustrating them. Hopelessly overrun and without any solution, highways become ruins, their promise of Deleuzean fluidity gone forever. In this highways embody the ruins of all infrastructure. The master plan is gone forever, replaced instead by perpetual stalemate and increasing tolls.

2   Tony Smith, "Talking with Tony Smith," interview by Samual Wagstaff Jr., *Artforum* (December 1966): 18–19.
3   Joan Didion, *The White Album* (New York: Simon and Schuster, 1979), 83.

Distribution Centers

As we turn to the landscape for relief during the perpetual traffic jams that characterize today's highways, we see massive distribution centers off of which cities feed.

Distribution centers have replaced farmyards along the rural countryside. Where the latter still exist, as in California's Harris Ranch (colloquially known as "Cowschwitz"), they increasingly adopt the logic of distribution centers. At such factory farms, hundreds of thousands of hormone-injected and antibiotic-fed animals are kept in tight confinement until ready for slaughter and shipment to the appropriate distribution centers.

Built to facilitate the unpacking and reorganization of goods from shipping containers to their next destination at minimal expense, distribution centers are largely devoid of aesthetics and can be distilled down to three main programmatic functions of loading, receiving, and storage. Staffing within distribution centers is equally minimal. Automated warehouse management and logistics systems enable more efficient and expedient turnovers of commodities with limited storage and down time. A single distribution center can support multiple, even competing, vendors with minimal separation between clients.

The most advanced distribution centers respond directly to online shopping. Much like a massive, distributed version of Cowschwitz, consumers increasingly order products online, never having to leave their comfortable homes as their arteries steadily clog with fat. In operations like the FedEx Logistics Distribution Centers, products go directly from the factory to consumer thereby simplifying the supply chain and eliminating the need for retail venues and intermediary storage. When products break down, if they are not discarded, they can be sent back for "factory" repair, repairs often done not in the factory but in a shipper-operated repair center located on the premises of the distribution center.

During the Grand Tour aristocrats purchased the exotic goods that would bring quality and authentication to the rest of their lives. Today, the role of things and people are reversed in an animistic practice. It is objects that now dominate our lives, touring the world to visit us.

Data Centers

Where distribution centers coalesce consumer goods, data centers reorganize the immaterial world into a more streamlined network. Data hotels such as One Wilshire allowed corporations to become immaterial, reducing their operations to assemblies of servers interconnected with servers from other corporations in a single building. Today, however, facilities like Google's massive center at The Dalles, Oregon, reduce the materiality of the corporation even further. Housed in massive horizontal structures holding countless numbers of cheap off-the-shelf processors and hard drives working together to emulate a single massive computer on which space can be rented, the contemporary data center undoes any need for separate servers at all. Multiple corporations simply rent parcels of its virtual space.

Increasingly, software applications are migrating to the Web as well. This is attractive for individuals since licenses are often free in exchange for precious demographic data that would otherwise be unavailable—hence, no more need to pirate. Corporations embrace such services since leases of software can be more conveniently written off than outright purchases. Social networking applications allow us to reconnect, never losing touch with friends better left forgotten long ago, while social content applications allow us to create meaningless content that can then be watched endlessly by individuals with little better to do. But after three decades of the means of production drifting downward into our hands, they are given up to centralization, to big computing that exists with minimal human intervention. Old meshworks are breeding new hierarchies.

If the PC was a device for production, applications based on data centers are much more clever. The Internet becomes a place in which we strive to appear, our need for publicity so great and our faith in brands so intense that corporations can rely on consumers to produce their own viral ad campaigns and shoot down the competition viciously. The data center is the modern temple, the place in which we hope to dwell telematically, our Google shadow intense, our presence maintained on archive.org long after we are gone.

Historically, cities were the place where capital appeared, where operations of investment were made visible, and where production occurred. Today the most advanced forms of capital hide in the network, leaving cities to maintain themselves through speculation and shopping. Instead of the place in which capital appears, cities are now the place in which capital disappears. The yuppie of the 1980s who defined himself through work as well as his consumption has been phased out by the hipster, whose source of income is vague but whose life focuses on consumption and blogging about that consumption. Meanwhile reverse commuting, the emergence of hipster parenthood, and the permeation of cities by malls and mall stores has effectively equated the city core with the suburb; we are all hipsters, we are all suburbanites. The only movement that matters is that of finding the most fashionable neighborhood before anyone else. This is done through a Situationist game in which potential becomes an identity in and of itself. Once a blog announces that an area has potential (the next "Greenpoint") hipsters kill it, obliterating any of the area's authentic, local features. On a global scale, a formless, unaccountable mass of NGOs, multinational conglomerates, and investment firms move from city to city, following crisis and opportunity in order to capitalize on speculation.

The contemporary city becomes a place of wonder, a moment to marvel at conditions that are seemingly impossible, most likely unsustainable or destructive, yet intensely desirable. Like the Romans, we live in an Empire driven not only by power but by magic. Much like the urban fiction of today (such as Jonathan Safran Foer's *Extremely Loud and Incredibly Close,* Dave Eggers's *A Heartbreaking Work of Staggering Genius* or Alice Sebold's *The Lovely Bones),* Empire itself is a book of wonders, providing comforting outcomes and explanations for the anxiety produced by a city without attachment or alienation. Empire is a constructed myth that allows us to imagine order behind a power that should not, cannot exist. The multitude, whose home is the city, is a hipster dream state that speaks to our desire for the emotional substantiation of an empty experience.

Cork model of the so-called Tomb of the Horatii and Curiatii at Albano Laziale, near Rome, made by an unknown model maker, late eighteenth century. Photograph by Hugh Kelly. Courtesy the Trustees of Sir John Soane's Museum.

This model shows a tomb of the first century B.C. located on the Via Appia south of Rome. An excursion to the tomb of the Horatii and the Curiatii was an essential part of any visit to Rome in the eighteenth century, and it was frequently depicted by artists. Measured plans of the tomb, which might have served as the basis for the construction of the model, were published by Bartoli and Piranesi. Soane mentioned the tomb in his tenth Royal Academy lecture as an example of the commemoration of heroic deeds through monuments. The accompanying lecture illustration has a note on the back reading "from a model by Turnerelli." This probably refers to the sculptor Peter Turnerelli (1774–1835), who may have been the maker, or, perhaps more likely, the previous owner of the model. The lecture illustration shows how models could also be used in the creation of *vedute* (views) of antique ruins. The model takes up almost the entire surface of the board on which it stands, has a rough finish, and has been blackened to heighten the appearance

of antiquity. It is of less fine quality than cork models by the leading Italian makers, such as Giovanni Altieri, and it is possible that it was manufactured in England, perhaps by Richard Dubourg, who made and exhibited cork models in London in the late eighteenth century. Soane visited Dubourg's "museum" on March 11, 1785, and it is possible that some of the other cork models in his collection came from this source. — *Helen Dorey*

RUINS of the TOMB of the HORATII & CURIATII.

For more on Sir John Soane, see page 46. For additional images from Sir John Soane's Model Room, see pages 26 and 92–93.

Cork model of the Monterisi-Rossignoli tomb in Canosa, made by Domenico Padiglione (architecture) and Raffaele Gargiulo (vases and stucco reliefs, attributed) in Naples, early nineteenth century. Photograph Hugh Kelly. Courtesy the Trustees of Sir John Soane's Museum.

This model is one of four models of ancient tombs excavated in the Kingdom of Naples, around 1800, which were in Soane's collection by 1825. Sadly, one of the four does not survive. Like the Paestum models, the tomb models were made by Domenico Padiglione in Naples. Their internal furnishings and decoration were made by another employee of the museum in Naples, the vase conservator Raffaele Gargiulo. From the outside, the models look like plain cork boxes. However, opening the lids reveals their sophisticated interments. Each tomb contains a skeleton surrounded by vases and other items that, despite their minute size, have very detailed decoration.

The models show famous excavations of the period and were intended to demonstrate the find context of classical vases, which were popular among collectors and still described as "Etruscan" in the early nineteenth century. Such models are known to have been used as adjuncts to vase collections, as when the King of Naples presented a large number of ancient vases to Napoleon Bonaparte in 1802. He sent with them a model of a tomb, meant to be displayed with the vases to explain their original context.

Soane mentioned such tombs in his first Royal Academy lecture, in which he compared different kinds of ancient sepulchral chambers and singled out Etruscan tombs for their interesting and varied decoration. —H. D.

The cork model attributions (pp. 93, 170, 171) and much of the information about the individual cork models comes from Professor Valentin Kockel of Augsburg University, whose book on the Soane Museum cork models will be published in 2008.

Aaron Betsky

We have a romantic notion of airplane travel. It takes us to other places and does so at amazing speed. Even if today the complexities of negotiating security systems and the compression of space on the airplane itself have taken a great deal of the beauty out of the experience, it remains one that is exotic and strange, if nothing else. We are suspended in midair, very close to strangers we do not know, and we use this system to supercede the natural unveiling of landscapes as we travel, engaging instead in something like the quick cut of the film: we are there and then we are someplace completely different.[1]

As such, the airplane is a destroyer of many of the aspects of architecture we have held dear. It does not respect place and it hovers impossibly in nothing. Most architects might even define the airplane interior as the antithesis of architecture, as Le Corbusier so polemically did in his 1935 book *Aircraft*.[2] And yet it is a bounded space with private and public zones that creates a relationship between ourselves, the world around others, and us. It is a structure and a spatial envelope. But the airplane interior has something more to offer. Unless we become very ill, the place where we are most cocooned by technology during our lifetime is in an airplane. It is also the environment where we are most resolutely thrust into a public space, sharing narrow confines for extended periods, finding ourselves regulated by rules of safety and propriety without any chance to seclude ourselves. The airplane is also the space where we are most clearly nowhere and anywhere at the same time, hovering somewhere in transit in an atmosphere that would kill

us if we became exposed to its thin makeup. In this way, the banal act of being in an airplane makes three of the most fundamental aspects of our modern lives spatially present and intimately felt: the importance of technology to mediate between us and a world most of us experience as uncomfortable, if not inimical, without machinery's intercession; the loss of boundaries between the private and the public sphere, or between one's body and the social network of which one is part; and the loss of a clearly defined sense of place. The airplane is the space of sprawl condensed and raised up, a placeless cocoon of technology creating an artificial society without permanence. It is just as environmentally destructive as sprawl. Yet the airplane's interior is also a place of liberation and sensuality, a place redolent of the excitement of travel—however dimly—and at its best designed to conform completely to pure bodily comfort and safety. Might the airplane interior not be a model that we could use as we try to develop efficient, safe, and exciting social spaces?

Of course architecture has a long tradition of looking at the confines of vessels for inspiration. Le Corbusier, long before he was seduced by both the form of aircraft and the ease with which they turned him into the first international architect,[3] famously felt that we could learn from boats and from cars.[4] In more recent times, both Michel Foucault[5] and Peter Sloterdijk[6] have held the boat up as an emblem not so much of how one can most efficiently organize and encase space as of a fragment of society, unmoored from the systems in which it was embedded, free and thus a catalyst for change in other systems, whether they be social, economic, cultural, or

sexual. The ancient "ship of fools" thus flipped into a quasi utopia to match the postulation of idealized spaces in the finely crafted ship.

Yet no philosopher so far has written about airplanes in the same manner, and this is despite the fact that these two modes of transportation come out of this legacy, are equal technological marvels, and can have analogous social effects. Certainly contemporary architects continue to look at the airplane and the rocket ship as symbols of technological logic and condensation when applied to spatial containment, but usually only in the sense of science fiction. From Archigram to Future Systems, architects have thought that the fuselage, with its tremendous economy of surface and the presence of so much condensed technology, presented an extreme version of the modern building, with its integrated environmental and safety systems. In more recent times, architects have looked toward that same logic with a certain amount of irony, producing such projects as LOT-EK's various attempts to repurpose airplane interiors as art gallery–based cocoons. Yet none of these architects or their followers have ever attempted to take the actual environment of the airplane seriously.

When airplanes began to carry passengers and not just pilots or mail in the 1920s, their interiors were strongly based not so much on the design of ships, however, as they copied railroad cars.[7] The emphasis was on the compartmentalization of space into berths, or, as travel became more affordable, and there was less space to devote to each passenger, the arrangement of people in rows. Unlike a ship, which had provided, at least for the passengers,

THE BRANDED COCOON
Architecture at Ten Miles Up

more traditional living spaces, the airplane was to create an environment where human beings could be stored with a modicum of comfort and as much efficiency as possible during transit. Early planes used the accoutrements of railroad and even horse-drawn coaches much in the same way that cars accentuated plush upholstery with wood trim.[8] Airline designers created a serial configuration within what they saw as a box. While the exterior of airplanes had a strong influence on the design of everything from cars to pencil sharpeners to "Airstream" trailers, the interiors trailed behind for decades—as did the design of the interiors of homes and cars.[9]

The idea that the aircraft interior is influenced by but separate from the exterior and its streamlined forms still underlies most cabin design. What has changed has been principally the replacement of wood and metal by plastic and metal alloys that create the possibility of molding the fuselage more closely around its structural elements, along the way incorporating storage while at the same time responding more precisely to the human body.[10] Only recently, with the development of the Boeing 777 and now the Airbus A380, has open and multiuse space, which was considered as a potential when the first generation of Boeing 747s began flying,[11] made its entry as a factor in the design of the commercial airplane interior. What this tube of suspended place provides is an environment flowing around its structure on the one side and acting as a mold of the human body on the other. Strangely enough, it is thus also a realized example of what some architects and designers think of as the destiny of their disciplines: to dissolve into the completely fluid response to both what we are as human beings and what we make as an artificial world around us.

In reality, most of what defines the design of a commercial airplane interior derives from the most stringent regulations—though one might say that this is also just an intensification of the same codes of life safety and optimized material use that govern the manufacture of most products and buildings.[12] FAA and IATA regulations[13] define not only the narrow range of materials that can be used in an airplane interior, they even define the color ranges to be used (in order to make sure that exit instructions are clear). What is not defined by such agencies is the result of the market research airline manufacturers and airlines do: gray is good not only because it is soothing, but because it is the color of business suits. White is not acceptable because it reflects the colors of the sky, reminding passengers that they are actually up in the sky.[14] The configuration of the chairs is the result of ergonomic and human factors research, those quasi-sciences that pretend that they can establish the absolutely most comfortable and appropriate response to the human body.[15] Lighting and air become part of a program meant to make people find themselves in the space, escape from the space when necessary, concentrate on their space, feel at ease there, and then revive when it comes close to the time for landing, all while using the minimal amount of energy possible. The airplane's interior design has special constraints that are much more intense than one finds in most architecture, but it also works much harder by controlling light, air, temperature, and all other environmental factors continually while also taking care of every single inch of three-dimensional space.

And so one sits, in an extremely expensive and completely calibrated environment, tied to one particular place, one's light and air and space defined for one. It sounds like pure fascism, but there is another side to it. All of these devices and systems are in fact meant to make one feel that the most absolutely minimal space is in fact one's own and responds perfectly to what one needs. And if one gets up to business or even first class, one finds that the whole cocoon creates a quasi-utopian version of the kind of cocoon that, to Peter Sloterdijk, is the real essence of our culture.[16] This cocoon, however, has a particular character, and is, in fact, designed.

The most dominant aspects of the airplane interior are curves and the overwhelming tubularity that those curves both complement and try to counteract. The curves start from the tube itself, but then peel off into the fixed objects or built-ins that inhabit these spaces. Whereas in previous generations of airplane designs elements such as the luggage storage bins, the toilets, and the kitchens owed their appearance more to their terrestrial counterparts and thus were predominantly square, in the Boeing 777 and Airbus A340 they themselves became curves, with a sweep and elongation that attempted to visually deny their bulk while extending their interior volume. The tendency is thus toward a kind of minimalism not unlike one that has dribbled down from Miesian ideals to loft design to the restaurants, shops, and hotels inhabited by the same people who are the airlines' most profitable audience: the globally oriented businessperson. That same sensibility is evident in the detailing of these elements as well. Here again the square latch has given way to the recessed ovoid, the bar of lighting and air shoots have become smooth and embedded in the lower surface of the luggage compartment, and even the lettering in both the newer Airbus and Boeing models tends toward a computer-oriented variation on Helvetica.

The seats, meanwhile, have lagged behind in this march toward repressive minimalism. To a large extent this is because there are simply too many demands on that piece of equipment: its various components must move to accommodate the body, must unfold into horizontal surfaces, and must have outlets for power or screens for the display of video material.[17] Even here, though, the reduction of elements is clearly a goal for most airlines. Lufthansa's new chairs in this sense are instructive. In 1995, Frog Design designed the last generation of chairs to deliberately recall the romance of flying while articulating its various elements. Thus the sides of the chairs in business class and first class were covered with aluminum-painted plastic that was ribbed to recall old German airplanes such as the Messerschmitt, and the seats had backs that blossomed into semicircular elements. Every element, down to the paper wrapper of the cutlery, recalled these ribs and referred to rivets and other mechanical aspects of airplanes.[18] In the newer version of Lufthansa's interior design scheme, first put into place in 2005 and created by an anonymous in-house design team, all that is gone. Now the emphasis is on long, lazy curves, completely smooth surfaces, and a minimum of articulation. Again the excuse for this redesign is mainly functional: in business class the chairs are now of the "lie-flat" variety, which means they do not unfold and telescope from chair to recliner, but rather form themselves into a vaguely bed-shaped arc at about 160 degrees. This ergonomic rationale does not in itself generate the arched molds of the chair surrounds and the smooth surfaces of the backrests that accommodate the television screens.

Another excuse for the elimination of elements is cost. Even minute amounts of reductions in the weight of a chair or a latch can aggregate into substantial savings in fuel costs. Yet at the other end of the spectrum from the elaborate amenities to be found in business class, the no-nonsense design of the budget airlines again makes a rhetorical point out of this parsimoniousness. In the EasyJet cabin, even the lettering seems smoothed out into the most direct statement of the brand, while there is a sense that every surface is the product of one single mold. In more stylish off-shoots of this movement, such as JetBlue in the United States and Vueling in Europe, the aesthetic is deliberately one of surfaces that have the matter-of-factness of an iPod or some other electronic gadget, while the graphics tend toward what one might see when large corporate brands try to address

a younger audience.[19] If the model for the high end seems to be W Hotels and Armani (if not John Pawson and Ross Lovegrove), then in the cheap world the model may be Zara and Ikea, with Karim Rashid or Jonathan Ive of Apple as the inspiring figures.

If it is true, as Rem Koolhaas likes to proclaim, that "all conditioned space is conditional," then certainly one pays a price, both literally and figuratively, for all of this comfort and containment. One has to "buy into" the world the airline presents to one in the airplane interior, and in so doing follow not only its rules and regulations, but also its semantic cues.

What is remarkable is the amount of identity the airlines are able to develop within such a standardized environment, though they are most successful at the upper (or front) end of the cabin. The most radical company here is Virgin Atlantic. Having started as a rock-and-roll airline, they have now become an exemplar of Cool Britannia. In their latest Upper Class interiors, the chairs and partitions swerve and curve with all the abandon of Marc Newson's furniture or Zaha Hadid's architecture (at least within the restraints within which they have to operate), and what the in-house designers, under the direction of Joe Ferry, were not able to accomplish with actual forms they implied by recessing the edges of planes or, most ingeniously, with a color scheme that extends into the mood lighting that varies from a shocking purple to an icy blue, depending on the flight's phase. Against this expressive integration Singapore Airlines uses the reactionary sarong-based skirt to abstract the flight attendants' bodies, along with the application of a strange puce with some fake gold trim, which seems almost so out of date as to be knowing, perhaps getting us ready for a revival of the 1980s.

What we are seeing, in other words, is the most all-around branding one can encounter anywhere. Even the car interior, which designers have worked hard to make both more responsive to "human factors," or ergonomics, while at the same time conveying the character of the company that sells the car, have not been as successful in creating an environment in which every single element is both the product of refined design aimed at making the space as comfortable and as cheap as possible, and a small signal that helps reinforce the sense that one is inhabiting a space that is Delta, United, Emirates, or Air France.

And yet the branding is not overt, the way it is in the logos one sees on clothes or the aspirational shaping of cars. The airlines do not pretend to make you part of their company, but rather hope to reinforce, through subliminal means, your preference for their company. They must be subtle about this, because consumers choose for time and price as well as loyalty, especially when it comes at such an expense, and the almost inevitable irritations of modern travel can instantly ruin all good associations. The irony is that, at the very moment that the branding becomes so "deep" that it creates a complete universe around you, it almost disappears. In this as well, airplane interiors are leading the way in the world that attempts to influence consumer behavior: the attempt now is to go beyond the brand into a place where, like Google or the iPhone (as a cover for AT&T), the actual service becomes so pervasive that it is invisible.

The brand becomes a network and an overall reality. It becomes a cocoon. The cocoon, it turns out, is not just that which becomes a shell drinking in those forces—mainly of a technological nature, allowing us to inhabit our modern world in such a way that they seem to respond to the human body while forming a mold of that body—but it is also the most perfect brandspace in which we do not just assemble a reality by purchasing separate objects, but in which we consume a complete world. It is an ideal Apple would love to achieve, as would consumer conglomerates such as Proctor & Gamble, but nobody but the airlines has come even close to achieving it with such a degree of thoroughness.

A final development within the airplane interior is the ever-increasing segregation between the various classes. While more and more people are crammed together into tighter and tighter spaces at the "back of the bus" (note the historical overtones of that phrase), the wealthy enjoy ever more real estate toward the front. Especially remarkable are the sci-fi-like "pods" that were introduced, starting with British Airways' version in 1997, in first class. For the first time since the inception of the modern aircraft interior, a stand-alone architectural element has appeared. Usually placed at a diagonal to the fuselage, these pods are self-contained units geared to allow individuals to work, relax, dine, sleep, and isolate themselves from their surroundings. They are molded plastic ovoids that completely cocoon the inhabitant, becoming almost prosthetic in the way they answer to every bodily need.[20]

The situation is an intensified version of what is happening in the spatial politics of the urban environment; with the wealthy isolating themselves into larger and larger mansions in luxury laagers while the less fortunate must make do with smaller and smaller spaces. In the airplane, it is a question of inches, not feet, and it shows that the fight is ultimately about the space one can control with one's body. Creature comfort, visual and aural isolation, and the ability to either escape into a fantasy world or to be connected to information all come together to create the rich person's cocoon. In the Airbus A380, several airlines have taken the next logical step, making separate rooms that recall the private cabins of ships and trains, though one wonders how long these spaces will last, given the economic pressures on each square inch of even the largest airplanes. It is noteworthy that early promises of public spaces in the A380, including bars, fitness centers, and stores, have so far remained unfulfilled. Instead, all available space is filled with seats. In fact, the next generation of planes, having exhausted the possibility of growing in length, might extend out (the so-called "delta wing design") into amphitheaters where only a very small percentage of the population will have access to a window or an aisle. The answer to the claustrophobia

this might produce is to ramp up the fantasy, surrounding each occupant with the ability to loose him- or herself in the other worlds of film, television program, or commercial advertisement.

Despite some countervailing trends, such as the much larger windows in the new Boeing 787, the movement is away from the reality of the airplane as an object containing a coherent space and toward the production of isolated or collective cocoons defined by brands. What we do not see in such environments is the technology that makes all this possible. Nor do we experience the constraining structures, what we might call the architecture of these spaces. Finally, airplanes less and less frame the outside world as an experience to be had even at a far remove, and do not take us into an exotic locale in and of itself. Instead, the airplane interior takes us into what might be a not-too-distant future, in which we will aspire to inhabit something that is between our body and the world, something between our clothes and a building, something that seems to be completely designed for us and yet places us in a world over which we have no control.[21] Notions of place-making, but also utopian thoughts of the liberating potential of the merger between body and building through the mediation of technology, seem particularly irrelevant in this respect.

1   The romance of flying has a long tradition in literature (beyond the dreams of Icarus), ranging from Saint-Exupéry (who wrote "L'Aviateur" in 1926, seventeen years before *The Little Prince*) to Walter Kirn's *Up in the Air*, a more caustic and world-weary musing on the ennui and obsession it produces. There has not, however, been an analysis published of the effect of flying on aesthetics in the manner of Leo Marx's seminal *The Machine in the Garden* and its treatment of the effect of train travel.
2   Le Corbusier, *Aircraft*, trans. Anna Foppiano (1935; reprint, Milan: Editrice Abitare Segesta, 1996).
3   Le Corbusier, *Aircraft*, 10.
4   Le Corbusier, "Eyes That Do Not See," in *Towards a New Architecture*, trans. Fredercik Etchells (1927; reprint, New York: Praeger, 1974), 81–138.
5   Michel Foucault, "Other Spaces: The Principles of Heterotopia," *Lotus* 48–49 (1986): 10–24.
6   Peter Sloterdijk, *Im Weltinnenrauym des Kapitals: Fuer eine Philosophische Teorie der Globaliserung* (Frankfurt: Suhrkamp Verlag, 2004).
7   The most complete analysis of the historic development of the airplane interior is provided by Barbara Fitton Hauss, "A Trip through Time in the Aircraft Cabin," in *Airworld: Design and Architecture for Air Travel*, eds. Alexander von Vegesack and Jochen Eisenbrand (Weil am Rhein: Vitra Design Museum, 2004), 82–123.
8   For an analysis in spatial and mechanical terms of the development of the railroad cabin and its influence on early aircraft interior, see Sigfried Giedion, *Mechanization Takes Command: A Contribution to Anonymous History* (1948; reprint, New York: W. W. Norton, 1969), 439–68.
9   See Jeffrey Meikle, *Twentieth Century Limited: Industrial Design In America, 1925–1939* (Philadelphia: Temple University Press, 1979), 134ff. It is worth noting that Le Corbusier in *Aircraft* never mentions

the interior of the machines he glorifies.
10   Mary Edwards and Elwyn Edwards, *The Aircraft Cabin: Managing the Human Factors* (London: Aldenshot Publishers, 1990).
11   Hauss, "Trip through Time," 112.
12   Lori Erenaker Kovarik, R. Curtis Graeber, and Peter R. Mitchell, "Human Factors Considerations in Aircraft Cabin Design," in *Handbook of Aviation Human Factors*, ed. Daniel J. Garland (New York: Lawrence Erlbaum Associates, 1998), 389–404.
13   Kovarik et al. list at least eleven major U.S. regulatory advisories and regulations applicable in the year they wrote their text.
14   In an article I wrote in the mid-1990s, I noted experiments to create all white interiors had failed for this reason. Aaron Betsky, "Changing Flight Patterns," *Metropolis* (September 1994): 33–37.
15   Jochen Eisenbrand, "More Legroom Please: A Historical Survey of the Aircraft Seat," in von Vegesack and Eisenbrand, Airworld, 124–43.
16   Peter Sloterdijk, *Sphaeren* (Frankfurt: Suhrkamp Verlag, 1998).
17   Eisenbrand, "Legroom," 137; Kovarik et al., *Human Factors*, 392.
18   See www.frogdesign.com/case-study/lufthansa-brand-experience.html.
19   It should be noted that airlines, like many corporate entities, do not like discussing or even disclosing the designers of their cabins. A more thorough investigative analysis of the sources, development, and authorship of modern aircraft interiors is called for.
20   Eisenbrand, "Legroom," 140.
21   This is a world Reyner Banham had already foreseen, though he saw the instigator as being the more extreme environment of the spacecraft. Reyner Banham, *The Architecture of the Well-Tempered Environment* (1969; reprint, Chicago: The University of Chicago Press, 1984), 290ff.

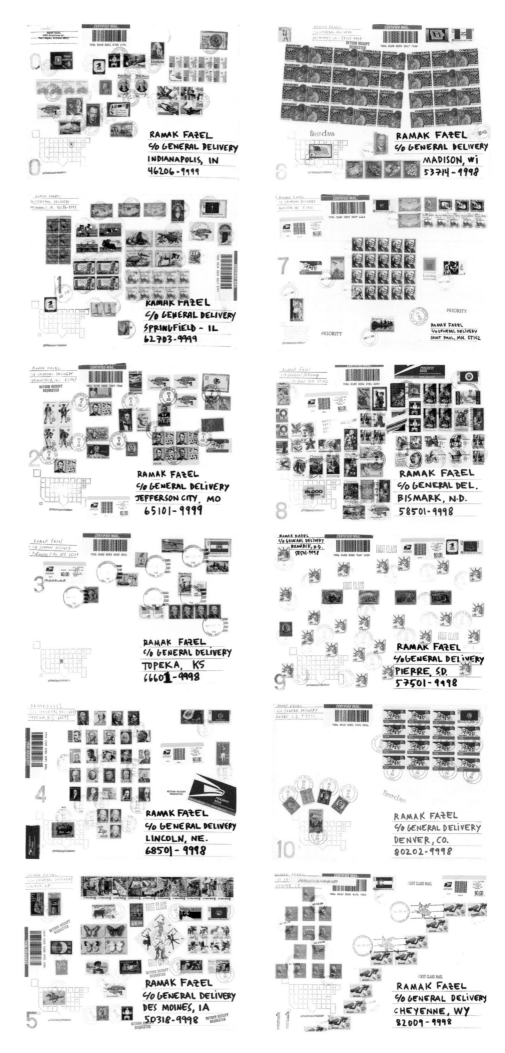

For additional images by
Ramak Fazel, see pages 54–56
and 60–61. For an interview with
Ramak Fazel, see pages 57–59.

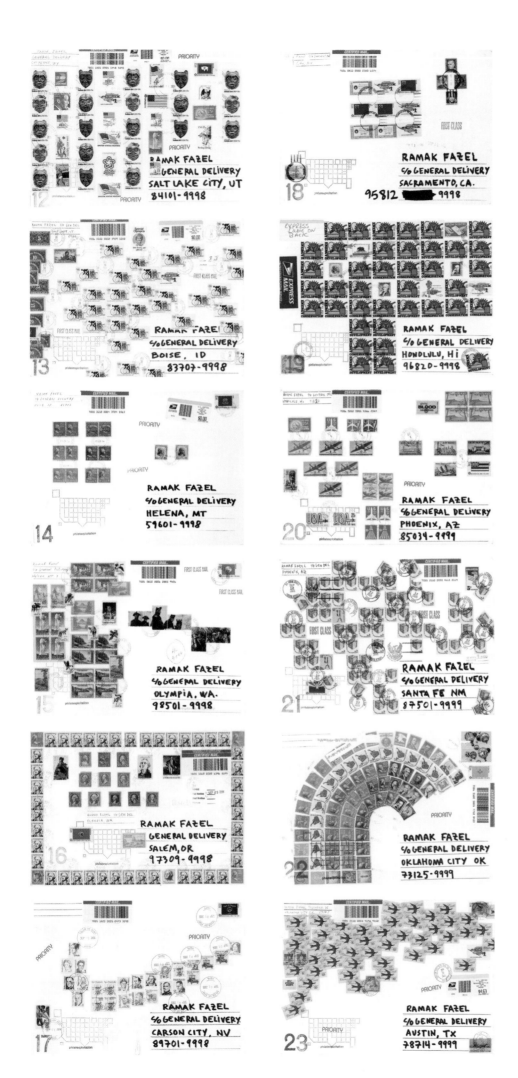

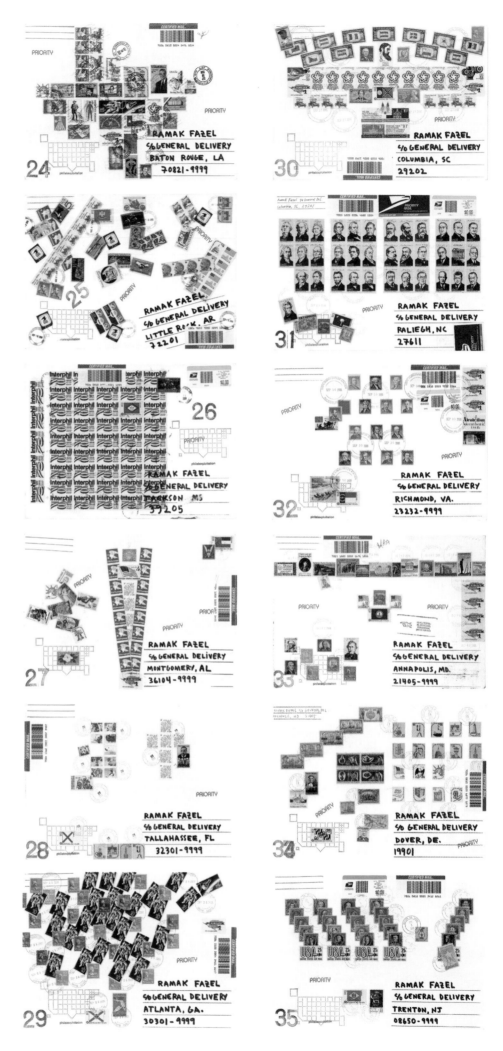

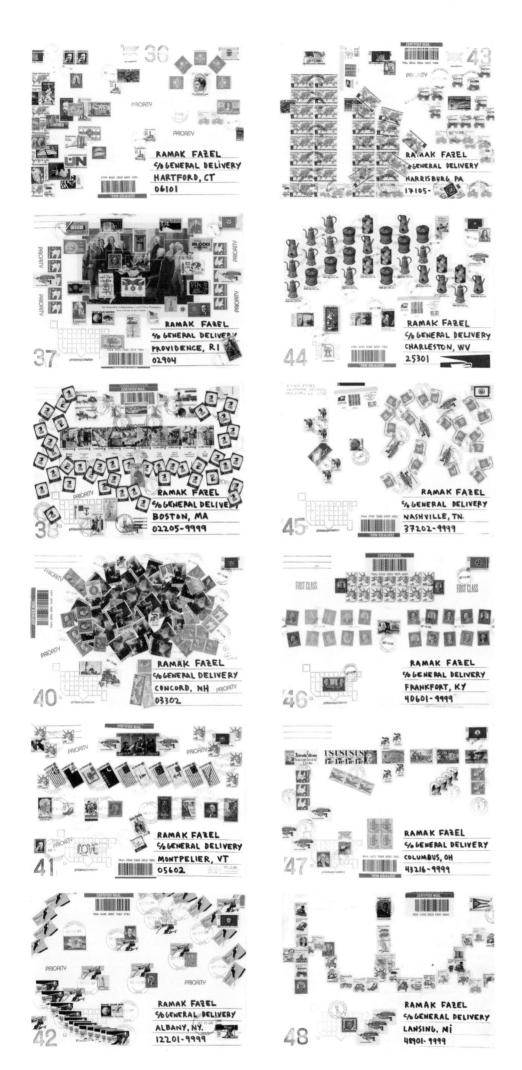

RAMAK FAZEL
c/o GENERAL DELIVERY
HARTFORD, CT
06101

RAMAK FAZEL
c/o GENERAL DELIVERY
HARRISBURG, PA
17105-

RAMAK FAZEL
c/o GENERAL DELIVERY
PROVIDENCE, RI
02904

RAMAK FAZEL
c/o GENERAL DELIVERY
CHARLESTON, WV
25301

RAMAK FAZEL
c/o GENERAL DELIVERY
BOSTON, MA
02205-9999

RAMAK FAZEL
c/o GENERAL DELIVERY
NASHVILLE, TN.
37202-9999

RAMAK FAZEL
c/o GENERAL DELIVERY
CONCORD, NH
03302

RAMAK FAZEL
c/o GENERAL DELIVERY
FRANKFORT, KY
40601-9999

RAMAK FAZEL
c/o GENERAL DELIVERY
MONTPELIER, VT
05602

RAMAK FAZEL
c/o GENERAL DELIVERY
COLUMBUS, OH
43216-9999

RAMAK FAZEL
c/o GENERAL DELIVERY
ALBANY, NY.
12201-9999

RAMAK FAZEL
c/o GENERAL DELIVERY
LANSING, MI
48901-9999

Postcards. James Gamble Rogers Papers, Manuscripts and Archives, Yale University Library.

The architect James Gamble Rogers is best known for designing Yale's collegiate Gothic campus, built in the 1920s and 1930s but meant to evoke the medieval atmosphere of seventeenth-century Oxford and Cambridge. When Rogers received his first commission at Yale, for the dormitories known as the Memorial Quadrangle, he had never visited Oxford or Cambridge. His experience included five years at the École des Beaux-Arts in Paris and projects in Chicago and New York that combined historical styles with modern programs and construction techniques. To develop his interpretation of collegiate Gothic, Rogers relied in part on his collection of architectural postcards (now at Yale University Library).

The postcards, which depict Gothic, Renaissance, and Baroque architecture, are a collection of architectural fragments that, taken together, form a lexicon of architectural styles. Their images of highly articulated friezes, fan vaults, column capitals, and statuary are curiously flat, devoid of spatial, contextual, and programmatic information. Indeed, one can see where Rogers has literally clipped the cards to remove this information, resulting in oddly shaped snippets. These clippings reflect Rogers's pragmatic understanding of architectural style, not as ideological program but rather as detail that could be cut, copied, and pasted from one project to another.

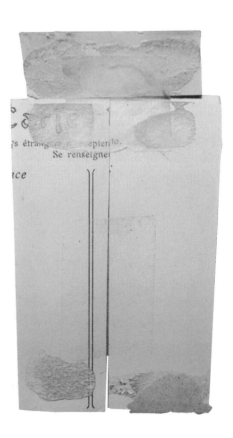